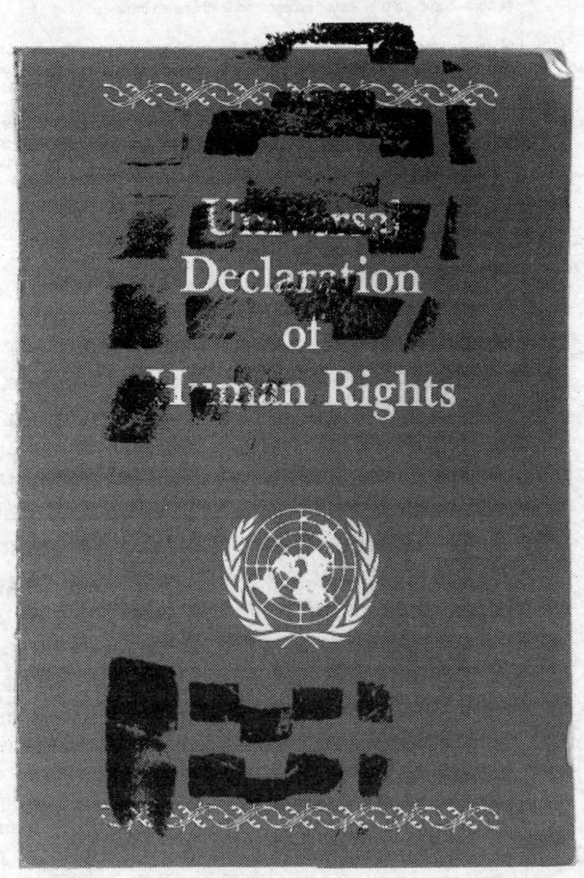

INDEX ON CENSORSHIP 3 1998

INDEX ON CENSORSHIP

WEBSITE NEWS UPDATED EVERY TWO WEEKS

www.indexoncensorship.org
contact@indexoncensorship.org
tel: 0171-278 2313
fax: 0171-278 1878

Volume 27 No 3 May/June 1998 Issue 182

Index on Censorship (ISSN 0306-4220) is published bi-monthly by a non-profit-making company: Writers & Scholars International Ltd, Lancaster House, 33 Islington High Street, London N1 9LH. *Index on Censorship* is associated with Writers & Scholars Educational Trust, registered charity number 325003

Periodicals postage: (US subscribers only) paid at Newark, New Jersey. Postmaster: send US address changes to *Index on Censorship* c/o Mercury Airfreight Int/ Ltd Inc, 2323 Randolph Avenue, Avenel, NJ 07001, USA

UNESCO has supported this publication. The authors are responsible for the choice and the presentation of the facts contained in this book and for the opinions expressed therein, which are not necessarily those of UNESCO and do not commit the Organization. The designations employed and the presentation of material throughout this publication do not imply the expression of any opinion whatsoever on the part of UNESCO concerning the legal status of any country, territory, city or area or of its authorities, or concerning the delimitation of its frontiers or boundaries.

EDITORIAL

Hands off the document

Only eight people made up the Drafting Committee, chaired by the formidable Eleanor Roosevelt, of the Universal Declaration of Human Rights. Drawn up after the barbarities of the Holocaust, moral universals were for the first time manifested as rights for individuals. It is an extraordinary document, aspirational, crystal clear – and battle-stained.

No doubt the fierceness of the arguments over Article 19, on the right to freedom of opinion and expression, came out of the unspoken recognition that free expression is the touchstone for all other freedoms, the tool with which individuals can defend their basic human rights. And this is implicit in every article in this issue of *Index*, which celebrates the 50-year-old Declaration: in Shada Islam's exposure of the secrecy behind asylum laws, for instance; in Alex de Waal's arguments over the erosion of the Genocide Convention; in Michael Ignatieff's discussion of 'rights talk' as a threat to authoritarianism.

How does the Declaration stand up at the end of the century? Is it worth the paper it's written on? The Palestininans, on whom Edward Saïd reports, would say no. The Bangladeshi women who tell Naila Kabeer of their determination to give their daughters education might say yes. What becomes clear is how much it is lack of will by those in power, not the words of the Declaration itself, which is to blame for its failures.

Even so, the Declaration should not be treated as a sacred text. Fifty years on, there are some striking absences: nothing on minority rights, nothing on environment or disability, only *his* home, family, privacy, reason, conscience, not *hers*. And there have been enormous changes since it was written – for instance, the media revolution. So how should Article 19 be expanded and reapplied to deal with the restrictive powers of the new media conglomerates?

Cynics might say that, since the demise of communism, two new opposing ideologies have emerged, the free market and human rights – a duality which the Declaration in some ways reflects. In practice, for example, it has emphasised civil and political rights and has not lived up to the equal concern for economic and social rights. But governments could do a lot worse than start implementing the Declaration properly, instead of diluting it with double standards and selective application. Fifty years on, it is still a good basis for the arguments – and the listening – to begin.

contents

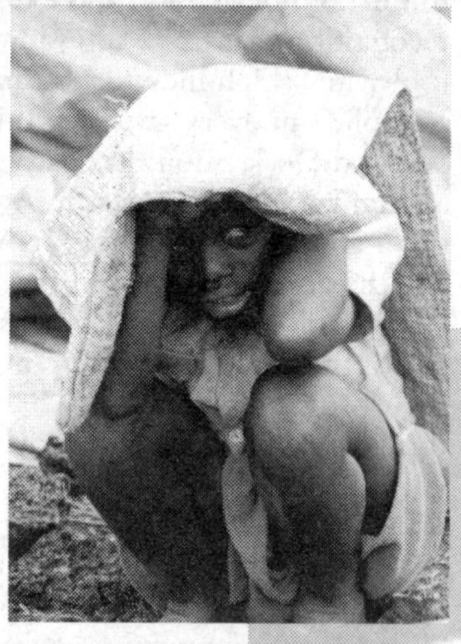

Article 1 'All human beings are born free and equal in dignity and rights. They are endowed with reason and conscience and should act towards one another in a spirit of brotherhood.'

JO GLANVILLE

Babel: First witnesses

On 15 April 1945, the British army entered Bergen-Belsen Camp in north-west Germany. The soldiers who liberated the camp, and the medical staff who came to assist them, were among the first to convey the horror to the world outside.

Their letters home and the diaries written in Belsen are little known, yet they remain as fresh, immediate and shocking as when first written. There is an urgency and eloquence in these accounts, many written by very young men desperate to bear witness to what they had seen, but fearful they would not be believed.

When the British entered Belsen, they were faced with 10,000 corpses, 60,000 internees in varying stages of starvation and a typhus epidemic. Contrary to appearances, Belsen had not been designed as an extermination camp, but as a detention camp for Jewish prisoners who were to be exchanged for Germans prisoners in the USA and the UK. This changed when the Nazis began to evacuate the camps in the east; many of the inmates and SS staff were transferred to Belsen and a former commanding officer at Auschwitz, Josef Kramer, was put in charge. By April 1945, rather than evacuate the infected population, the Germans made a truce with the British and handed the camp over to their control. The SS camp staff remained, along with a regiment of Hungarians, while the Wehrmacht were returned to German lines.

Two years later, in 1947, when the commission of 18 nations met to discuss the draft of the UN Declaration of Human Rights, outrage at the barbarism of the Holocaust informed much of their debate. A number of the subsequent Articles, including those on slavery, the right to life and on torture, were shaped with images of the camps fresh in mind.

Belsen April 1945; Volunteer medical students – Credit: Imperial War Museum

*From the diary of **Dr Michael Hargrave**, April to May 1945. Michael Hargrave was one of 97 volunteer medical students who assisted in the Belsen relief operation.*

'I was allotted Hut 1 Laager 1 (Men) - located the hut on the map of the Camp and then set off to find it.

I now began to see the Concentration Camp proper, the first thing that struck me was the amazing bleakness of the Camp – the huts had once been painted red – but this had faded to an indiscriminate pink – and otherwise there was no colour at all in the Camp, everything was grey or slaty brown. The next thing was the dust, this was everywhere and even as you walked you left clouds of dust behind you.

Then the Internees – they looked thin, brown and dirty and they shuffled along in a purposeless sort of way, dressed in their blue and white striped slave clothing. They were not in the least interested in anything and took no notice of us at all as we walked by.

Found my hut with some difficulty, but on going inside with Russell Barton who was also sharing the hut, we found that it was comparatively clean – that it contained 3-tier bunks and that all the men inside it seemed capable of walking, and therefore capable of getting their own food and eating it.

So we reported back to the Office and we were told to try Hut 224 Laager 1 (Women). We found by looking at the map that this was right at the other end of the Camp. We set off towards it and noticed another striking thing about the Camp – the Smell – this was a hot, humid smell mixed up with the smell of burning boots, dirty clothing and faeces and once smelt was never forgotten! [...]

We eventually came into the Women's Laager, where the Smell increased in intensity – we found Hut 224, which was painted the usual pink colour with the Red Cross which the Germans had had the nerve to paint on each hut.

We went into the hut and were almost knocked back by the smell, but we went into one of the two main rooms.

The sight that met us was shocking – there were no beds whatsoever and in this one room there were about 200 people lying on the floor. In some cases they wore a few battered rags and in some cases they wore no clothes at all.

They were all huddled together one next to the other. In many cases 1 blanket having to cover 3 people. The floor was covered in faeces and soaked in urine and the people lying on the floor were in just the same state – as they all had extremely severe diarrhoea and were all too weak to move.

Next to each person was a tin can or old mug and various small pieces of bread which they were carefully hoarding up – this latter lying on the floor and when they felt like it they took a bite out of it – irrespective of what it had been lying in. Their hair, hands, faces and feet were all covered in a mixture of dry faeces and dirt. At least ¾ of them had hacking coughs and the other ¼ were just lying. Here and there a dead person could be seen lying between two living ones, who took no notice of her at all and just went on eating, coughing or just lying, and these were all women whose ages varied from 15-30.'

Lieutenant Colonel Mervin Willett Gonin DSO, TD. *This account appears to have been delivered as a talk*

'We met every evening at 9 o'clock to discuss the difficulties, which at times seemed insurmountable, which had arisen during the day. Some twenty officers, three or four nursing sisters, Red Cross workers, St. John's members, U.N.R.A. [United Nations Relief Agency. Ed] would collect, the problems particular to the ladies would be discussed first, about eleven oclock they would be dismissed, gin, brandy and champagne would appear and we would finish our business by twelve or one in the morning – and it was not a party but damned hard work which those meetings produced. I am very certain that it was the very considerable quantities of liquor that we got through at those meetings that kept those of us who were responsible for the administration of the place from going as mad as most of the internees in the Horror Camp. [.....]

I can give no adequate discription of the Horror Camp in which my men and myself were to spend the next month of our lives. It was just a barren wilderness, as bare and devoid of vegitation as a chicken run. Corpses lay everywhere, some in huge piles where they had been dumped by other inmates, sometimes they lay singly or in pairs where they had fallen as they shuffled along the dirt tracks. Those who died of disease usually died in the huts, when starvation was the chief cause of death they died in the open for it is an odd characteristic of starvation that it's victims seem compelled to go on wandering till they fall down and die. Once they have fallen they die almost at once and it took a little time to get used to seeing men women and children collapse as you walked by them and to restrain oneself from going to their assistance. One had to get used early to the idea that the individual just did not count. One knew that five hundred a day were dying and that five hundred a day were going on dying for weeks before anything we could do would have the slightest effect. It was, however, not easy to watch a child choking to death from diphtheria when you knew a tracheotomy and nursing would save it, one saw women drowning in their own vomit because they were too weak to turn over, and men eating worms as they clutched a half loaf of bread purely because they had had to eat worms to live and now could scarcely tell the difference between worms and bread.

Piles of corpses, naked and obscene, with a woman too weak to stand proping herself against them as she cooked the food we had given her over an open fire; men and women crouching down just anywhere in the open relieving themselves of the dysentery wich was scouring their bowels, a woman standing stark naked washing herself with some issue soap in water from a tank in which the remains of a child floated. [...]

It was shortly after the B.R.C.S. [British Red Cross Society. Ed] teams arrived, though it may have no connection, that a very large quantity of lipstick also arrived. This was not at all what we men wanted, we were screaming for hundreds and thousands of other things

and I dont know who asked for lipstick. I wish so much that I could discover who did it, it was the action of genious, sheer unadulterated brilliance. I believe nothing did more for those internees than the lipstick. Women lay in bed with no sheets and no nightie but with scarlet lips, you saw them wandering about with nothing but a blanket over their shoulders, but with scarlet lips. I saw a woman dead on the post mortem table and clutched in her hand was a piece of lipstick.

Do you see what I mean? At last someone had done something to make them individuals again, they were someone, no longer merely the number tatooed on the arm. At last they could take an interest in their appearance. That lipstick started to give them back their humanity.

Perhaps it was the most pathetic thing that happened at Belsen, perhaps the most pathetic thing that's ever happened, I dont know. But that is why the sight of a piece of lipstick today makes my eyes feel just a little uncomfortable.'

Private Emmanuel Fisher. *A Soldier's Diary of Belsen 7406789 Pte Fisher E. 32 C.C.S. [Casualty Clearing Station], R.A.M.C. [Royal Army Medical Corps]. British Liberation Army*

17/4/45

To whom it may concern:

'I served breakfast at 8:30 am – tea and a slice of dry bread. Every room I entered told the same story. The men pleaded for food, clothing (they were all naked), for bandages, for more blankets, medical treatment. I could do nothing but tell them to be patient. All would come in time. They were in no frame of mind to listen to any explanation I might give of the enormity of our task. I couldn't bear their frenzied shouts any longer – so after a while I shut my mouth and adopted a poker-face. If those men only knew how many years I had aged that day, they would have been sorry for me instead of vice-versa.

After my lunch, always a hurried affair, I came back to find my only efficient nurse weeping. She couldn't carry on, she said. The men had rioted during my absence – had run about, naked, searching for food. They had entered the doctor's room and stolen some biscuits I had given him. They had even snatched a large, quite meatless bone. The whole place was in an uproar. 'Food, food, food,' was all I heard. Some

Credit: Imperial War Museum

of the men were quite out of their minds.

A similar incident had occurred in the neighbouring house, [temporary German barracks cleared for patients. Ed] where four men had lain, stark naked since midday, on the concrete floor, under the table used for serving meals, waiting for the next meal to appear.

My R.A.M.C. comrades saw my anxious face and told me not to 'take it to heart'. There was nothing I could do about it, they said. At tea-time, I asked the chief nurse to dole out the food herself, since I would not be coming back again, thanks to my leave being due on the morrow. She pleaded with me to accompany her. She was afraid that as soon as she made an appearance with the bread, the men would 'tear her to pieces' in their efforts to grab the food. I insisted – saying that she *had* to get used to doing it herself until one of our English nursing sisters started working there. I watched her mount the stairs and listened. After a few seconds there broke out a tremendous uproar. I dashed upstairs - entered the room and saw half of the occupants, stark-naked, scuttling back to their beds. Absolute silence greeted my stern countenace. I reprimanded them and told them to be patient - we were doing our best.

That evening I wearily made my way back to Camp, feeling years older, afraid that my family would notice my grey hairs, afraid of what those men, reduced by the Germans to animal level, might do during my absence.

I am going on leave tomorrow, to London, which I have not seen for 11 months. I should be full of spirit, and happy in anticipation – but I am not. I simply feel tired, spiritually weak and depressed.....'

The accounts above, reproduced with their original spelling and syntax intact, are part of an archive at the Imperial War Museum. Index *would like to thank the Trustees of the Imperial War Museum for allowing access to the collection and the Department of Documents for their permission to publish the extract from Dr M J Hargrave's papers. Thanks are also due to the Reverend Chris Gonin for permission to publish the extract from Lieutenant Colonel Gonin's papers and to Emmanuel Fisher for permission to publish the excerpt from his own diary.* ❑

***Jo Glanville** is a freelance journalist living in London. She selected and edited the excerpts.*

Article 19 'Everyone has the right to freedom of opinion and expression; this right includes freedom to hold opinions without interference and to seek, receive and impart information and ideas through any media and regardless of frontiers.'

BILL ORME

Rhetoric and reality

Compelling but not binding, Article 19 is a 'fine piece of aspirational rhetoric' still more widely honoured in the breach than the observance

It is succinct, unambiguous, and wonderfully prescient. Even Internet communications are protected by Article 19 which, along with the rest of the Universal Declaration, is having its fiftieth birthday commemorated in ceremonies and symposia around the world.

Its plainspoken promise of freedom of 'information and ideas' for all provides the perfect umbrella text for those of us in the press freedom business. We take refuge in its universality, reminding governments that they, too, are signatories to this expansive document. European free-expression advocates neatly sidestep the multiple lacunae in their own national and regional free expression guarantees. US press freedom advocates avoid First Amendment parochialisms (while still reminding themselves and the world that the Declaration's godmother was a quintessentially US internationalist). In emerging democracies, civil libertarians can cite Article 19 as a kind of international norm to which their societies are ethically obligated to conform.

Ethically, that is, but not legally. The Universal Declaration of Human Rights is a fine piece of aspirational rhetoric, but the governments that signed it never thought of it as binding. They never would have endorsed it otherwise. There was to be no global court striking down prior restraint rules or state broadcasting takeovers on the basis of the Universal Declaration. Only a minority of the original signatories – the founding members of the United Nations – were by any reasonable measure democratic states. Even those governments that were popularly elected in 1948 restricted information in ways we wouldn't tolerate today. Neither the Soviet bloc nor its western opponents would have then permitted direct communications to its citizens from the other side 'through any media and regardless of frontiers' (short-wave radio was grandfathered in as the technologically unavoidable exception).

In the USA 50 years ago, public figures could and did threaten critical newspapers with devastating libel suits. The post-war, Cold War US press was especially circumspect in its national security coverage. Not until the Pentagon Papers case two decades later would US newspapers dare print anything classified as 'state secrets'.

At the half-century mark, Article 19 remains more poetry than reality. On the first day of 1998, at least 129 journalists were held in prisons in 24 countries for exercising their ostensibly guaranteed right to freedom of expression. Their criminal offences were typically linked to purportedly seditious or revolutionary or counterrevolutionary 'propaganda'. These inclued not just articles of opinion but straightforward news reporting.

There are scores of other writers, artists and political dissidents imprisoned around the world on similar charges. And most of the world's governments continue to impose some political control on outgoing and incoming publications and news broadcasts.

The prosecutions and censorship of journalists are justified by governments under the terms of the 'other' Article 19: not the original article of the 1948 Universal Declaration of Human Rights, cited above, but Article 19 of the International Covenant of Civil and Political Rights, or the ICCPR, as it is known in UN shorthand.

Drafted under UN auspices in 1966 and ratified in 1976, it is the ICCPR that signatory governments in theory do consider binding, and which should properly be the focus of freedom of expression activism organized around the fiftieth anniversary of the UDHR. For it is the ICCPR that represents the multilateral betrayal of the Declaration. The ICCPR version of Article 19 restates the basic free-expression promise of its progenitor and then buries it under a cascade of caveats, exemptions and pretexts for government interference in the media.

The right to freedom of expression 'carries with it special duties and responsibilities', the ICCPR states, and 'may therefore be subject to certain restrictions as are provided by law and are necessary: (1) For respect of the rights or reputations of others; (2) For the protection of national security or of public order, or of public health or morals.'

If that weren't sufficient juridical cover for censorship-minded autocrats, the ICCPR continues with Article 20, not found in any form in the Universal Declaration. Article 20 outlaws 'any propaganda for war' and 'advocacy of national, racial or religious hatred that constitutes incitement to discrimination, hostility or violence'.

At first blush, these prohibitions may seem unobjectionable: who can defend incitements to genocide, or terrorism? Yet this loosely worded article in effect bans the essential public discussion of cultural and ethnic conflicts that are central to the political lives of scores of nations around the world. It has been used to ban direct citations from (and even indirect references to) the official statements of insurgent or separatist movements that enjoy substantial internal and international legitimacy.

The ICCPR allows the Turkish government to suppress media coverage of the quest for Kurdish autonomy, and the Chinese government to squelch any open press debate about Tibet. It sanctions, implicitly, the tragicomic past censorship of Gerry Adams by the UK government, and the not at all comic suppression of Ken Saro-Wiwa's championing of the cause of his fellow Ogonis in Nigeria. Under the ICCPR it is legitimate for the Milosevic government to suppress news about armed Albanian insurgents in Kosovo today, just as the Somoza government claimed it was following domestic and international law when it censored coverage of the Sandinista rebels two decades ago. In the Middle East, Netanyahu, Arafat, Hussein and Mubarak can all find ample refuge under the ICCPR when attempting to limit press coverage of their enemies.

The counterpart of the ICCPR's gutted and pernicious Article 19 is Article 10 of the European Covenant of Human Rights, also with similarly broad 'exceptions' to its guarantees of press freedom. Article 10 is in turn being used as a new legal guideline for the constitutions of emerging democracies of the 1990s. The World Press Freedom Committee recently conducted a valuable research experiment. They showed that hundreds of press freedom abuses denounced through the International Freedom of Expression Exchange (IFEX) network could be legally defended under the standards of Article 10.

An official of the European Union complained that the cases cited were mostly from other continents and therefore could not be interpreted as an indictment of the European Covenant. He rather missed the point. Western Europe is rightly considered a model of democratic development, and a literal reading of Article 10 – as of Article 19 of the ICCPR – shows that it is apparently permissible for democracies to suppress press freedom for any number of reasons. It would be an oddly obtuse or uncreative regime that could not find ways to justify censorship under the terms of Articles 19 or 10.

In the search for global norms and guarantees, we still end up back at the Universal Declaration. It is perfectly defensible, strategically and ethically, to cite the original, unfettered Article 19 in remonstrations to repressive governments – or at least I have persuaded myself that this is so, having done it literally hundreds of times in letters sent by the Committee to Protect Journalists. But we must keep in mind that the original Article 19 still represents a quest, an ideal, that certainly should be universal honoured, but manifestly is not. Texts, binding and otherwise, only go so far. It is the perceived legitimacy of dissent within a national culture that is the ultimate determinant of freedom of expression; and that legitimacy is won internally, gradually and painfully by a steady succession of local political battles, not by the force of some external mandate.

Look at the British Commonwealth. Among the varied legacies of British colonialism are some of most horrific press laws in the world: Official Secrets Acts, seditious libel statutes, onerous prior restraint powers invested in appointed courts. Much of CPJ's daily work is combating the tenacious power of this legal heritage in Africa, Asia and the Middle East. Yet it is also true that former British colonies harbour some of the most independent-minded news media cultures in the world: go to a newsstand in Lagos, Abacha notwithstanding; or New Delhi; or Hong Kong. This may be because part of the political culture bequeathed by Britain was a subterranean disdain for repressive legal texts and the belief that such laws and the people who enforce them can and should be openly opposed.

James Madison had it right: the best press law is no press law. He crafted the First Amendment pre-emptively to prohibit any future attempt to legislate restrictions to freedom of expression. But it wasn't until the US press – at significant risk though also with significant public support – challenged official attempts to restrict those rights in the second half of the twentieth century that the promise of the First

Amendment was fully realised. (Almost fully: legislative and court battles continue today.)

In that spirit, until the rest of the world's legislatures are also constitutionally enjoined against curtailing press freedom, we shall continue to cite the Article 19 of 50 years ago as the best international articulation of what Americans are fortunate and unusual to have enshrined in law as an inalienable right. But those freedoms will ultimately be won on the ground, by writers and their readers, not in fiftieth-anniversary ceremonies, or through appeals to sacred texts. ❑

***Bill Orme** is executive director of the Committee to Protect Journalists in New York*

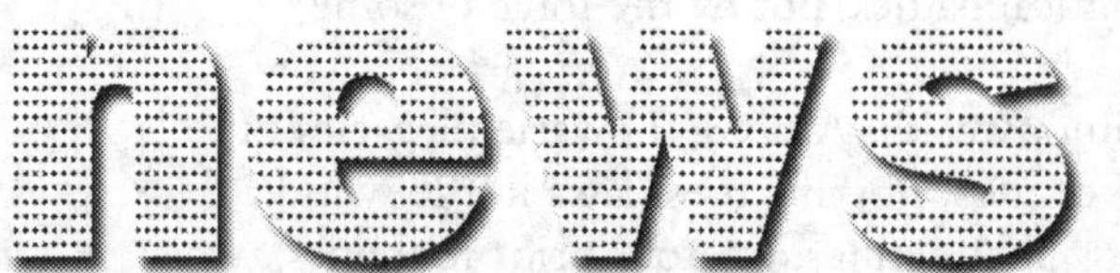

USA

'The news is what we say it is

Suzanne Fisher

A husband and wife, both reporters with Fox TV, filed a lawsuit in Tampa on 2 April against Fox's local subsidiary, WTVT, alleging that they were fired because they refused to broadcast a story they knew to be misleading.

The lawsuit revolves round whether Fox had the right to dilute a script by Steve Wilson and Jane Akre in order to give viewers a milder assessment of the danger of synthetic recombinant bovine growth hormone (rBGH), an artificial hormone used to boost milk production from cows. The drug is manufactured by Monsanto Company in the US. According to Wilson and Akre, Fox pressured them to include pro-Monsanto product claims 'without documentation of accuracy' and asked them not to mention the link between rBGH milk and cancer.

Fox had planned to air Wilson and Akre's uncut programme in February 1997 but changed its mind after Monsanto wrote a letter threatening litigation. But it refused to kill the story, the journalists claim, lest word leak out. Wilson and Akre were ordered to write and rewrite the story more than 73 times.

Wilson and Akre quote the Fox general manager as saying: 'We paid US$3 billion for these stations, we'll decide what the news is.' Fox TV is owned by Rupert Murdoch's News Corporation.

MICHAEL IGNATIEFF

Out of danger

Cast in the shadow of World War II and Nazi atrocities, the Universal Declaration of Human Rights was shaped more by the fear of evil than the expectation of good. Fifty years on, it has become the individual's defence against the excesses of power and, even when challenged by dictators and demagogues, the universal language of human rights everywhere

In *If this be a Man*, Primo Levi describes being interviewed by Dr Pannwitz, chief of the chemical department at Auschwitz. Levi had been a chemist by profession. Securing a place in the chemical department might save him from extermination. As Levi stood on one side of the doctor's desk, in his concentration camp uniform, the doctor looked up at him as if he were gazing at a fish in an aquarium. Levi had never been looked at in this manner before, and he never forgot its significance. Any history of the moral imagination of our era would have to provide a genealogy of Dr Pannwitz's 'aquarium look'. Here was an encounter between two human beings recast as a meeting between two different species.

The Universal Declaration of Human Rights of 1948 was the work of the first generation to take the measure of Auschwitz. If Dr Pannwitz could look at a man and see only another species, how was it possible to believe in moral universalism ever again? The Declaration implies a certain trust in our species. What trust is possible?

Before 1945, the only rights individuals had under international law were in the treaties abolishing the slave trade, the Geneva and Hague conventions regulating the conduct of war and the minority rights treaties concluded after Versailles. But these were rights held only by virtue of membership in particular groups and in specific situations. It is

only since 1945 that the individual acquired legal personality in international law. This simple fact matters more than the rights enumerated in the Declaration. The year 1948 represented the moral birth of this particular type of individual as a global entity.

Between 1945 and 1951, this universal individual was enfranchised, not just in the Universal Declaration, but in the UN Charter; Nuremberg case law; the Genocide Convention; the Geneva Conventions; the European Convention on Human Rights; and the UNESCO statement on race, in which prominent anthropologists undertook a scientific exorcism of Dr Pannwitz's 'aquarium look'.

All of these documents bear witness to a faith in moral universals. Yet some consciousness of Dr Pannwitz kept breaking in. The Universal Declaration itself incorporated barbarity into its preamble: 'Whereas disregard and contempt for human rights have resulted in barbarous acts which have outraged the conscience of mankind'. Barbarity had not figured in the Declaration of the Rights of Man and the Citizen of 1791. Our post-1945 heritage is steeped in it.

Beyond this, what common ground did the Declaration put under our feet? The Universal Declaration universalised rights talk. This at least allows people to speak the same language, but it doesn't mean they will say the same things. Human rights universals do not end arguments: they begin them. Indeed, most conflicts in the world today are conflicts of rights, and the fact that both sides understand the language of rights does not necessarily make them any more amenable to resolution. It is not merely that different cultures and ideologies disagree about the content and application of universals. There remains substantial conflict between the universal principles themselves.

The UN Charter was addressed to states while the Universal Declaration addressed the individual. In the past 50 years, all regimes practising human rights abuses have taken refuge behind the UN Charter's guarantees of state sovereignty and non-interference. In response, there now exists a presumption in favour of human rights over state sovereignty in humanitarian emergencies where the violations are gross, visible or genocidal in character. But this remains a presumption only, as the dolorous litany of failure – Rwanda, Kurdistan, Bosnia – continues to attest.

The second tension between universals is between the laws of war tradition in the Geneva Conventions and the rights tradition of the

Berlin, 1945 – Credit: Rex/Sipa

Universal Declaration. The Geneva Conventions accepted war as a normal, even lawful means of resolving human disputes, while the Universal Declaration tacitly treated war as an intrinsic infringement of moral norms. The Universal Declaration's Article 1 speaks of human beings as being obliged to 'act towards one another in a spirit of brotherhood'. Whatever war is, it is not an act of brotherhood.

'the Declaration implies a certain trust in our species. What trust is possible?'

The third tension has been between the civil and political rights traditions of the western democracies and the social and economic rights traditions of the communist world. Both traditions flowed from the Enlightenment Rights of Man and both laid claim to its emancipatory heritage. The Universal Declaration was written while the Cold War was locking itself into place with the division of Berlin, the establishment of communist governments in Eastern Europe and the formation of NATO. In this context, shared universals were quickly turned into a weapon in the ideological battle between the superpowers. For 20 years after 1945, each side used the Universal Declaration to denounce each other while protecting its own rights regimes behind the UN Charter's guarantee of state sovereignty.

By the 1970s, the Cold War had evolved into a system of complicity, in which the West agreed to keep silent about human rights abuses in return for Soviet co-operation in the maintenance of geopolitical order. The Helsinki Final Act of 1976 was intended to ratify this regime of complicity. The West acquiesced in a Soviet sphere of influence in Eastern Europe in return for guarantees of human rights protection within the Soviet area of influence. At Helsinki the communist world finally acknowledged that there were not two human rights cultures in the world but one. This ideological concession was meant to be symbolic only, but it had unexpected results. First in Poland, then in Czechoslovakia and finally throughout Eastern Europe, rights groups sprang up to demand that their regimes keep the promises made at Helsinki. Human rights language enabled Eastern Europeans to hoist their rulers by their own petards.

To support these groups and to break down the collusion between governments, a host of civil-society actors entered the fray. Amnesty International, *Index on Censorship* and Human Rights Watch came into being and, by the 1980's, the Universal Declaration had enlisted a huge constituency of global human rights activists. The Declaration had enfranchised the individual against the state; now it was engendering its own indigenous constituency of support, a global network of activists adept at using the publicity of shame. For the first time in history, repressive governments around the world began to discover that repression had its costs. Thanks to this pressure from below, human rights had forced its way onto the agenda of international politics.

During the 1980s, human rights pressure from without and within hastened the moral decay of communism. In a real sense, the collapse of the Soviet Empire was the work of the human rights revolution begun in 1948.

Since Helsinki, there has been a single human rights culture in the world. But this does not mean that it is not challenged without and embattled within. Nation states with indigenous human rights traditions – France, Britain and the United States for example – are often guilty of what might be called rights narcissism. They find it disagreeable to have their own human rights record brought before the scrutiny of international bodies. Rights narcissism makes the British resistant to appeals against judgements made in British courts being heard by the European Court of Human Rights. Rights narcissism also makes pro-death penalty Americans indignant when the capital punishment statutes of US states are denounced by international rights bodies.

Another observable phenomenon, besides rights narcissism, is rights inflation. Originally, the founding fathers and mothers of the Declaration envisaged a succinct document incorporating only those rights that could command universal assent. There are now dozens of international conventions and human rights instruments amplifying and specifying the terms of the Universal Declaration. Sometimes, these conventions, for example, those relating to women and children, add useful detail and clarification to the general principles set down in the Universal Declaration. Sometimes, though, the proliferation of rights documents seems to weaken the currency of rights language itself. Proliferation of rights is a natural enough response to disagreement. In the face of the Cold War stand-off between the civil and political and social and economic rights traditions, the solution was to incorporate both into separate conventions, ie, to go for inclusion rather than argue the list down to a central core. The inflation of rights language – everything desirable in the world is now posited as a right – has the effect of reducing the value and legitimacy of rights terminology in general.

Besides rights narcissism and rights inflation, there is the phenomenon of rights trading. Powerful states, like the UK, France and the USA, soften human rights criticisms of other powerful nations, like China or Iran, for the sake of trade or other economic benefits. Rights trading not only violates the premise of universality and universal application, it also misunderstands the essential priority of rights as a moral claim. The point about rights language is that it is supposed to be a moral trump card. Rights ought not to be traded against other goods. If so, why call them rights at all?

All of these betrayals – rights inflation, rights trading and rights narcissism – are practised, not by the enemies of the human rights traditions of the Enlightenment, but by its ostensible friends. With friends like these, human rights hardly needs enemies.

But there are states that directly challenge the universality of rights norms themselves, China being the most egregious and powerful example. Although the Chinese regime claims that the individualism of rights norms is antithetical to the civilization of China, the reality is that human rights poses a challenge not to the civilization of China, but to the regime. In turn, the regime is adept at making the Chinese people believe that its survival is essential to theirs. The heart of the Chinese case against human rights is that individual rights threaten the cohesion of the nation itself. Once these rights are granted, political pluralism and competition must follow; once these follow, the country will divide, split and sunder into civil war. Behind the ideological opposition to human rights, therefore, lies the spectre of China's pre-communist past.

Authoritarianism usually conjures up such spectres to defend itself, and it is not mistaken to believe that rights talk threatens its survival. Once people believe they have the right to speak freely, they are likely to demand the right to chose their governors. Rights of free expression are, in many ways, the precondition for all other rights, and while free expression does not necessarily entail democracy, in practice it often does. It is significant, in fact, that China continues to claim that rights talk is antithetical to its traditions: cultural relativism is the last refuge of authoritarianism everywhere. The government may claim that the thousands of Chinese activists who have risked imprisonment and death in defence of the Universal Declaration are in the grip of some western individualist fantasy, but the truth seems to be that they are defending an idea of dignity as autonomy that has become universal.

China is not the only formidable opponent of global rights culture. While some parts of Islam have made peace with human rights and indeed have argued that the terms of the Universal Declaration were anticipated, centuries ago, in various articulations of Quranic wisdom, there has always been a strand of Islam that opposes the secular individualist bias of rights talk. This criticism was heard from the outset. During the debates on the Universal Declaration in 1948, Saudi Arabia led the Islamic nations' objections to Article 16 on equal marriage rights and Article 18 on the right to change religious belief. While other nations with substantial Muslim populations such as Syria, Turkey and Pakistan did vote for the Declaration, Saudi Arabia eventually abstained, laying down a marker for future Islamic resistance to the universalising claims of the Declaration.

'every time a ceiling of human rights expectation is reached, another level becomes visible above it. Are we going anywhere?'

In the 1950s, most emerging nations were so anxious to sign up to the modernising project that they ratified international human rights treaties in somewhat the same way that they sought to have their own airlines: as part of a general wager on modernisation. But when modernisation and state building ran into difficulties, a cultural backlash against the individualist bias of human rights language began. The Iranian Revolution of 1979 provided the focus and the leadership for this revolt.

But as the two languages – Islamic law and human rights discourse – have encountered each other in the 1980s and 1990s, a process of hybridisation has taken place. In Afghanistan, for example, women use western human rights talk to defend their right to education and health care, while insisting that they wish to be faithful to Muslim traditions in the domestic sphere. Attachment to human rights no longer needs to imply the purchase of the whole package of modernity: secularism, western dress and sexual mores, advanced technology. Hybridisation permits complex forms of accommodation between the unquestionably individualising bias of western moral discourse and the communal and family impulses of traditional society. To call the penetration of rights talk into traditional society a form of imperialism is to miss the point that these languages have become indigenous. The universal has married the local and settled down into a complex dialogue between modernity and tradition

Even in 1948, European powers were aware that their colonial writ no longer ran around the world. The Universal Declaration was not in fact dominated by Anglo-American and French rights traditions. A serious attempt was made to incorporate non-western legal and philosophical traditions; and the global influence of the Declaration in the 50 years since would be incomprehensible if rights talk was seen only as a hegemonic European discourse. In the 50 years since 1948, rights talk has become the vernacular with which individual victims of traditional society defend their claims against the claims of community. The legitimacy of human rights has become its capacity to become a moral vernacular for the demand for freedom within local cultures.

Fifty years since the Declaration, the story of human rights can be told as a story of progress: the global ratification of human rights standards; the creation of an international network of rights activists; the hybridisation of human rights values with customary norms; and, finally, the existence of more democratically elected governments nominally committed to the observance of human rights norms than at any time in history.

The same history could be understood, however, in more pessimistic terms. A cynic might say that the period from 1945 to 1948 merely set down the breviary of a conscience whose terms the behaviour of most states has flouted ever since. On such a reading of the history of the past 50 years, the so-called setbacks that human rights activists lament are not setbacks at all but the norm of human rights behaviour around the world. History is not a narrative of moral progress: we are not, strictly speaking, heading anywhere at all, or at least we are not heading in a single direction. Human rights work, on this reading, is a battle against engulfing darkness, rather than a long march towards a better future.

At every point, we can tell one of two stories. Yes, there is an International Tribunal at The Hague and at Arusha. But no, they have not managed to indict the major perpetrators of crimes against humanity or to break the cycle of impunity that prevents either the former Yugoslavia or Rwanda from freeing themselves of their genocidal past. Yes, there is more explicit human rights protection for women and children than ever before. But no, it has not stopped abuse and degradation. Indeed, human rights activity is driven by the logic of insatiability:

the more that is accomplished, the more there remains to be done. New statutes and campaigns render visible abuses which were previously undefined, unreported or unknown. Every time a ceiling of human rights expectation is reached, another level becomes visible above it. Are we going anywhere? Or are we engaged in a labour of Sisyphus?

The most we can say is that rights talk has legitimised individual selfhood and authenticated every form of discontent with injustice, ascribed and inherited status. Rights language has been central not simply to the protection, but also to the production of modern individuals. There are many ways – western and non-western, secular and religious – to become an individual, but the desire to be one on one's own terms is a universal aspiration. To the degree that it has helped to legitimise and empower that aspiration, human rights has allied itself with a need shared by several billion of our fellow creatures.

We cannot be certain that the role of human rights language in the production of modern individuality is a good thing. What the history of human rights, after the Holocaust, demonstrates is that human rights activism must sustain itself without the sunny metaphysical optimism that History once provided the men and women of Victorian times. We do not know where the story is headed: we do not know whether human rights language is here to stay or whether we will look back on it one day, as we do the vanished minority rights treaties of the League of Nations, as a monument to our illusions.

But it can hardly be said that the Universal Declaration arose because we wished to tell ourselves agreeable fables. Human rights arose in the post-war era not as an attempt to deny the reality of human aggression or to sing us a moral lullaby about our better natures. Human rights arose because we saw Dr Pannwitz's gaze and in that gaze we saw who we truly were. In this sense, the Universal Declaration was built not upon trust in ourselves, but on fear, and however paradoxical it may sound to say so, we build better when we mistrust our natures than when we give way to hope. ❑

Michael Ignatieff *is a writer and broadcaster. His most recent book is* Warrior's Honour: Ethnic War and the Modern Conscience *(1998)*

WEI JING SHENG

The taste of the spider

Wei Jing Sheng, in conversation with Yang Lian, talks of politics culture and the role of China's intellectuals

Yang Lian *My sister Yang Cui is the same age as you, one of the generation on whom youthful revolutionary dreams were thrust. Her memoirs,* The Spider Eaters, *takes its title from a saying of Lu Xun (leading writer of the 1920s; died 1936) 'We should be grateful to the first person who ate crab. But equally, we should not neglect those who first dared to eat spider: thanks to them we know how poisonous they are.' You are a spider eater. How do they taste?*

Wei Jing Sheng Not good! I grew up in a home of good card carrying Party members and even ardently believed in the Communist Party myself. I adored Mao Zedong, I hoped to come through our struggle - not only to deliver China but to rescue the whole world. At that time the rhetoric was of 'Democracy' and 'Freedom' and everyone swarmed together towards progress. Who was to know that we were gorging on spider and not succulent crab. Even though it lacked a couple of legs, it took us a long time to tell them apart.

Like the spider, the Communist Party is a great swindle. Its real motivation was despotic rule - the very thing people had spent almost 200 years resisting. If we were to win our freedom, they told us, we needed a dictatorship; and in the name of this dictatorship we revived autocratic rule. Our fine ideals were appropriated, we allowed terrible things to be done in the name of our aspirations. The means had become the end. This spider is so seductive yet so vile to swallow. Once we came to our senses, we felt only nausea, most of all with ourselves. How could we

Article 19 'Everyone has the right to freedom of opinion and expression; this includes freedom to hold opinions without interference and to seek, receive and impart information and ideas through any media and regardless of frontiers'

have been so thoroughly duped?

The Communist Party is a past-master at appropriating language for its own ends. For instance, the phrase 'people's democracy': who are the 'people' for you?

For me 'people' is synonymous with 'person'. In the first instance, 'person' refers to the people we know – our family and friends extending out to ever more distant connections until the relationship is lost. The Communist Party operates in this way: beyond its family and friends, people are simply tools. Those well placed within close Party circles are treated with kindness while inferiors or outsiders are treated with great savagery. It's currently the fashion for people to write books on Mao Zedong's humane treatment of the people around him. Everyone has a human side; these views are irrelevant. There is a saying 'Even the tiger does not devour its own child'. But if the tiger identifies you as a source of food he can be extremely vicious.

Then comes the somewhat abstract notion of 'person' that carries the sense of equality. In fact, this is a sham philosophy since each person is nothing more that part of an undifferentiated and idealised mass. This does nothing to further democracy. So many fearful things founded on this empty concept were done during the Cultural Revolution. The Chinese have struggled for democracy for 100 years, but the true nature of humanity, the individual person, has been overlooked.

It was only bitter experience, recalled in tranquility long after events, that taught us that though we may wish people to be perfect, in reality we must acknowledge their imperfection; recognising that people are capable of terrible crimes, fail to live up to our expectations. Even so, they remain human and deserve rights and dignity. Democracy is fought for real people with all their failings. We differ from the Communist Party in recognizing that when we fail to guarantee another person's human rights we undermine our own rights in the process.

How does this relate to events in modern China?

The killers in Tiananmen Square were soldiers. They could only do what they did because they failed to recognise that in suppressing the rights of others they were also destroying their own. More people recognise this today, including many in the army. The situation has changed: the army doesn't want to be simply a tool of political power, new social classes have emerged. The rulers will have to give way a little.

The path towards better government for ourselves and our descendants is long and arduous. There are no shortcuts to democratic rights: a neat coup d'état or an uprising may appear to be a quick fix but who will ensure the new system? In any case, this has been tried in China many times without success. The longer we leave it the higher the price we shall pay. The time to strive is now.

Power is sliced up from the top down to the humblest doorman or Neighbourhood Committee; everyone takes a slice no matter how small. The 'people' share in power and are corrupted by it. The Party has ensured that power is the only value recognised by society. Rulers and ruled share the same ethos. Even if the roles were reversed, nothing else would change. This is the fundamental problem 'democracy' faces in China.

China's ancient rulers discovered that violence alone is not enough to achieve submission. There needs to be a culture that allows as many people as possible to participate in it. They created a culture that had a monopoly on employment and used it to control society by controlling its means of livelihood. The culture and the political system were intimately intertwined. We have to rid people's minds of this idea before we can build democracy.

We have the right to a decent life and to political, economic and cultural rights. Chinese people today are completely different from the charac-

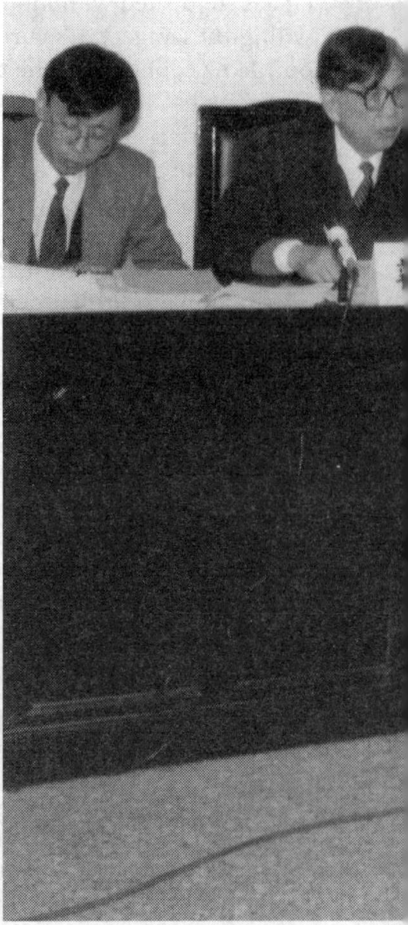

Wei Jing Sheng being sentenced to 14 years, 1995, Beijing – Credit: Agence Chine/SIPA/Rex

ters in old romances and fiction. The gap between their thinking and that of many overseas Chinese is even greater. Overseas Chinese live in democracies but retain their traditional way of thinking as part of their precious links with the homeland. But within China expectations have changed: even an illiterate peasant understands that he should not be set upon by the village head, should not have his food confiscated. This kind of expectation can form the real foundation of democracy in China.

When the Communist Party seized power it offered substantial promises as

well fine slogans - 'Down with the landlord', 'Distribute the land' and so on. What promises could a democratic China offer?

No grand promises: simply the rule of law and the acceptance of personal – not collective,– responsibility. We were fooled because we were greedy and the dictatorship took advantage of our greed saying, support us and we will distribute the riches of the wealthy among you. The poor consented and the rich were deprived of their wealth and of their rights. But the rights of the poor were appropriated in turn. The Chinese people have been had many times: now the government is trying it on with western governments who are perfectly prepared to go along with it. Although democratic societies are not paved with gold, they offer fair competition, the chance to strike out and make a life for yourself. The law exists to defend people against encroachments on their rights; every individual pays for this by accepting personal responsibility.

Has your life-long struggle for human rights in China been worthwhile?

Western journalists repeatedly ask me if I ever regretted my actions while I was in prison. They have been brought up in democratic societies; in China our only experience is thousands of years of authoritarian rule and we have no choice but to take this path despite the cold hearted cynicism and brutal methods of the authorities.

In 1989, everyone saw they were prepared to kill the people. If one tool is not doing the job it must be thrown out, like replacing an old pair of pliers or a wrench. I knew from the outset that we would have to pay a very high price; I've always been quite clear about this. I don't feel hard done by or wronged. Oppressors will always suppress dissent.

Political authority still poses a threat, but the market is a great enticement. Aren't your chances of success limited?

The chances were even slimmer in 1979 than now. Most people didn't agree with us; the Democracy Wall was just a novelty that satisfied people's curiosity. Yet even then we had confidence. So many countries had achieved democracy and freedom, why not China? If people are unwilling to pay the price, we ourselves become the price. And we will continue to pay, generation after generation.

This issue goes beyond toppling the Communist Party. It is more a question of whether traditional Chinese culture can be transformed into a modern society. Communism itself is only one of many twentieth century experiments aimed at achieving this. But again and again, the conflict over political ideas became nothing more than a naked struggle for power fought over the bodies of its victims. As China's, maybe the world's most famous 'prisoner of conscience', how do you see the relationship between power and ideology?

The need to change people's way of thinking is at the heart of our struggle for democracy. So far, we haven't achieved this. The Communist Party keeps tight control of culture. The 'Yan'an Forum on Art and Literature', 'the Cultural Revolution', 'the Anti Spiritual Pollution Campaign', even Liu Shaoqi's outrageous doctrine of 'the docile tool': all these 'cultural' movements set out to brainwash. They were not without success. The entire value system of the Chinese people was affected. Our traditional notion of virtue has been destroyed; the virtues of modern western civilisation have not been established. We live in a state of 'no thought', a moral and intellectual vacuum.

One of the worst legacies of the Communist Party is that even the opposition has inherited its language and obsession with power.Its ideas may be different but the nature of power will not change.

Purging the legacy of their cultural control is hard. Every one of us is a slave to it. We have yet to learn to think for ourselves, draw our own conclusions. Why did so many intellectuals of an earlier generation jump on the Communist Party bandwagon? Whenever they had a choice, instead of defending the rights of the people, they sprang to the defence of the Party. This is what I mean by 'intellectual dependency'. Without even being aware of it they do the ruler's thinking for him. They tell him how he might govern better, but never get down to saying 'now this is what *we* want'.

That kind of dependent thinking is deeply engrained in our intellectual tradition. If it is not transformed, our intellectuals and thinkers will never take on a leading role.

If China is to be transformed it must create a culture that puts the individual

at the centre of its value system. Can it do this?

Chinese tradition is not monolithic: there are figures like Confucius, Mencius, and free-thinkers such as the Daoist Zhuang Zi are central to it. If Chinese culture were purely slavish and offered no space for expression or for the development of personal freedom then it could not possibly have survived so long. But the Communist Party has introduced a system that offers no personal freedom. We have no choice but to fight for a free and democratic system: to take the best of traditional Chinese culture and combine it with the positive elements of western culture to create a vibrant new culture.

What is Communist Party culture?

An ugly and hateful culture that has eliminated the finer elements of traditional culture and absorbed the worst of western culture – those elements that even the West rejects.

Choice has become part of everyday experience. in 90s China. The popularity of business life, shares trading and the stock exchange show that at one level new and genuinely interesting things are happening in China. Yet spiritually, intellectually, its culture remains impoverished. What sort of contribution can Chinese intellectuals make to changing this ?

Western thinkers push society forward, continuously develop their thinking; they contribute to the creation of the enviable social system they have today. But Chinese intellectuals are not exempt from the intellectual dependency we talked about earlier. As Han Wudi [Emperor Wu of the Han dynasty] put it over 2,000 years ago, 'I have caught all the able men under heaven in my net'. The Communist Party has done the same: if you want a living, come into the fold, serve the Party. Intellectuals had little choice but to submit; they never played an important part in the democracy process.

Is there, then, no hope for our intellectuals?

China's intellectuals fall into three groups. First and worst, there are those who are at the beck and call of the Party and fall in with its every wish.

Then there is a new generation, independent and able, mainly young but also to be found in increasing numbers among the middle-aged intellectual community. They have been educated and, while not all can be called 'intellectuals', even workers peasants and those who are now in business have acquired a level of independence and can think for themselves. Their numbers are growing and they may prove to be important in China's future.

Finally there is a group that sits somewhere between these two. While their thinking remains tied to the government line, they can, when their interests are threatened, strike out on their own account. There's not much the government can do about this and we should encourage it. If these people can swell the ranks of the independent thinkers and the democracy factions there is hope for China yet.

Will you continue to publicise the true taste of the spider?

Of course. Not everyone has taken it on board yet. How do we bring about changes in political rights? From inside as well as outside the country. I spent long dark years in prison but I never acknowledged their right to curtail my freedom of speech. By standing firm for years, I won small victories: they allowed me to have some books and newspapers. Even as an insignificant political prisoner, in a small way I achieved something. We Chinese people need to hold on to our demands, keep up our pressure on the government. At some point, even the Communist Party will have to concede some ground.

And we must keep up the pressure on the international front. That's my job now. In the past, we've neglected this and have lost out. Western countries are making public overtures to the Communist Party. This is partly because their governments are shameless, but mainly because we don't make much effort to speak out, either because we're afraid or because we expect others to do it for us.

We should look after our own needs, maintain our independence in the face of everyone whether they agree with us or not. ❑

***Wei Jing Sheng**, who was released from prison in China last November on the grounds of ill health, now lives in the USA.* ***Yang Lian**, a poet, has lived in the UK since 1996*

Article 23 'Everyone has the right to work, to free choice of employment, to just and favourable conditions of work and to protection against unemployment.'

VIVIENNE WALT

Down Mexico way

As the women of Tijuana have discovered, the much lauded North American Free Trade Agreement operates one law for the north and quite another south of the border

Driving from San Diego to Tijuana these days is as good a measure of the end of the millennium as you can hope to take on this planet. From the lush breeziness of southern California's beach towns, with their cappuccino bars and designer malls, you zigzag through the US Border Patrol's barrier system – an obstacle course designed to prevent high-speed car chases – and straight into the cacophony of Tijuana, one of Mexico's most sprawling cities.

Dividing the two worlds, a tall, concrete barrier is rammed into the earth, stretching into the horizon. Tiny portholes here and there provide Mexicans with a peek into the promise beyond. The structure looks as impenetrable as the Berlin Wall probably did in early 1989. And like that one, its unbreachable facade is increasingly an illusion.

It's just a short ride across Tijuana to the trailer home of Ana Luisa Armenta, who works the night shift at the Panasonic speaker factory on the hill above her rickety abode. Like most women in this city, she's barely heard of the North American Free Trade Agreement, even though the 1992 trade pact with the United States and Canada has helped to transform Tijuana into a magnet for foreign companies. But late last year, one issue in Armenta's life suddenly collided head-on with NAFTA's officials: her job depends on proving she's not pregnant.

It's not hard to see the attractions of Tijuana. Corporations like RCA, Matsushita, Sanyo and Zenith, whose factories line the newly built roads around the city, find an abundant supply of Mexican women, generous tax benefits under NAFTA and, best of all perhaps, labour conditions that are almost unheard of just a few miles north of here.

For years, attorneys and human-rights groups have claimed that the 2,700 or so border factories screen out pregnant applicants and that many women who fall pregnant on the job are coerced into resigning, a violation of America's labour laws, as well as NAFTA's own anti-discrimination clauses. No-one seems able to agree on whether it violates Mexican law. Under the law, companies are required to give generous maternity benefits to anyone who's worked there for less than seven months; after that, government benefits kick in. In interviews, several American corporate officials defended their practice of screening out pregnant women, saying, in the words of a General Motors official, 'It's perfectly common and legal.'

Yet early last winter Mexican women crossed the border to Brownsville, Texas, to testify at a US government hearing on the issue. Those who'd fallen pregnant on the job recounted how they'd been switched to heavy-duty manual tasks, inevitably forcing them out. Others had simply been asked to leave. Four years into NAFTA, the hearing was a first: an attempt to tackle the criticisms against the free-trade agreements by dealing with human-rights violations. 'Women depend on these jobs,' says Irasema Garza, secretary of the US National Administrative Office in Washington which was set up under NAFTA to hear complaints from across the border. 'If they're being excluded from work, it's fairly egregious.'

Garza's little-known office has heard only seven cases since 1994; all the other hearings have concerned the right of Mexican workers to form independent unions. But as Bill Clinton tries to persuade Congress to broaden free trade into Latin America, long-held practices like pregnancy discrimination have become key issues in the political fight. The Democratic representatives managed to scuttle Clinton's plan last year. 'The Mexican government neither has the funding nor the will to enforce laws that are on their books,' says one Congressional staffer. Their strategy now is to show companies operating across the border in a way unacceptable to many Americans. 'All these companies are getting away with doing things they'd never get away with here,' says LaShawn Jefferson of Human Rights Watch in Washington, who's twice released reports showing widespread discrimination against women in the border factories. 'They'd never be able to defend it at a shareholders' meeting.'

Despite that, the practice is so common south of the border that no one seriously thinks to question it. Armenta, who at 25 would already be an older mother around here, has taken pregnancy tests at every job she's held. 'If you're pregnant, you just don't think of applying,' she says. Outside the factories at dusk, when the shifts change, hundreds of women pour in and out of the doors. Among them, few thought the issue worth fighting hard for: it was a fact of life they'd long lived with. And in the scheme of things, there are more serious issues.

Up against the border wall, Dulce Guttierez Rodriguez stands in the crisp sunlight, and tells of one of those more dire matters. About a year ago, when she was 13, she began to work the night shift at a Korean-run factory that makes power switches for General Electric washing machines. Around her fourteenth birthday, her boss began calling her into his office, closing the door and demanding sex from her. Incredibly, Dulce, a petite girl with long hair, in blue jeans and sneakers, finally tired of battling his advances, and went to a labour support organization in Tijuana who helped her bring criminal charges against him.

For the labour group here, her story was hardly new. Two years before, women working in the Tijuana plant of National O-Ring, a Southern California company, won an out-of-court settlement against the company after charging that the local managers were requiring the women to parade before them in swimsuits.

After 20 years of refusing work to pregnant women, General Motors last year put out an advisory to its Mexican managers, asking them to stop administering pregnancy tests. 'We decided it was the right thing to do,' says one official, 'and we hope other companies will do the same.'

But that might be some time coming. Zenith, Panasonic and Thomson Consumer Electronics officials all say they reject pregnant applicants mostly because their competitors do too. And as of April this year, officials at General Motors' plants in Mexico were quietly ignoring the directive from El Norte to stop the practice.

As a measure of how difficult it might be to change the practice, Garza's office heard the women's stories in Brownsville, then requested a meeting to discuss the issue with top Mexican government officials. Four months later, the meeting had still not taken place. The case of those in Washington arguing against new free-trade agreements may now be stronger. ❑

***Vivienne Walt** is a contributing editor to* US News & World Report, *based in Los Angeles, and a member of* Index*'s US committee*

CARLOS FUENTES

Unjust land

Juan Zamora had a nightmare, and when he woke up to find that what he'd dreamed was real, he went to the border and now he's here standing among the demonstrators. But Juan Zamora doesn't raise his fists or spread his arms in a cross. In one hand he carries a doctor's bag. And under each arm, two boxes of medicine.

He dreamed about the border and saw it as an enormous bloody wound, a sick body, mute in the face of its ills, on the point of shouting, torn by its loyalties, and beaten, finally, by political callousness, demagoguery, and corruption. What was the name of the border sickness? Dr. Juan Zamora didn't know and for that reason he was here, to relieve the pain, to give back to the United States the fruits of his studies at Cornell, of the scholarship Don Leonard Barroso got for him fourteen years earlier, when Juan was a boy and lived through some sad loves...

On his white shirt, Juan wears a pin, the number 187 canceled by a diagonal line that annuls the proposition approved in California, denying Mexican immigrants education and health benefits. Juan Zamora had arranged an invitation to a Los Angeles hospital and had seen that Mexicans no longer went there for care. He visited Mexican neighborhoods. People were scared to death. If they went to the hospital – they told him – they would be reported and turned over to the police. Juan told them it wasn't true, that the hospital authorities were human, they wouldn't report anyone. But the fear was unbearable. The illnesses too. One case here, another there, an infection, pneumonia, badly treated, fatal. Fear killed more than any virus.

Parents stopped sending their children to school. A child of Mexican origin is easily identified. What are we going to do? the parents asked. We pay more, much, much more in taxes than what they give us in education and services. What are we going to do? Why are they accusing us? What are they accusing us of? We're working. We're here because they need us. The gringos need us. If they didn't, we wouldn't come.

Standing opposite the bridge from Juárez to El Paso, Juan Zamora remembers with a grimace of distaste the time he lived at Cornell. He doesn't want his personal sorrows to interfere with his judgement about what he saw and understood then about the hypocrisy and arrogance that can come over the good people of the United States. Juan Zamora learned not to complain. Silently, Juan Zamora learned to act. He does not ask permission in Mexico to attend to urgent cases, he leaps over bureaucratic obstacles, understands social security to be a public service, will not abandon those with AIDS, drug addicts, drunks, the entire dark and foamy tide the city deposits on its banks of garbage.

"Who do you think you are? Florence Nightingale?"

The jokes about his profession and his homosexuality stopped bothering Juan a long time ago. He knew the world, knew his world, was going to distinguish between the superficial – he's a fag, he's a sawbones – and the necessary – giving some relief to the heroin addict, convincing the family of the AIDS victim to let him die at home, hell, even having a mescal with the drunk...

Now he felt his place was here. If the U.S. authorities were denying medical services to Mexican workers, he, Florence Nightingale, would become a walking hospital, going from house to house, from field to field, from Texas to Arizona, from Arizona to California, from California to Oregon, agitating, dispensing medicines, writing prescriptions, encouraging the sick, denouncing the inhumanity of the authorities.

"How long do you plan to visit the United States?"

"I have a permanent visa until the year 2010."

"You can't work. Do you know that?"

"Can I cure?"

"What?"

"Cure, cure the sick."

"No need to. We've got hospitals."

"Well, they're going to fill up with illegals."

"They should go back to Mexico. Cure them there."

"They're going to be incurable, here or there. But they're working here with you."

"It's very expensive for us to take care of them."

"Its going to be more expensive to take care of epidemics if you don't prevent diseases."

"You can't charge for your services. Did you know that?"

Juan Zamora just smiled and crossed the border.

Now, on the other side, he felt for an instant he was in another world. He was overwhelmed by a sensation of vertigo. Where would he begin? Whom would he see? The truth is he didn't think they'd let him in. It was too easy. He didn't expect things to go that well. Something bad was going to happen. He was on the gringo side with his bag and his medicines. He heard a squeal of tires, repeated shots, broken glass, metal being pierced by bullets, the impact, the roar, the shout: "Doctor! Doctor!"

the gringos came (who are they, who are they, for God's sake, how can they exist, who invented them?

they came drop by drop,

they came to the uninhabited, forgotten, unjust land the Spanish monarchy and now the Mexican republic over-looked,

isolated, unjust land, where the Mexican governor had two million sheep attended by twenty-seven hundred workers and where the pure gold of the mines of the Real de Dolores never returned to the hands of those who first touched that precious metal,

where the war between royalists and insurgents weakened the Hispanic presence,

and then the constant war of Mexicans against Mexicans, the anguished passage from an absolutist monarchy to a democratic federal republic:

let the gringos come, they too are independent and democratic,

let them enter, even illegally, crossing the Sabinas River, wetting their backs, sending the border to hell, says another energetic young man, thin, small, disciplined, introspective, honourable, calm, judicious, who knows how to play the flute: exactly the opposite of a Spanish hidalgo

his name is Austin, he brings the first colonists to the Río Grande, the Colorado, and the Brazos, they are the old three hundred, the founders of gringo texanity, five hundred more follow them, they unleash the Texas fever, all of them want land, property, guarantees, and they want freedom, protestantism, due process of law, juries of their peers,

but Mexico offers them tyranny, catholicism, judicial arbitrariness

they want slaves, the right to private property,

but Mexico abolished slavery, assaulting private property, they want the individual to be able to do whatever the hell he wants

Mexico, even though it no longer has it, believes in the Spanish authoritarian state, which acts unilaterally for the good of all

now there are thirty thousand colonists of US origin in the río grande, río bravo, and only about four thousand Mexicans,

conflict is inevitable: "Mexico must occupy Texas right now, or it will lose it forever," says Mier y Terán,

Desperate, Mexico seeks European immigrants,

but nothing can stop the Texas fever,

a thousand families a month come down from the Mississippi, why should these cowardly, lazy, filthy Mexicans govern us? this cannot be God's plan!

the pyrrhic victory at the Alamo, the massacre at Goliad:

Santa Anna is not Gálvez, he prefers a bad war to a bad peace,

here are the two face-to-face at San Jacinto:

Houston, almost six feet tall, wearing a coonskin cap, a leopard vest, patiently whittling any stick he finds nearby,

Santa Anna wearing epaulets and a three-cornered hat, sleeping his siesta in San Jacinto while Mexico loses Texas: what Houston is really carving is the future wooden leg of the picturesque, frivolous, incompetent Mexican dictator,

"Poor Mexico, so far from God and so close to the United States," another dictator would famously say one day, and in a lower voice, another president: "Between the United States and Mexico, the desert" ❑

From The Crystal Frontier *by* ***Carlos Fuentes*** *published in May by Bloomsbury.*

Apologies: who's sorry now?

The fashion for 'apologies' is growing. For the offenders they draw a line under the past. But reparations are seldom discussed

1988 USA The Civil Liberties Act 'apologises on behalf of the people of the United States' for the internment of Japanese-Americans during World War II

1993 USA Public Law 103-150 'To acknowledge the 100th anniversary of the January 17, 1893 of the Kingdom of Hawaii, and to offer an apology to Native Hawaiians on behalf of the United States for the overthrow of the Kingdom of Hawaii'.

1995 Switzerland The International Red Cross apologises for the agency's 'moral failure' in not openly denouncing the atrocities committed against the Jews during World War II. 'We have taken another look at our own share of the responsibility for the almost complete failure by a culture, indeed a civilisation, to prevent the systematic genocide of an entire people and of certain minority groups'.

1995 Japan In June, the Japanese parliament passes a resolution intended to atone for the atrocities committed by the country in World War II. Prime Minister Tomiichi Murayama says: 'I would like to say that Japan is deeply remorseful for its past and strives for world peace'. In July, the government apologises to the 200,000 'comfort women' (*Index* 3/1995) forced into military-run brothels during WWII and starts a compensation fund as 'an expression of atonement on the part of the people of Japan to these women'.

1996 Germany/Czech Republic German officials apologise for the invasion of Czechoslovakia in 1938 and establish a fund for the reparation of Czech victims of Nazi abuses: 'The German side is aware of the fact that the National Socialist violence against the Czech people helped to create the basis for the post-war...expulsion and forced resettlement [of ethnic Germans living in Sudetenland]'. The Czech Republic apologises for the expulsion of the Sudeten Germans in 1945-46. 'The Czech side is sorry that by the post-war expulsion, as well as by the forced resettlement of Sudeten Germans from then Czechoslovakia, by expropriating and revoking citizenship, much suffering and injustice was caused to innocent people'.

1997 USA President Bill Clinton issues an official apology to the survivors of a government experiment that infected 399 black men with syphilis without their knowledge. The While House spokesperson says: 'The President feels we have a moral obligation'.

1997 Ireland The Christian Brothers apologise for the cruelty and sexual abuse suffered by students in their schools over many years. 'Children and their families have been hurt and betrayed by abusive behaviour...'.

1997 France The French Catholic bishops apologise for their complicity in the Holocaust at the site of the Drancy transit camp from which many Jews were sent to Auschwitz. They say the French Church displayed 'a narrow vision of its mission,' and its leaders were guilty of 'loyalism and docility far beyond traditional obedience' to the Vichy regime.

1998 Canada 'As a Country we are burdened by past actions that resulted in weakening the identity of Aboriginal people, suppressing their languages and cultures, and outlawing their spiritual practices. The Government of Canada today formally expresses to all Aboriginal people in Canada our profound regret for past actions...'.

1998 Japan Ryutaro Hashimoto, Japanese Prime Minister, offers his 'heartfelt apology' to the UK government and expresses 'deep remorse' for Japan's treatment of POWs in WWII.

1998 Australia The Anglican Church apologises for its participation in the policy of forcibly removing aboriginal children from their mothers: 'I suggest that to Aboriginal people an apology carries a weight that many white Australians have scarcely begun to understand'.

1998 The Vatican apologises for its silence and inaction in defence of the Jews during WWII, but stops short of criticising Pope Pius XII. 'This is more than an apology...this is an act of repentance...since as members of the Church we are linked to the sins as well as to the merits of all her children'.

1998 USA President Clinton on the 1994 genocide in Rwanda: 'The international community, together with nations in Africa, must bear its share of responsibility for this tragedy as well. We did not act quickly enough after the killing began. We should not have allowed the refugee camps to become safe havens for killers'. In Uganda on the slave trade: 'The United States has not always done the right thing by Africa...European Americans received the fruits of the slave trade and we were wrong in that'. ❑

Compiled by ***Emily Mitchell***

Article 26 'Education shall be directed to the full development of the human personality and to the strengthening of respect for human rights and fundamental freedoms'

SABUROU IENAGA

Turning the page

Japan's refusal to admit to the atrocities committed by its troops in World War II still undermines its standing in Asia and the world. Recently retired from a long-running campaign for greater academic openess, Professor Ienaga explains his personal mission to bring the grisly germ experiments of Unit 731 into the light of day. His barrister Kinju Morikawa explains why the fight must still go on.

I have been struggling to stop the school textbook authorisation system for more than three decades. I didn't start this litigation by being concerned about whether I could win or lose. That was not my first objective. If I had finished with the first ruling on my first lawsuit given by the Supreme Court in 1993, it would have left me with a unacceptable feeling. So, even if it was not my original intention, I feel very happy to have come up to this point where the Supreme Court said the Ministry had gone too far in ordering deletion, because the atrocities of Unit 731 have now been established beyond question.

I received many letters from Japan and abroad, and more than 150 foreign media covered the ruling. It attracted far more attention than my other two lawsuits, especially from Asian countries. It was also a success. The court ruled that the government had abused its administrative powers. I had often been intimidated by ultra-rightists in the past, but this time no threats were made, except for one anonymous postcard.

When I first filed a lawsuit in 1965, I was of the opinion that the screening system itself violated the Constitution of Japan and the Fundamental Law of Education. So I appealed in my message: 'Confronted with the reality of the process of screening to trample down the spirit of the Constitution of Japan and the Fundamental Law of Education, I, who went through those two decades of traumatic experiences, just cannot overlook this.'

In 1970, in my second lawsuit, the Tokyo District Court ruled that screening, if it interferes with the content of textbooks, constitutes censorship and consequently is unconstitutional and illegal. Though this decision was later overturned, I believe that, having once made such remarkable decision, the court retains a precious spiritual and cultural heritage.

After the landslide victory of the Liberal Democratic Party in 1980, some scholars and LDP members started criticising textbooks as biased, which invited severe foreign and domestic criticism. As a result, the Ministry of Education finally came to approve the description of 'aggression' of the Japanese Imperial army in Asia.

In those days I already had two lawsuits pending and it felt a little hard to file yet another, but the members of my counsel were eager to do so. And I think it was important because of the potential for results, having had the first case getting the worst final ruling and the second case turned away at the gate of the courts. My basic motive is that I have always felt morally responsible for having abstained from expressing my view that I am against war. To avoid repeating my regrets, I determined to resist against illegal interference by the government.

In summer 1997, the Supreme Court ruled that the screening conducted by the government on my descriptions of Unit 731 in China and the Nanking Massacre were illegal. It was a partial victory. But I am especially pleased that, on 22 April 1998, Yokohama District Court also ordered the Ministry of Education to pay damages of ¥200,000 to Professor Nobuyoshi Takashima who had been forced to integrate changes to his textbook under the revamped authorisation system. It made it abundantly clear that the screening system still has fatal flaws.

Professor Takashima is the second person after me to file a suit over the textbook censorship system. I hope that more and more people will start appealing to the government to eliminate this unconstitutional system. ❑

Saburou Ienaga *is professor emeritus at Tokyo University of Education. Translation by Katsutoshi Namimoto.*

DESCRIPTION IN PROFESSOR IENAGA'S MANUSCRIPT:

'A unit specialising in bacteriological warfare called the 731st Unit was stationed on the outskirts of Harbin and, until the Soviet Union entered the war, it engaged in such atrocious acts as murdering several thousand Chinese and other non-Japanese in biological experiments.'

Screening examiner's comment Delete entire passage. No credible scholarly research exists concerning Unit 731. It is premature, therefore, to takeup this matter in a school textbook.

Professor Ienaga's argument The historical facts concerning Unit 731 have been corroborated by innumerable records and documents. By demanding the deletion of this passage, the government is trying to conceal in academic studies the truth about its forerunner's criminal activities.

Outcome The textbook was approved after all references to Unit 731 were deleted.

DESCRIPTION IN PROFESSOR IENAGA'S MANUSCRIPT:

'When the Japanese Army occupied Nanking, they murdered large numbers of Chinese soldiers and civilians and many of the Japanese officers and soldiers violated Chinese women.This incident came to be known as the Nanking Massacre.'

Screening examiner's comment 'Delete the passage referring to rape by Japanese troops. As it is common throughout the world for troops to rape women during war, it is not appropriate to refer only to the acts of the Japanese Army. Too much emphasis is placed on specific incidents.'

Professor Ienaga's assertion 'The nature of war and the character of the Japanese Army were reflected in acts of rape by the Japanese Army. The study of such incidents will help students understand more profoundly the intrinsic nature of wars and armies.' ❑

When Professor Ienaga filed his suit in 1965 against the Minister of Education over the constitutional legality of censoring school textbooks, I was head of his counsel. The lawsuit, composed of three separate cases, was fought for 32 years and the Supreme Court's decision, given in August 1997, ended this long legal battle.

The most controversial point in the case was whether screening school textbooks infringed the freedom of speech guaranteed under Article 21 of the Japanese Constitution and Article 19 of the Universal Declaration of Human Rights. Article 21 guarantees freedom of speech, prohibits censorship and forbids bugging, or any other violation of means of communication.

In no other developed country can such a system be found as in Japan, where the Ministry of Education screens the contents of all textbooks used in primary, junior and senior high schools and forces authors to delete or revise the content if it is deemed 'inappropriate'. Several years ago, I visited the UN in Geneva and asked if any country had ever brought the screening issue to the attention of the Human Rights Committee. I was told that the only reference had been in a Japanese context in 1982.

Then the Ministry of Education had repeatedly insisted on the replacement of 'aggression' by the words 'military advance', saying that the term had 'negative ethical connotations'. As a consequence, Japan was severely criticised by Asian countries, especially by China. One of Ienaga's lawsuits had arisen out of the Ministry's order to delete references to the army's rape of Chinese women during World War II.

Professor Ienaga claimed that the textbook authorisation system violated Article 19 of the UDHR. In documents submitted to the Supreme Court in July 1997, the Ministry responded that the right to freedom of expression was suspended when it violated 'the rights or reputations of others' or endangered 'national security, public order or public health or morals'. The concept of 'public welfare' is also enshrined in the Constitution, which provides for restrictions of freedom of speech 'within the limits of the reasonable and the bare minimum' if it is endangered.

The Ministry further argued that since pupils under18 are not 'capable of criticising the contents' of their classes, equal opportunity of education is required and the education must be 'fitted' to the development of every pupil. For these reasons, it claimed, textbook authorisation was essential. And since screening protected the rights or reputations of others and was attentive to the needs of 'public order', it could not be said to infringe either Articles 19 or 24.

On 29 August 1997, the Supreme Court ruled that the screening of Ienaga's textbook did not indeed constitute censorship, which is prescribed by the Constitution, because it does not prohibit the book from being published commercially. The court found that freedom of speech is restricted by the 'public welfare' to the extent of the reasonable and necessary limit.

We think that these views, maintained by the Japanese government and Supreme Court, violate both the Constitution and the UNDHR and are similar to the ones which controlled people's minds before the Second World War. That is why we intend to file our case with the UN Human Rights Committee. ❑

***Kinju Morikawa**, a barrister, was president of Japan's Civil Liberties Union from 1947 to 1962. Translation by Katsutoshi Namimoto.*

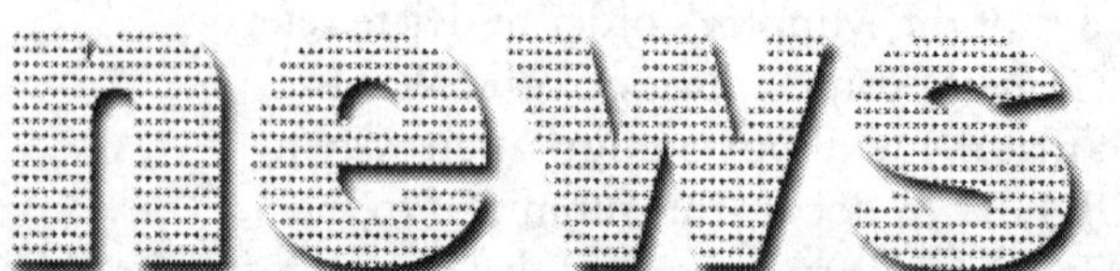

BELARUS

Critics panned

Vera Rich

Aleksi Shidlovsky, a 19-year-old student at State University in Minsk, and schoolboy Vadzim Labkovich, 16, were sentenced in late March to 18 months' imprisonment for writing 'anti-presidential' graffiti on city monuments. The state prosecutor accused the youths of hooliganism with 'special insolence and extreme cynicism'.

Labkovich's sentence was suspended for two years, subject to 'good behaviour'. He is unlikely to comply with this condition. 'If we don't get involved in politics in this country,' he explained,' they will simply lock everyone up!'

The graffiti were, for the most part, unexceptionable slogans such as 'Long live Belarus' and 'Belarus! Land of our fathers'. Only one could be deemed scurrilous: a crude couplet which translates roughly as: 'Let Belarus to Europe make its way/Flush Lukashenka down the pan straightaway!'

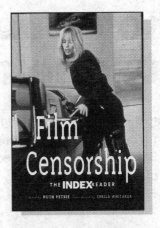

ISMAÏL KADARE

Who owns the battlefield?

History in the Balkans is a commodity used and traded by all sides in furtherance of competing claims. The fourteenth century Battle of Kosovo has become central to Serbia's present claims to Kosovo

The great crimes of humanity are always backed by a great lie. Politicians, diplomats, historians and writers rush en masse to the support of the murderers. They provide a backup force that often first incites people to crime and then justifies it.

The drama that is being played out in Kosovo today is a typical illustration of this phenomenon. It is a tragedy long foretold, fostered and exacerbated by the chauvinism of this backup force. Without their support, things could not happen the way they do.

Earlier this year, television screens around the world showed the long line of 70 covered corpses lain out on the ground in a Kosovan village. The Serbian government claimed these were the bodies of slain 'terrorists'. Yet journalists on the spot admitted that the dead included over 30 women and children. Given their monstrous lie, how does the Serbian government succeed in retaining the slightest credibility?

A massacre has been carried out in Kosovo before our eyes: savage, mediaeval, intolerable. The murder of a whole family, 11 of them: parents, children and those as yet unborn. The crime symbolised the destruction of one ethnic group by its rival and revolted world opinion.

But what is truly staggering is that even after the massacre, voices here and there were still ready to attempt a convoluted 'explanation' of what had happened by 'putting it in its historical, nostalgic context, and looking at it from an Orthodox point of view'. In other words, there were still people anxious to justify these acts of barbarism in whatever way they could.

In pursuit of this, defenders of the crime have recourse to myths and legends stemming from a remote historical past. Any discussion on Kosovo today begins with the cliché: 'sacred territory for the Serbs'; 'the cradle of the Serb nation'; 'the Battle of Kosovo in 1389...'.

In brief, the core of the mythology goes as follows: at the time of the battle in 1389, the Serbs were in a majority in a region that was at the heart of their kingdom; the Albanians only came into the territory after the battle. This is a crude distortion and its effect in any public discussion of the subject on TV or elsewhere is to pre-empt any Albanian from putting across a different view or attempting some clarification of history. And this is where another cliché rears its head: there is a statute of limitations on how far back we can delve in history. In other words, we can allow the 'historical memory' and 'nostalgia' of the aggressor, but not that of the victim.

This is precisely what happened in a discussion on France's TV channel *Canal Plus* in the presence of the French foreign minister, Hubert Védrine soon after the massacre. After the usual opening cliché that 'Kosovo is the cradle of Serbia', an Albanian student, who attempted to give another version of events, was prevented from speaking. They could not allow two different approaches to the problem. It is, indeed, a pity that one has to plunge so far back in history to throw light on today's problems. But when the criminals themselves have recourse to history to justify their crime, then their distortions of history must be exposed once and for all.

On 10 March, the leading French daily *Le Monde* published a piece entitled 'A holy land for Balkan Orthodoxy' by its religious correspondent, Henri Tincq. It had a strongly pro-Orthodox bias and followed the line more or less those familiar to all Serbs: Kosovo the cradle of the Serb nation; the significance of the Battle of Kosovo; the arrival of the Albanians in Kosovo only after the battle... However, Tincq concedes one thing: he admits unequivocally that 'Albanians and Valaks were living in the Balkan peninsula before the arrival of the Slavs in the sixth century'. This is the view accepted by all serious historians and confirms that the Albanians were already there, on their land, before the arrival of the Serbs.

But this statement contradicts a later assertion by Tincq in the same article: 'with the blessing of the Turks, the Albanians spread into Serbia in the fifteenth century'. A simple question: if it is agreed that the Albanians were in Albania before the arrival of the Serbs, why would they not also be in Kosovo? Why would they have left the land that adjoins Albania empty? Why would they have waited for the Turks before establishing themselves on land that was fertile and unoccupied? One has to be more than gullible to believe that the Albanians have not, from time immemorial, been exactly where they are today.

It is in his attempt to explain the late arrival of the Albainians in Kosovo that Tincq's article becomes truly grotesque. On the one hand he claims that it was the Turks who encouraged the Albanian expansion; on the other, that 'the demographic imbalance became more marked in the twentieth century'. In other words, it was mainly in this century that the Albanians became the majority. However, by then there were no Turks around to encourage them! Tincq gives a figure of 600,000 Albanians at the outbreak of World War II and this seems reasonable. But when he claims that 'their expansion continued under Tito' he is piling insult upon injury. Because he is forced to admit that the Albanians arrived in Kosovo from somewhere, he would have us believe they came from Albania in the communist era.

I am forced to ask another question: where did these Albanians come from? Did they fall from the heavens or make their way from Albania? Tincq should have been aware that the borders of communist Albania were so tightly and cruelly sealed that at least half of the 200 or 300 people who tried to escape in Enver Hoxha's time were killed by their own countrymen, the Albanian frontier guards.

It is true that a great many Serbs have left Kosovo in recent years, but 10 times more Albanians have fled. Those in Germany, Switzerland, Belgium and the USA alone add up to more than 500,000, driven out by poverty and Serb repression.

As to the Battle of Kosovo, this central element in the Serb mythology: there are none so blind as those who will not see. In recounting their own version of events, these historians allow themselves to be blinded by distortions. The Battle of Kosovo was not a confrontation solely between Serbs and Turks. It was a battle fought by all the peoples of the Balkans united against an invader. All the histories list the names of the Balkan peoples who fought alongside one another against a

Serb monument commemorating the battle of Kosovo – Credit: Melanie Friend

common disaster. Serbs, Bosnians, Albanians and Rumanians were led by Prince Lazarus of Serbia, King Tvrko of Bosnia, Voïvode Mircea of Rumania and the Counts Balsha and Jonima of Albania. The battle, which should have been preserved in memory as a symbol of friendship between the Balkan peoples, was appropriated exclusively by criminal Serbs to serve their purposes. And became the starting point of a future crime.

The tragedy that is playing out in Kosovo presents a challenge to the conscience of many. Instead of listening to justifications of the crime, the world should put a stop to it. The falsification of history is an aberration; manipulating it to whitewash a crime is even more serious. ❑

***Ismaïl Kadare** is an Albanian writer and poet living in Paris. This article was first published in* Le Monde *on 14 March 1998*
Translated by Judith Vidal-Hall

***Correction:** In Index 2/98 we inadvertedly printed an inccorrect photo-caption on page 63, in an article about the women of Srebrenica. The person photographed is Kada Pasic, not Kada Hotic as stated. Also, the individual in the uncaptioned photograph on pages 3 and 34 is Almasa Alic.*

CHINA

Disappeared

Michael Griffin

According to official figures, there were 2,026 people in China's prisons for 'political crimes' at the end of 1996, and a further 230,000 undergoing re-education.
Despite the high-profile release of Wei Jing Sheng in November 1997, and Wang Dan in April this year, Chinese jails continue to house thousands more anonymous individuals, jailed for their opposition to the Communist Party. Human Rights in China (HRC), a US-based group run by Chinese exiles, has issued a list of 158 names from Beijing of people who are serving lengthy sentences for their participation in the 1989 pro-democracy movement.
The list was mainly compiled by Li Hai, a Beijing student, who was arrested in 1995 for making the list public and subsequently sentenced to nine years in prison.
The persons on this list,' HRC told the *International Herald Tribune* in late April, 'and the many other "nameless" individuals jailed in China in connection with the 1989 crackdown, might not be as internationally well-known, but their lives and liberty are equally important.'

EUROPAS KULTURZEITUNG
Lettre
INTERNATIONAL

WEIMAR
1999
kulturstadt europas

SHADA ISLAM

Castle perilous

In secrecy and in haste, the European Union is fortifying its borders against refugees, asylum seekers and all who seek to penetrate its defences

It was the European Union's first 'crisis' of the year. EU officials making their way home from the Christmas break in early January 1998 were greeted with near-hysterical warnings that Europe was being overrun by a 'massive influx' of illegal Kurdish immigrants.

Media reports referred to ship-loads of poverty-stricken Kurds disembarking in Italy, ready to use the country as a staging post for entry into other, richer parts of Europe. Those who bothered to take a closer look discovered there was little reason for panic: the 'enormous wave' turned out to be little more than a trickle.

A total of 3,000 Kurdish asylum-seekers did arrive in Italy by boat, fleeing persecution in Turkey and Iraq. They were received calmly enough by an Italian government that promised to grant them access to traditional asylum procedures.

The response was quite different in other parts of Europe, however. Politicians in Germany, France and Austria warned against an 'invasion' by the Kurdish 'boat people.' German interior minister Manfred Kanther fumed against the 'threatening situation' created by the Kurds, warning grimly that Germany would not and could not tolerate a 'criminal wave of immigration.' Kanther and other German officials demanded that Italy 'stamp out' the Kurdish problem or accept responsibility for the collapse of the 1995 Treaty of Schengen that promised a passport-free Europe. France and Austria reinforced the manpower on their borders with Italy.

Under pressure from its Schengen partners, Rome fell into line. National asylum laws were toughened. Previously illegal immigrants caught by the authorities were given two weeks in which to go home.

each state. Everyone has the right to leave any country, including his own, and to return to his country.' Article 14 'Everyone has the right to seek and to enjoy in other countries asylum from persecution'

The Italian Parliament quickly abolished the 15-day grace provision for refugees; 'retention centres' were hastily set up to prevent asylum-seekers whose cases were rejected from 'escaping' to other lands.

Meanwhile, EU governments, spurred by fears that Europe's long-time goal of eradicating frontier controls was under threat, worked frantically to draw up an 'Action Plan' aimed at stemming the flow of Kurds.

In the end, Schengen survived – expanded even. Italy and Austria became full members of the treaty on 29 March this year, abolishing all controls on sea and land travel with their seven Schengen neighbours (Belgium, the Netherlands, France, Germany, Spain, Luxembourg and Portugal). Frontier checks for air travel between the two new members and the rest of Schengen-land were eliminated last October. Once the EU's new Amsterdam Treaty is ratified, asylum policy will shift from the realm of inter-governmental cooperation to full Community competence and Schengen will be integrated into mainstream EU law. The secrecy presently surrounding the EU's procedures on asylum will become more transparent and open to public scrutiny.

Meanwhile, Europe's passport-free travel arrangements have been saved at a high price: the EU has violated the spirit and in many cases the letter of the Universal Declaration of Human Rights which, among other things, guarantees everyone the right to seek and enjoy asylum from prosecution in all countries. As a result, the EU's reputation as a defender of human rights, a place where the world's persecuted can find shelter and succour has been tarnished, probably permanently. EU leaders still routinely lecture their Asian, African and Latin American counterparts on the importance of protecting human rights; but their own niggardly response to the plight of the Kurds is a keen reminder that Europe's commitment to certain key tenets of the UDHR has worn dangerously thin.

Europe's reaction to the arrival of the Kurds was 'control-oriented, short-term and disproportionate to the numbers involved,' says the European Council on Refugees and Exiles (ECRE). Instead of taking up their responsibility under international law to admit asylum seekers and investigate their applications, EU governments retaliated with an arsenal of measures designed to create a fortress. The focus was on stepping up controls at Europe's external borders, intensifying police cooperation and controlling the movement of the 'illegal immigrants.' There was no attempt to help a people in need of shelter and asylum.

A closer study of the 'Action Plan on the Influx of Migrants from Iraq and the Neighbouring Region', drawn up by EU governments in the wake of the Kurdish 'crisis', reveals startling violations of the internationally recognised right of asylum as embodied in the UDHR and the 1951 Geneva Conventions. The Plan is not about protecting Kurdish refugees: it is about protecting Europe from Kurdish asylum-seekers. By referring specifically to Kurdish 'migrants' rather than asylum-seekers, the EU blueprint effectively rejects any possibility that the people in question are fleeing human rights violations and persecution in Iraq and Turkey. By utilising the term 'influx', meanwhile, governments actually end up encouraging a xenophobic reaction to the Kurdish arrivals.

'the EU has violated the spirit and in many cases the letter of the Universal Declaration of Human Rights'

Most significantly, the Plan's entire focus is on measures designed to prevent the Kurds from leaving Turkey or on forcing them to return there. Given Turkey's poor human rights record, this is hardly appropriate. As Amnesty International points out, by taking steps that directly or indirectly force people to go back to or stay in a country where they are at such risk, EU governments are in flagrant breach of the fundamental principle of 'non-refoulement' that is binding on all states both through their ratification of the Geneva Convention and as a matter of customary law. EU plans to return even non-Kurdish asylum-seekers to Turkey – because that was their first port of call before entering EU territory – are equally dangerous. Although it is a signatory to the Geneva Convention, Turkey only applies it to refugees from Europe. As a result, there is a real danger that people who come to Turkey from Iran, Afghanistan and elsewhere in the hope of eventually reaching safety in other countries in Europe, will be sent back forcibly to their countries of origin.

The Kurdish Action Plan may be particularly striking in its disregard for international asylum practice but it is only one instrument in a long line of restrictive EU moves in this area. Over the years, winning asylum in Europe has been getting much harder. Little by little, EU countries have reinforced the bricks and raised the walls of fortress Europe (*Index* 3/1994). Many of the restrictions are the result of tougher EU rules on

Safe haven

I said good-bye to my wife, Josie and my nine-month-old son, Taro, in London on 28 March 1996 and departed for the 'safe haven' in northern Iraq. I wanted to help my three brothers, Kadir, Mohamad and Kawa, escape and seek asylum in Europe. First I had to locate Iraqi passports with Turkish visas to travel into Turkey from the Kurdish region – this cost me US$2,000.

By 11 May we were in Turkey, terrified of being arrested. Kurdish refugees are always in danger of being ripped-off, imprisoned, tortured and then deported back to Saddam's Iraq. After 10 days, we got visas to Ukraine – another US$500. Flying out of Istanbul is a high risk business, but we had no choice. In Kiev we went into hiding to avoid the police. Smugglers took us across into Germany.

Asylum is an expensive business: this cost a further US$3,500 for each brother. This time we travelled by train. I went on ahead and waited. After two weeks we were reunited. My poor brothers had endured the journey across Eastern Europe – by train, minibus, lorry and taxi – only to be arrested at the border by German guards. They tried to claim asylum but were refused and deported back to the first 'safe' country – the Czech republic. There, too, they tried to claim asylum, but were given visas for only three days and told to leave before they were deported back to Iraq.

What could we do? We seemed to be stuck in an immigration loop. We decided to avoid those 'Schengen' countries, as they would not accept my brothers after their deportation from Germany. I had to pay US$1,000 for false Greek passports. If you have money there are many ways: none guarantee success.

From Amsterdam we managed to get a flight to London on 20 June 1996. My brothers claimed asylum on arrival while I waited nervously inside. Almost inevitably, they were refused. The Home Office wanted to return them to Holland even though they had tried and been refused there. They ended up in a UK prison for 10 weeks, waiting for their appeal hearing.

Finally, after many appeals, many hours in court and waiting, always waiting, my three brothers were given permission to remain and seek asylum on 2 July 1997. Even now, two years after their arrival in this country, they are waiting to hear if they will be accepted as asylum seekers and granted full political refugee status; or remain subject to Home Office policy to Kurds escaping from that western dream, the 'safe haven'. ❑

Karzan Krekar

Kurdish refugees on the French-Italian border – Credit: Jobard/Rex

migration and a desire to keep out people coming to Europe to escape poverty rather than fleeing persecution. The United Nations High Commission for Refugees has warned, however, that in its zeal to keep out false asylum seekers, the EU is denying access to genuine refugees whose lives and freedom are in danger at home.

However, the higher walls around Europe are also the direct result of its drive to create a frontier-free EU zone. The benefits of a borderless EU are meant to be enjoyed by European citizens alone. As a result, the elimination of passport controls within Europe has gone hand in hand with a range of so-called 'compensatory measures' including stepped-up controls on the EU's external frontiers, increased police cooperation and restrictions on the movement of non-EU nationals including asylum seekers. Part of the price for Schengen has been a dramatic extension of police powers to undertake 'hot pursuit' and make arrests across national frontiers. Schengen has already launched the first trans-Europe database of some 8 million names of suspected criminals, drug traffickers, terrorists and illegal immigrants. Countries in the zone are ringed with border-guards and sensors. Central European countries seeking to join the EU have been told to tighten up their own borders before they can join the club.

Both Schengen, and the Dublin Convention that entered into force in September 1997 with 12 signatories, compared with Schengen's nine, contain elements that run counter to Europe's international asylum obligations. UNHCR, Amnesty and ECRE have voiced concern that the Dublin Convention allows European governments to expel asylum seekers to so-called 'safe third countries' outside the EU, even though there is no common acceptance in international law of such a concept. EU governments are under no obligation to verify that the third country is a party to the Geneva Convention, that the refugee will be given access to proper asylum procedures or that his/her life and freedom will not be threatened.

Without such safeguards, implementing the 'safe third country' doctrine poses a serious risk to the institution of asylum and to the fundamental principle of non-refoulement.

Both Schengen and the Dublin Convention also seek to ensure that applicants for asylum are not referred successively from one member state to another. They establish a system under which only one member of the club is responsible for examining an asylum application. In theory this aims to put an end to the creation of 'refugees in orbit' where asylum seekers are shuffled from country to country. In practice, however, human rights groups have warned that since there are no EU-wide minimum standards on asylum procedures, countries can pass the responsibility for examining asylum requests to another state with weaker safeguards.

Lack of EU-wide harmonisation of asylum rules means that there is a plethora of dangerous concepts in force in many parts of Europe. For instance, some European countries have established the notion of 'safe country of origin'. Asylum seekers from such countries are not recognised as genuine refugees. In Germany, any person who has transitted through a country considered 'safe' is not given the right to asylum. He or she is sent back to that country.

Even more worrisome is an EU joint position adopted in November 1995 that gives a highly restrictive interpretation of the Geneva Convention by accepting that only those who fear persecution by a state are entitled to refugee status. This interpretation creates an anomalous situation in which someone targeted by a government can gain asylum abroad, but victims of persecution by non-state agents – rebel groups or extremist organisations – have no right to asylum. The UNHCR stresses that persecution that does not involve the state is still persecution: the Geneva Convention applies when the state is unable – as well as unwilling – to protect its nationals. Yet victims of generalised violence, civil rights and human rights abuse are often refused EU asylum on the grounds that they do not individually face a threat from the state. Austria deported 43 Bosnians in this way in 1994 in direct violation of the principle of non-refoulement.

European governments are also examining concepts like the 'internal flight alternative' under which someone who fears persecution should first try to find refuge in a safe area of his or her country. On the pretext that a more familiar cultural environment is less traumatic, asylum-seekers would be forced to remain within their country of origin.

Further, and in spite of opposition from the UNHCR and human rights agencies, a protocol suppressing the right of EU nationals to seek shelter and asylum in another EU state has been annexed to the Treaty of Amsterdam. The Geneva Conventions guarantee unqualified access to asylum; as long as the EU does not constitute a single state and accede as such to the Conventions, its member states remain individually bound by their international obligations under the Conventions. Amnesty has warned that on the eve of the EU's enlargement by up to 10 countries, this decision erodes the system of international protection for refugees and asylum seekers. By weakening the universality of the Geneva Conventions, it may encourage other countries to follow suit.

So far the EU has refused to change its ways. As far as its member governments are concerned, years of clamping down on asylum demands is proving effective. But as the UNHCR points out, it is weaving a net so tight that many legitimate refugees cannot pass through. In doing so, European governments are violating the same international covenant on human rights they insist must be respected by others. ❑

***Shada Islam** is a freelance journalist based in Brussels specialising in European issues*

SPAIN/ARGENTINA

Extra-territorial justice

Dolores Cortés

On 7 October 1997, Judge Baltasar Garzón sentenced Argentine naval officer Adolfo Scilingo to two years in prison for his role in the 'disappearance' of some 600 Spanish passport-holders during the dictatorship of 1976-83, a period in which more than 30,000 people vanished without trace. Since 1996, Garzón's highly charged enquiry has ordered the arrest of another 10 high-ranking officers, including former army chief General Eduardo Massera.

Driven by public outrage in Buenos Aires, on 9 February President Carlos Menem signed into law decree 111/98, dissolving the 1987 extradition treaty between Spain and Argentina. Under the controversial Full Stop and Due Obedience laws promulgated in 1986 and 1987, military personnel were granted retroactive immunity for acts committed during the period of dictatorship. The laws were derogated on 25 March but those most in need of protection remain immune from prosecution.

Though popular with the Spanish public, Garzón's crusade to exorcise the ghosts of Argentina's past is not without critics. Judge Eduardo Fungairiño told the Chilean newspaper Mercurio in October 1997 that 'Spain lacks the legal jurisdiction to judge what happened in Argentina and Chile'. The inquiry continues, but the jury remains out on whether its judgements can be enforced.

SUPPORT FOR INDEX

Index on Censorship and the *Writers and Scholars Educational Trust (WSET)* were founded to protect and promote freedom of expression. The work of maintaining and extending freedoms never stops. Freedom of expression is not self-perpetuating but has to be maintained by constant vigilance.

The work of *Index* and *WSET* is only made possible thanks to the generosity and support of our many friends and subscribers world-wide. We depend on donations to guarantee our independence; to fund research and to support projects which promote free expression.

The Trustees and Directors would like to thank the many individuals and organisations who support *Index* and *WSET*, including:

Anonymous
The Arts Council of England
The Bromley Trust
Danish International Development Agency (DANIDA)
Demokratifonden
The European Commission
The Ford Foundation
Fritt Ord Foundation
The JM Kaplan Fund
The Goldberg Family Trust
The Lyndhurst Settlement
The Open Society Institute
Pearson plc Charitable Trust
The Prins Claus Fund
The Ruben and Elisabeth Rausing Trust
CA Rodewald Charitable Settlement
EJB Rose Charitable Trust
The Royal Literary Fund
The Royal Ministry of Foreign Affairs, Norway
The Alan and Babette Sainsbury Charitable Fund
Scottish Media Group plc
The Stephen Spender Memorial Fund
Tom Stoppard
Swedish International Development Co-operation Agency (Sida)
UNESCO
United News and Media plc

If you would like more information about *Index on Censorship* or would like to support our work, please contact Dawn Rotheram, Director of Development, on (44) 171 278 2313 or e-mail dawn@indexoncensorship.org

Article 18 'Everyone has the right to freedom of thought, conscience and religion; this right includes freedom to change his religion or belief, and freedom, either alone or in community with others and in public or in private, to manifest his religion or belief in teaching, practice, worshipand observance.'

FRANK NORDHAUSEN & LIANE V. BILLERBECK

Sect crime

Eminent scientologists in the USA cry 'Foul!' But Germany's treatment of its sect members is haunted by the past and the pre-eminence of pseudo cults and religions under the Nazis

In February 1997, Germany experienced a new kind of political theatre. In a full-page, open letter to Chancellor Helmut Kohl in the *International Herald Tribune*, 34 Hollywood celebrities alleged that scientologists were being hounded in modern Germany, much as the Jews were during the Third Reich. Among the signatories were actors Dustin Hoffman and Goldie Hawn, and the director Oliver Stone. Chancellor Kohl responded that these stars 'knew nothing about Germany' and dismissed the matter out of hand. Politicians of all parties, as well as the German Jewish Council, expressed their indignation. 'In comparing their treatment in Germany to the Holocaust,' remarked foreign minister Klaus Kinkel, 'Scientologists are falsifying history.'

But the attack was well targeted, professionally produced and found ready ears. The US State Department's 1997 report, the UN's Human Rights Commission and the KSZE (the German Congress for Security and Collaboration in Europe) all criticised Germany's alleged discrimination against a 'religious minority'. US senators and members of the House of Representatives had complained to the State Department about the behaviour of German authorities towards the US sect as far back as summer 1996; by the time US Secretary of State Madeleine Albright visited in February 1997, the Scientology affair was high on the German agenda.

Since the early 1990s, former scientologists have testified to brainwashing, brutal exploitation and punishment camps for recalcitrant members. Revelations of plans for economic and social infiltration had alarmed politicians across the board. Scientologists now control a large share of real estate in Hamburg and hand over millions of marks to the sect every year. In 1995, a former high-ranking German scientologist, Tom Voltz, revealed secret strategy papers in which the leaders of the sect defined 'global economic dominance through Scientology' as their chief aim. Another former manager in the sect, Gunther Träger, revealed recently that, since the fall of the Berlin Wall, senior scientologists had forged plans to overthrow the government and install 'Clear *Deutschland*'. ('Clears' are those who have reached Scientology's highest level of psychological attainment.) This is just what founder L Ron Hubbard had always trumpeted: 'To hell with society - we're building a new one!'

German politicians have actively addressed the issue since 1993. When Scientology appeared on the agenda of the German Law and Order Conference, it was described as an organisation that 'combines elements of corporate crime and psychological terror under the auspices of a religious order'. Political parties drafted legislation to bar scientologists from becoming members, and reports in 1995/96 concluded that Scientology was 'a new form of political extremism… founded on basic principles that are totalitarian and incompatible with a democratic constitution.'

In 1997, the German *Bundestag* (Lower House) launched an inquiry with the intention of drafting legal measures to provide better protection for the public. In June, the interior ministry placed Scientology under surveillance after finding 'sufficient indications' that its activities were at odds with the democratic principles of Germany's Basic Law. In an opinion poll in February 1997, 59.2 per cent of respondents agreed that the intelligence services should conduct covert surveillance of the sect.

The US media, as well as politicians such as Senator Alfonse d'Amato, see surveillance by government agents, as well as the exclusion of Scientologists from political parties, as a kind of witch hunt. Even in Germany, there have been warnings of 'sect hysteria' and fears that the freedom of religion guaranteed under the German Constitution is in danger. But for German critics of Scientology the problem lies in the past: their experience of National Socialism remains a constant reminder of the need for vigilance where 'fascist' movements are concerned.

Ironically, religious persecution has been raised on TV talk shows so often it has provided scientologists with a platform. What this public debate conceals, however, is that the cries of 'religious discrimination' are also a method of disinformation. 'I don't care what anyone thinks or

War in cyberspace

TILMAN HAUSHERR loves a joke. The software specialist finds it even more amusing to reveal the secrets of that most enchanted of businesses, Scientology. Surfers used to find quirky versions of Scientology logos side by side with anti-Scientology articles on his homepage. In January this year, the on-line server CompuServe blocked Hausherr's site on the orders of the sect which successfully claimed infringement of copyright. 'Scientologists don't have a sense of humour,' said the computer nerd from Berlin.

Scientology has been waging a bitter cyberspace campaign against its critics for years. The stimulus was an on-line news group, *alt.religion.scientology*, where critics of Scientology had published information about the sect's victims of since 1991. Without warning, in 1994, the group's announcements were illegally removed and scientologists mobilised their lawyers against anyone reproducing Scientology texts on the net: everything that their founder and guru, L Ron Hubbard, had ever written was protected by copyright.

The first victim was Dennis Erlich, a former scientologist from Caifornia who had published Hubbard's writings on the Internet. In January 1995, the sect's lawyers obtained a search warrant and, in a raid on his apartment, confiscated 360 diskettes and downloaded data. A San José court granted him permission to quote from Scientology documents, but it issued an injunction to prevent him publishing complete texts. Scientology also requested Erlich's server, Netcom, to delete the entire *alt.religion.scientology* group. Netcom refused but was promptly served with a writ and came to a settlement.

The conflict escalated when Scientology's 'secret service', the OSA, sent thousands of files to the site in an attempt to overload the system with a deluge of data. Scientologists' attempts to censor the Internet only fuelled the creativity of web-users further. alt.religion.scientology is now one of the most frequently visited sites on the Internet, while the search engine Yahoo! lists more than 100 sites put up by opponents of Scientology.

believes,' says Scientology critic Ursula Caberta. 'What I am concerned with are the dangerous practices of an extremist organisation'. In Caberta's hometown, Hamburg, there are around 50 religions; nation-wide not a single sect is banned. Scientologists claim that foreign observers simply lack the information to judge their complaints of alleged persecution.

Few Americans know, for example, that Scientology tactically disregards the fundamental concepts of a religion. In 1995, an advertisement for Scientology appeared in the Croatian newspaper *Vremja*. Running over several pages, the organisation presented itself not as a religion, but as a 'scientific ideology'. Former adherents recall L Ron Hubbard summarily declaring Scientology a religion at the beginning of the 1970s in order to claim tax incentives. A US cadre testified under oath that 'Hubbard never spoke of Scientology as a religion. In my experience, Scientology had to be considered a religion only to fulfil certain legal requirements'.

Scientologists in the USA highlight the fate of members who have allegedly been discriminated against in Germany. Few of the cases has withstood critical scrutiny. The absurdity of such claims was confirmed at a demonstration in Berlin on 27 October 1997 when, well protected by hundreds of police, US musical stars Issac Hayes and Anne Archer clamoured for 'Freedom!' Not even the German judiciary can operate uniform procedures when it comes to legal action against Scientology. A Berlin policeman used a standard Scientologist 'Personality Test' on applicants for the police force, then analysed the results with a Scientology computer programme. In 1996, he was fined heavily for contravening the data protection act, but an appeal court overturned the verdict in April 1998.

When it's an issue of the right to freedom of identity the law almost always sides with scientologists: if members are found guilty in court, it is because serious violations of the law can be proved. German labour laws, the court found, also apply to scientologists. In May 1995, the *Bundesarbeitsgericht*, the highest welfare tribunal in the land, ordered the Hamburg branch of Scientology to pay a former employee a basic minimum wage, backdated to the beginning of his employment. While a member, he had worked for up to 100 hours a week for a pittance.

It is a remarkable church that employs surveillance methods and private detectives to spy on its opponents and that spends millions of dollars a year on lawsuits to gag its critics. In 1993, the sect was regarded in the USA in much the same way as its German counterpart today – as a dangerous and demented organisation. In 1991, *Time* described Scientology as an 'immensely profitable swindle on a global scale'. And in 1992, when the US Claims Court maintained that Scientology had an obvious 'commercial nature', the sect felt as persecuted in the USA as it does in Germany today.

Yet in October 1993 and under circumstances which are still mysterious the Inland Revenue Service (IRS) granted Scientology the tax immunity status due to a 'Religious Order'. With this and with the aid of lobbyists in Hollywood, the scientologists managed to keep the matter of the alleged religious persecution of their German members on the US political agenda. The campaign reached its climax when, in October 1997, a US congressional commission chaired a hearing on 'religious discrimination in Germany'. In his testimony, actor and scientologist John Travolta alleged, wrongly, that political elements in Germany had called for the boycott of his film *Phenomenon*.

However, since the death of Lisa McPherson at the Scientology headquarters in Clearwater, Virginia in December 1995, when the sect withheld access to life-saving treatment, the US media and politicians in Washington have adopted a more critical attitude to the sect. In November 1997, the US House of Representatives threw out a motion to censure Germany because of its discrimination against religious minorities. And earlier in the same year, UN special observer Abdelfattah Amor spoke of Germany's 'culture of tolerance' towards religion. The Tunisian lawyer characterised the scientologists' claim that their persecution resembled that of the Jews under Hitler as 'shocking', 'banal' and 'childish'. ❑

***Frank Nordhausen** and **Liane v Billerbeck** are the authors of* Psycho-Sekten: Die Praktiken der Seelenfänger *(Ch. Links Verlag Berlin 1997)*
Translated by Syra Morley

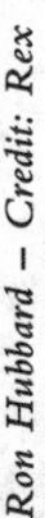

L Ron Hubbard – Credit: Rex

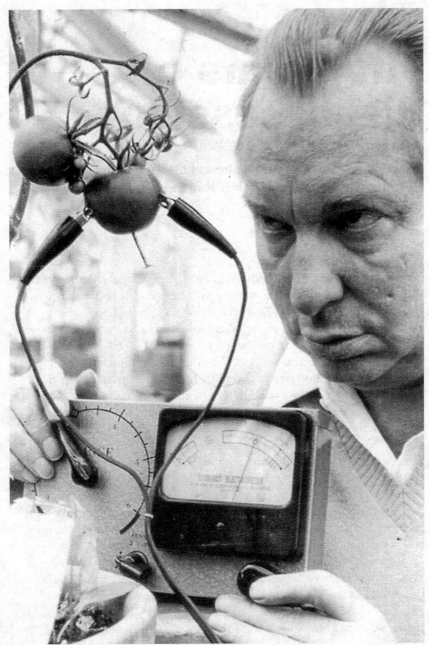

EDWARD SAID

Fifty years of dispossession

Peace is not now and Israel shows no sign of honouring the Oslo Accords of 1993. The only way forward is for Palestinians to renew the struggle

In the United States, celebrations of Israel's 50 years as a state have tried to project an image of the country that went out of fashion since the Palestinian *intifada* (1987-92): a pioneering state, full of hope and promise for the survivors of the Nazi Holocaust, a haven of enlightened liberalism in a sea of Arab fanaticism and reaction.

On 15 April, for instance, CBS broadcast a two-hour prime-time programme from Hollywood hosted by Michael Douglas and Kevin Costner, featuring movie stars such as Arnold Schwarzenegger, Kathy Bates – who recited passages from Golda Meir minus, of course, her most celebrated remark that there were no Palestinians – and Winona Ryder. None of these luminaries are particularly known for their Middle Eastern expertise or enthusiasm, although all of them in one way or another praised Israel's greatness and enduring achievements. There was even time for a cameo appearance by Bill Clinton, who provided perhaps the least edifying, most atavistic note of the evening by complimenting Israel, 'a small oasis', for 'making a once barren desert bloom', and for 'building a thriving democracy in hostile terrain.'

Ironically enough, no such encomia were intoned on Israeli television, which has been broadcasting a 22- part series, 'Tkuma', on the country's history. This series has a decidedly more complicated and, indeed, more critical content. Episodes on the 1948 war, for instance, made use of archival sources unearthed by the so-called revisionist histo-

Article 7 'All are equal before the law and are entitled without any discrimination to equal protection of the law.' Article 17 'No-one shall be arbitrarily deprived of his property.'

rians (Benny Morris, Ilan Pappe, Avi Schlaim, Tom Segev, et al) to demonstrate that the indigenous Palestinians were forcibly expelled, their villages destroyed, their land taken, their society eradicated. It was as if Israeli audiences had no need of all the palliatives provided for diasporic and international viewers, who still needed to be told that Israel was a cause for uncomplicated rejoicing and not, as it has been for Palestinians, the cause of a protracted, and still continuing, dispossession of the country's indigenous people.

That the US celebration simply omitted any mention of the Palestinians indicated also how remorselessly an ideological mind-set can hold on, despite the facts, despite years of news and headlines, despite an extraordinary, if ultimately unsuccessful, effort to keep effacing Palestinians from the picture of Israel's untroubled sublimity. If they're not mentioned, they don't exist. Even after 50 years of living the Palestinian exile I still find myself astonished at the lengths to which official Israel and its supporters will go to suppress the fact that a half century has gone by without Israeli restitution, recognition or acknowledgement of Palestinian human rights and without, as the facts undoubtedly show, connecting that suspension of rights to Israel's official policies.

Even when there is a vague buried awareness of the facts, as is the case with a front-page *New York Times* story on 23 April by one Ethan Bronner, the Palestinian *nakba* is characterized as a semi-fictional event (dutiful inverted commas around the word 'catastrophe' for instance) caused by no-one in particular. When Bronner quotes an uprooted Palestinian who describes his miseries, the man's testimony is qualified by 'for most Israelis, the idea of Mr Shikaki staking claim to victimhood is chilling', a reaction made plausible as Bronner blithely leapfrogs over the man's uprooting and systematic deprivations and immediately tells us how his 'rage' (for years the approved word for dealing with Palestinian history) has impelled his sons into joining Hamas and Islamic Jihad. Ergo, Palestinians are violent terrorists, whereas Israel can go on being a 'vibrant and democratic regional superpower established on the ashes of Nazi genocide.' But not on the ashes of Palestine, an obliteration that lingers on in measures taken by Israel to block Palestinian rights, domestically as well as in territories occupied in 1967.

Take land and citizenship for instance. Approximately 750,000 Palestinians were expelled in 1948: they are now four million. Left behind were 120,000 (now one million) who subsequently became Israelis, a minority constituting about 18 per cent of the state's population, but not fully-fledged citizens in anything more than name. In addition there are 2.5 million Palestinians without sovereignty on the West Bank and in Gaza. Israel is the only state in the world which is not the state of its actual citizens, but of the whole Jewish people who consequently have rights that non-Jews do not. Without a constitution, Israel is governed by Basic Laws of which one in particular, the Law of Return, makes it possible for any Jew anywhere to emigrate to Israel and become a citizen, at the same time that native-born Palestinians do not have the same right. Ninety-three per cent of the land of the state is characterised as Jewish land, meaning that no non-Jew is allowed to lease, sell or buy it.

Before 1948, the Jewish community in Palestine owned a little over 6 per cent of the land. A recent case in which a Palestinian Israeli, Adel Kaadan, wished to buy land but was refused because he was a non-Jew has become something of a *cause célèbre* in Israel, and has even made it to the Supreme Court which is supposed to, but would prefer not, to rule on it. Kaadan's lawyer has said that 'as a Jew in Israel, I think that if a Jew somewhere else in the world was prohibited from buying state land, public land owned by the federal government, because they're Jews, I believe there would have been an outcry in Israel.' (*New York Times*, 1 March 1998). This anomaly about Israeli democracy, not well known and rarely cited, is compounded by the fact that, as I said above, Israel's land in the first place was owned by Palestinians expelled in 1948; since their forced exodus their property was legally turned into Jewish land by The Absentees' Property Law, the Law of the State's Property and the Land Ordinance (the Acquisition of Land for Public Purposes). Now only Jewish citizens have access to that land, a fact that does not corroborate *The Economist*'s extraordinarily sweeping statement on 'Israel at 50' (25 April-1 May, 1998) that since the state's founding Palestinians 'have enjoyed full political rights'.

What makes it specially galling for Palestinians is that they have been forced to watch the transformation of their own homeland into a western state, one of whose express purposes is to provide for Jews and not for non-Jews. Between 1948 and 1966 Palestinian Israelis were ruled by military ordinance. After that, as the state regularised its policies on education, legal practice, religion, social, economic and political participation, a regime evolved to keep the Palestinian minority disadvantaged, segregated and constantly discriminated against. There is an eye-opening account of this shabby history that is rarely cited and, when it is, elided or explained away by the euphemism (familiar from South African apartheid) that 'they' have their own system: it is the March 1998 report, *Legal Violations of Arab Minority Rights in Israel*, published by Adalah (the Arabic word for justice), an Arab-Jewish organization within Israel. Especially telling is the section on the 'discriminatory approach of Israeli courts,' routinely praised by supporters of Israel for their impartiality and fairness. In fact, the report notes that the courts having delivered progressive and decent-minded decisions on the rights of women, homosexuals, the disabled etc. have 'since 1948 dismissed all cases dealing with equal rights for Arab citizens, and have never included a declaratory statement in decisions regarding the protection of Arab group rights'. This is borne out by a survey of criminal and civil cases in which Arabs get no help from the courts and are far more likely to be indicted than Jews in similar circumstances.

'policy towards the Palestinians clearly envisioned that community's disappearance'

It is only in the past year or two that investigations of Israel's political makeup, hitherto assumed to be socialist, egalitarian, pioneering, forward-looking, have turned up a rather unattractive picture. Zeev Sternhell's book *The Founding Myths of Israel* (Princeton 1998) is the work of an Israeli historian of twentieth-century right-wing European mass movements who finds a disturbing congruence between those movements and Israel's own brand of what Sternhell rightly calls 'nationalist socialism'. Far from being socialist, Israel's founders, and subsequently the polity they established, were profoundly anti-socialist, bent almost entirely upon 'conquest of the land' and the creation of 'self-realisation' and a new sense of organic peoplehood that moved steadily to the right during the pre-1948 years. 'Neither the Zionist movement abroad,' Sternhell says, 'nor the pioneers who were beginning to settle the country could frame a policy toward the Palestinian national movement. The real reason for this was not a lack of understanding of the problem but a clear recognition of the insurmountable contradiction between the basic objectives of the two sides.' After 1948, policy towards the Palestinians clearly envisioned that community's disappearance or its political nullity, since it was clear that the contradiction between the two sides would always remain insurmountable. Israel, in short, could not become a secular liberal state, despite the efforts of two generations of publicists to make it so.

After 1967, the occupation of the West Bank and Gaza produced a military and civil regime for Palestinians whose aim was Palestinian submission and Israeli dominance, an extension of the model on which Israel proper functioned. Settlements were established in the late summer of 1967 (and Jerusalem annexed) not by right-wing parties but by the Labour Party, a member, interestingly enough, of the Socialist International. The promulgation of literally hundreds of 'occupiers' laws' directly contravened not only the tenets of the Universal Declaration of Human Rights but the Geneva Conventions as well. These violations ran the gamut from administrative detention, to mass land expropriations, house demolitions, forced movement of populations, torture, uprooting of trees, assassination, book banning, closure of schools and universities. Always, however, the illegal settlements were being expanded as more and more Arab land was ethnically cleansed so that Jewish populations from Russia, Ethiopia, Canada and the USA, among other places, could be accommodated.

After the Oslo Accords were signed in September 1993, conditions for Palestinians steadily worsened. It became impossible for Palestinians to travel freely between one place and another, Jerusalem was declared off limits and massive building projects transformed the country's geography. In everything, the distinction between Jew and non-Jew is scrupulously preserved. The most perspicacious analysis of the legal situation obtaining after Oslo is Raja Shehadeh's in his book *From Occupation to Interim Accords: Israel and the Palestinian Territories* (Kluwer 1997), an important work that demonstrates the carefully preserved continuity between Israeli negotiating strategy during the Oslo process and its land-occupation policy established in the occupied territories from the early 1970s. In addition, Shehadeh demonstrates the tragic lack of preparation and understanding in the PLO's strategy during the peace process, with the result that much of the sympathy gained internationally for the Palestinians against Israeli settlement policy and its dismal human rights record was frittered away, unused and unexploited. 'All the support and sympathy,' he says, 'which it took years for Palestinians to rally, returned home, so to speak, with the mistaken belief that the struggle was over. The Palestinians, as much as the Israelis, helped in giving the false impression through, among other things, the highly publicised media image of theArafat-Rabin handshake, that the Israeli-Palestinian conflict was resolved. No serious attempt was made to remind the world that one of the main causes of the conflict after 1967, the Israeli settlements in occupied Palestinian territory, remained intact. This is not to speak of the other basic unresolved questions of the return of refugees, compensation, and the issue of Jerusalem.'

Unquestionably the moral dilemma faced by anyone trying to come to terms with the Palestinian-Israeli conflict is a deep one. Israeli Jews are not white settlers of the stripe that colonised Algeria or South Africa, though similar methods have been used. They are correctly seen as victims of a long history of western, largely Christian anti-semitic persecution that culminated in the scarcely comprehensible horrors of the Nazi Holocaust. To Palestinians, however, their role is that of victims of the victims. This is why western liberals who openly espoused the anti-apartheid movement, or that of the Nicaraguan Sandanistas, or Bosnia, or East Timor, or US civil rights, or Armenian commemoration of the Turkish genocide, or many other political causes of that kind, have shied away from openly endorsing Palestinian self-determination. As for Israel's nuclear policy, or its legally underwritten campaign of torture, or of using civilians as hostages, or of refusing to give Palestinians permits to build on their own land in the West Bank – the case is never made in the liberal public sphere, partly out of fear, partly out of guilt.

An even greater challenge is the difficulty of separating Palestinian and Israeli-Jewish populations who are now inextricably linked in all sorts of ways, despite the immense chasm that divides them. Those of us who for years have argued for a Palestinian state have come to the realisation that if such a 'state' (the inverted commas here are definitely required) is going to appear out of the shambles of Oslo it will be weak, economically dependent on Israel, without real sovereignty or power. Above all, as the present map of the West Bank amply shows, the Palestinian autonomy zones will be non-contiguous (they now account for only 3 per cent of the West Bank; Netanyahu's government has balked at giving up an additional 13 per cent) and effectively divided into Bantustans controlled from the outside by Israel. The only reasonable course therefore is to recommend that Palestinians and their supporters renew the struggle against the fundamental principle that relegates 'non-Jews' to subservience on the land of historical Palestine. This, it seems to me, is what is entailed by any principled campaign on behalf of justice for Palestinians, and certainly not the enfeebled separatism that movements like Peace Now have fitfully embraced and quickly abandoned. There can be no concept of human rights, no matter how elastic, that accommodates the strictures of Israeli state practice against 'non-Jewish' Palestinians in favour of Jewish citizens. Only if the inherent contradiction is faced between what in effect is a theocratic and ethnic exclusivism on the one hand and genuine democracy on the other, can there be any hope for reconciliation and peace in Israel/Palestine. Fudging, waffling, looking the other way, avoiding the issue entirely, or accepting pabulum definitions of 'peace' will bring Palestinians and, in the long run Israelis, nothing but hardship and insecurity. ❑

***Edward Said** is Professor of English and Comparative Literature at columbia University. His latest book is* Peace and its Discontents.

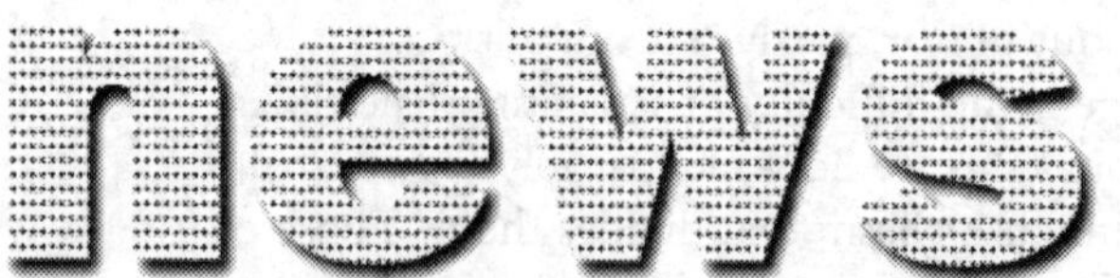

BURMA

Breaking a butterfly

Michael Griffin

Burma's military junta sentenced an elderly democracy advocate to 25 years in prison on 21 April for allegedly breaching the conditions of an amnesty granted for a previous treason charge.

Daw San San, a former deputy for the banned National League for Democracy, had given a telephone interview with the BBC World Service on 26 June last year which, in the view of the ruling State Peace and Development Council (SPDC), infringed the terms of her early release. An SPDC spokesman in Rangoon told Reuters: 'Due to fabrications and distribution of false information, domestically and internationally, to create instability and unrest in the country, as well as her participation in groups doing the same, the amnesty granted has been revoked.'

San San, in her late 60s, was arrested on 27 October 1997 and charged under the 1923 Official Secrets Act. Her earlier conviction for treason in 1990 arose out of participation in the1988 democracy movement.

includes freedom to change his religion or belief, and freedom, either alone or in community with others and in public or in private, to manifest his religion or belief in teaching, practice, worshipand observance.'

JUDY MABRO

Through a veil darkly

Seventy-five years ago, three Egyptian feminists returning from a women's suffrage conference in Rome removed their veils in public at Cairo railway statio. The veil, they said, was the most serious obstacle to women being educated and playing a full role in society. Today, in a society caught between Islam and the values of the West, their granddaughters are taking up the veil in pursuit of a new Egyptian identity

The traveller in the 'Women Only' carriages of the Cairo metro these days is confronted with a bewildering array of dress styles: modest western dress (jeans or skirt and blouse) with or without a headscarf; fashionable versions of the new Islamic dress (generally a long skirt and top) worn with headscarf or turban; the traditional long, patterned dress and black wrap worn by peasant and lower-class women; plainer versions of the new Islamic dress with a large headcover falling well past the shoulders and covering all the hair; and, finally, the severe and all-concealing *niqab* in black or other sombre colour. Not even the eyes are visible.

The elegant and expensive designer versions of 'Islamic dress', displayed complete with matching accessories in wealthy areas of the city, are not in evidence on the metro any more than the miniskirts once again in fashion among wealthier young women. The latter are confined to private functions like weddings and parties, or worn at clubs and summer resorts.

'Why do foreigners always want to discuss the *hijab* (the veil) when there are far more important issues – poverty, illiteracy, child labour, ill health, gender inequalities and so on?' I was asked several times in Cairo.

The West has been obsessed with the veil for centuries, but is it true, as my friends implied, that the *hijab* is no longer an issue? If so, why do people spend such an inordinate amount of time discussing it? Why did the minister of education attempt to ban the wearing of veils in primary schools in 1994 and again in 1996? And why do posters in the streets urge women to cover themselves? Are women and young girls being pressured into adopting a style of religious dress – the *niqab* – that has only recently come to Egypt from Saudi Arabia, along with petrodollars and returning migrants?

Clothes and fashion are a reflection of the cultural politics of their society, and the female body and dress are closely related to issues of national identity, cultural authenticity, political struggle and women's rights. The veil *is* important: it is a powerful symbol carrying widely varying messages to different people.

The phenomenon of young women choosing to wear a form of Islamic dress, while their mothers wear western dress, is not unique to Egypt. Asian girls and young women in Britain have made the same choice. In Istanbul recently, while women students demonstrated against a government ban on the wearing of headscarves on the campus, several hundred school teachers were under investigation for veiling in the classroom. In Germany, in Canada and, most famously, in France, young Muslim women of immigrant parents are wearing 'Islamic' headscarves.

In the 1980s, as the Islamic influence in Egyptian daily life strengthened, several explanations for the increased use of the *hijab* were proferred: it expressed the desire to re-establish an Egyptian identity to counter the influence of the western media and consumerism; it was a form of protest against the national government and the growing gap between rich and poor; and, of course, it was a sign of increasing religiosity. Women themselves, however, claimed the *hijab* was a way of avoiding male harassment in the streets, of saving the money they had been spending on their appearance and of facilitating their move into 'male space' in the university and the workplace – in government service and the professions, for example.

Since many of these women were often the first in their families to adopt the *hijab*, this was not a question of a 'return to the veil' or a retreat from the struggle for female autonomy of their mothers' generation. The choice of whether or not to wear the *hijab* cuts across generations and, to a lesser extent, across class. Middle-class women from liberal backgrounds, with no financial constraints and free to work as they choose, are also chosing to wear the *hijab*.

'I used to love fancy clothes and jewellery,' said Naila when I talked to her. Married with two children, she lives and grew up in a pleasant suburb of Cairo, studied at university and used to work in an office. Now she wears long clothes and a scarf covers her hair when she goes out. 'A few years ago I was going through a difficult period and my sister persuaded me to go along to a class on Islam being held at the local club. I agreed rather reluctantly, out of curiosity to see whether it was all brainwashing.'

What she discovered was that despite being a Muslim she knew nothing about Islam and became interested. She decided to wear the *hijab* and is happy with her decision. 'I don't need fancy clothes any more,' she says. 'Why should I dress for other men in the street?

Nobody persuaded me, I just wanted to.' I asked her about her teacher at the religious group. 'There is one thing she refuses to discuss at all in class and that is the *hijab*.'

Thinking of the ban by the minister of education, I ask whether young girls are being pressured to veil in school. 'If they do so it is because they like to imitate their mothers,' she replies. 'Islam does not require girls to veil until puberty.'

Her own mother, who enjoyed dressing up and going out with her daughter, was unhappy with the change in Naila. But having seen her happy, and discussed things with her friends, she accepts her daughter's decision. Naila is a lively and open woman who, through learning about Islam, has also learned about Egypt and the state of its poor. She works to raise money for the various activities organized by the religious groups, such as literacy classes, which the government is unable to provide. When she first went to the class on Islam there were about 10 older women who attended each week; now about 90 women of all ages regularly go along.

In a recent issue of the popular weekly *Rose el-Youssef* an article under the headline 'New Phenomenon in Cairo: the Return of the Miniskirt in the Time of the *Niqab*' considers the changes in women's dress over the past few decades. In the late-1960s, the ubiquitous miniskirt was considered an index of the openness of society and its liberal attitudes to women's rights. Next came the *hijab*, first worn among university students and a clear indication of the growing Islamisation of society. The *niqab* appeared in the 1990s along with the posters in the streets urging women to adopt this totally concealing dress. It was a form of political statement adopted in earnest after the Gulf War and the 1992 earthquake and is still used as such today.

'What makes a girl choose her style of dress?' asks *Rose el-Youssef*'s columnist. Apart from personal and religious reasons, it can be part of a group decision, as in the case of the women known as 'the earthquake generation'. They took the veil immediately after the 1992 earthquake in Cairo when the Islamic groups rather than the government provided immediate help to the victims. Veiling became a form of political protest against an uncaring and corrupt government. Some students have since adapted this dress to jeans, blouse and a scarf, complete with make-up.

Rose el-Youssef implies that girls and young women are free to choose what they wear. But, as in most societies, some are freer than others. In the words of one young woman: 'My father worked in Saudi and saw this as the ideal image of woman. He asked me to veil and I did.' Men increasingly stipulate in marriage contracts that their new wives must wear the *hijab*, even the *niqab*. A bride may be unwilling or unable to argue over this clause at the time but, should she later remove the veil, divorce would be instant.

Juggling the demands of daily life in a society where there is a struggle between two cultures – one pro and one anti-western – often makes women the pawns caught up in Egypt's search for identity. One young woman speaking in *Rose el-Youssef* describes the kind of dilemma this can bring: 'I wear the veil because my father is a *sheikh* and it is important for him that I do. But I work in a big company and I have to take off my veil in the lift every day when I arrive at work.' Other women may well be doing the opposite. Young women who wear miniskirts say it gives them a sense of freedom, but a 20-year-old student who said she liked to dress like that because she felt like the businesswomen she sees in foreign films, has stopped wearing them because she was harassed on the streets.

Whatever style they chose, young women must still be willing to adapt, to dress modestly when the need arises. The 1960s was a time of liberalism but, as in many other countries, the reactionary tide is dominant in 1990s Egypt. Just as in debates between 'new' and 'old' feminism take place between the 1960s and 1990s generations in the West, young women may find the values of their mother's generation irrelevant to their lives today. And, unlike their grandmothers, they know that there are many obstacles other than the veil that are holding back their development.

The veil is a powerful symbol and, once taken, the decision to adopt it is hard to go back on. Perhaps the question today is not so much whether women make a free choice in wearing it, as whether they are free to discard it. ❑

Judy Mabro *is a writer who visits Egypt regularly*

Landmarks: 1948-1998

Index's own chronology of free expression

1948

30 Jan	Mahatma Gandhi is assassinated
11 Feb	Sergei Eisenstein, director of *Ivan the Terrible*, dies
9 Apr	*El Siglo* office is destroyed in protest against the assassination of Colombian leftist leader Jorge Eliécer Gaitan
14 May	The State of Israel is proclaimed, with equal rights for Arab inhabitants
26 Jun	West begins the 328-day Berlin airlift to combat the Soviet blockade
28 Jun	Yugoslav Communist Party is expelled from the Cominform
23 Dec	Prime Minister Tojo, and six other war-time Japanese leaders, are hanged at Sugamo Prison in Tokyo

1949

10 Jan	Launch of seven inch vinyl disc
22 Jan	Mao Tse-Tung captures Beijing
Jan	Race riots leave 106 people dead in Durban
8 Mar	Peronista government expropriates paper production to curb the opposition papers, *La Nación* and *La Prensa*
27 Apr	Foundation of the Irish Republic, which refuses to join the Commonwealth in protest at the partition of Northern Ireland
13 Jul	The Pope excommunicates all members of the Communist Party
15 Jul	Cuban black activist singer Antonio Machín launches his first international tour
	James Joyce's *Ulysses* is allowed into Canada for the first time. Still prohibited are 505 books, including Faulkner's *Sanctuary* and *Tobacco Road* by Erskine Caldwell

1950

10 Jan	All books published before 5 May 1948 are banned in Czechoslovakia
16 Sep	260-strong UN naval armada lands on North Korean coast
21 Oct	Chinese troops invade Tibet
	China passes the Marriage Law of 1950 which bans polygamy, concubinage, child betrothal and the exaction of money or gifts in

connection with marriage

1951

14 May The Afrikaner nationalist majority votes to remove the coloured (mixed race) people from the electoral register
12 May First US H-bomb, 100 times more powerful than Hiroshima, is tested on Enwietok atoll
14 Aug William Randolph Hearst dies
23 Aug British forces withdraw from Iranian oil fields as Mohammed Mossadegh moves to nationalise the industry
24 Aug Birth of the Mau Mau Society in Kenya
19 Oct British troops take control of the Suez Canal

1953

5 Mar Stalin dies. The process of de-Stalinisation begins under Georgi Malenkov
8 Apr Jomo Kenyatta is jailed for seven years for leading the Mau Mau rebellion
25 Apr James Watson and Frances Crick isolate the double-helix structure of DNA
19 Jun Ethel and Julius Rosenberg are executed for selling secrets to Russia in 1951
19 Sep Charlie Chaplin interrogated as suspected 'subversive' by House Un-American Activities Committee

1954

27 Jul British forces pull out of the Suez Canal zone
17 May In *Brown vs. Board of Education*, the US Supreme Court rules that racially separate schools are inherently unequal
24 May IBM releases the first commercially available 'electronic brain'
A post-office in Providence, Rhode Island, blocks delivery of Lenin's *State and Revolution* to Brown University on the grounds that it is 'subversive'
1 Dec Serbian and Croatian cultural associations agree to produce a definitive Serbo-Croatian dictionary

1955

14 May Moscow establishes the Warsaw Pact, with Bulgaria, Czechoslovakia, Hungary, Poland and Romania as co-signatories
7 Sep Women in Peru are granted the right to vote

1956

26 Jul Nasser nationalises the Suez Canal Company
31 Oct British bomb Egyptian airstrips to secure the canal for

international use

11 Nov Counter-revolution is crushed in Hungry by Soviet troops, leaving over 3,000 dead, 13,000 injured and 2,000 executed

1957

Chairman Mao's Hundred Flowers Campaign encourages intellectuals to criticise the Communist party. Mao responds with a crackdown

24 Feb US journalist Helbert C. Matthews writes the first authentic account of the strength of Castro guerrilla movement in the *New York Times*

25 Sep Eisenhower calls in the National Guard to forcibly desegregate Central High School in Little Rock, Arkansas

1958

29 May Unrest in Algeria prompts return of General Charles de Gaulle as president

Jul Overthrow of the Iraqi monarchy

23 Oct 50,000 Czech Gypsies are ordered to settle down and become 'productive citizens' or face stiff penalties

23 Oct Boris Pasternak wins Nobel Prize for *Dr Zhivago*. It remains unpublished in Russia until 1980

1959

31 Jul Tibetan revolt against Chinese. The Dalai Lama had fled to India in April

Launch of the Great Leap Forward; 16 million people will die by 1961.

29 Sep Khrushchev visits the US: he is denied access to Disneyland on security grounds

1960

4 Jan Death of Albert Camus

24 Jan Pope John XXIII instructs Catholics not to watch 'unsafe' films or TV

13 Mar France explodes an atomic bomb in the Sahara over UN and US objections

21 Mar 56 shot in Sharpeville over the Pass Laws

22 May Mossad snatches Adolf Eichmann, architect of the Final Solution, in Argentina

20 May A tribute to poet Joan Maragall becomes a subversive act when the people sing the banned song 'El canto de la Senyera' in the Palau de la Musica, Barcelona

26 Sep Castro is called to order in his first UN speech, which lasts four hours and 27 minutes

2 Nov Old Bailey rules that *Lady Chatterley's Lover*, banned for 30 years, is not obscene

1961

13 Feb Deposed Congolese premier Patrice Lumumba 'dies in the bush'

India passes the Dowry Prohibition Act. Thirty years on, 4,785 women

	were killed for not having sufficient dowries
3 Aug	East Germany seals the border between east and west Berlin
12 Sep	Bertrand Russell jailed for anti-nuclear protest
18 Sep	UN chief Dag Hammarskjold dies in a plane crash while on a peace mission to Katanga

1962

17 Feb	James Hanratty sentenced to hang in the UK
3 Jul	Algeria becomes independent
28 Oct	Khrushchev promises missiles stationed on Cuba will be returned to the USSR
30 Sep	James Meredith enrols as Mississippi University's first black student
7 Nov	Nelson Mandela sentenced to five years for 'incitement'

1963

15 Jan	BBC ends ban on the mention of politics, royalty, religion or sex in comedy
13 Jun	Buddhist monk Quang Duc sets fire to himself in South Vietnam in protest at the unfair treatment by President Diem, a Catholic
27 Jun	President Kennedy makes his *Ich bin ein Berliner* speech at Tegel Airport
28 Aug	Martin Luther King delivers his 'I have a dream' speech
22 Nov	John F. Kennedy is assassinated in Dallas

1964

8 Jan	Adam Faith is banned from singing to a multiracial audience
10 Feb	London magistrate orders confiscation of *Fanny Hill* for obscenity
2 Mar	Communist Party announces a renewed drive to 'remove' religion from Soviet life
4 May	Pulitzer Committee decides there is no fiction, music or drama worthy of an award
28 Sep	Harpo Marx, the silent brother, dies
20 Nov	Vatican exonerates Jews of guilt for Christ's crucifixion
18 Dec	UK academic David Kitson is jailed in South Africa for 'revolutionary conspiracy'

1965

21 Feb	Malcolm X shot dead in mid-speech
31 Mar	President Johnson sends US Marines to Vietnam
Oct	Over 500,000 people perish in a communist uprising in Indonesia.
25 Nov	Joseph Desirée Mobutu seizes power in Congo and renames it Zaire

1966

14 Feb	Writers Andrey Sinyavsky and Yuri Daniel are sent to a labour camp for 'slandering the Soviet state'
20 Feb	An act of homage to Spanish poet Antonio Machado ends in violence between police and more than 2000 intellectuals
24 Feb	Kwame Nkrumah is overthrown by the army

16 May	Chairman Mao launches the Cultural Revolution against 'reactionary bourgeois ideas in the sphere of academic work, education, art and theatre and publishing'
1 Jun	Bob Dylan goes electric at Royal Albert Hall
3 Aug	Comedian Lenny Bruce dies of overdose

1967

10 May	Colonel Odemegwu Ojukwu announces the secession of the oil-rich Biafra. Government forces invade
5 Jun	Six Day War
	Laws forbidding the teaching of the theory of evolution in Tennessee schools are finally repealed
	UK legalises male homosexuality between consenting adults

1968

31 Jan	Tet offensive begins: CBS' Walter Cronkite reports that 'the Vietcong suffered a military defeat'
1 Feb	Bosnian Muslims are recognised as a separate 'ethnic group'
5 Mar	Czech government relaxes censorship as Prague Spring gets under way
16 Mar	US troops kill 504 villagers at My Lai
4 Apr	Martin Luther King is murdered in Memphis
May	Anti-war protests in Paris trigger nationwide strikes for radical reform
31 Jul	*Last Exit to Brooklyn* is cleared of obscenity charge in London
26 Sep	Soviet tanks stream into Prague
2 Oct	More than 300 students are killed in democracy demonstrations in Mexico City

1969

2 Feb	Nigeria bans Red Cross relief to breakaway region of Biafra
1 Nov	Thousands visit Copenhagen 'Sex Fair' as Denmark abolishes film censorship

1970

18 Jan	Marx's grave in Highgate, London is daubed with swastikas
3 Feb	Police in London seize Andy Warhol's film *Flesh*
17 Mar	*New English Bible* sells out
4 May	Four students are shot dead at an anti-war protest at Kent State University, Ohio
Sep	King Hussein evicts the PLO in what becomes known as 'Black September'

1971

3 Feb	Yasser Arafat appointed leader of the PLO
3 Mar	Winnie Mandela imprisoned for 'receiving visitors'
26 Mar	The secession of Bangladesh from Pakistan erupts in civil war
Aug	Idi Amin expels 50,000 Asians from Uganda
6 Nov	125 Tupamaru guerillas tunnel out of Montevideo prison

10 Dec	Chilean poet Pablo Neruda receives the Nobel prize

1972

30 Jan	British troops kill 13 and wound 17 Catholics in Londonderry's 'Bloody Sunday'
5 Sep	'Black September' guerillas massacre members of the Israeli Olympic team in Munich
3 Nov	Allende forms People's Front government in Chile
17 Nov	*Sunday Times* banned from printing articles on Thalidomide

1973

10 Jan	Luís Buñuel wins Oscar for *The Discreet Charm of the Bourgeoisie*, banned in Spain
28 Mar	Marlon Brando rejects Oscar in protest at treatment of native Americans
4 Apr	Vatican admits to wartime knowledge of Holocaust
6 Oct	Israel captures Golan Heights and Sinai Peninsula in Yom Kippur war

1974

13 Feb	Nobel winner Alexander Solzhenitsyn is exiled in the first forced deportation of a dissident since Trotsky in 1929
1 Mar	Jan Palach's ashes are are buried anonymously to prevent his grave becoming a pilgrimage site
25 Apr	The banned song Grandola, Vela Morena becomes the anthem of the revolution that replaces the 40-year military regime of Portugal's Oliveira Salazar
9 Jun	Exiled Guatemalan writer Miguel Angel Asturias wins Nobel prize for *The Buried Eyes*
30 Jun	Mikhail Baryshnikov leaps to freedom in Toronto
8 Aug	President Richard Nixon resigns after Watergate investigation
25 Nov	Greek generals oust President George Papadopoulos

1975

14 May	Frank Sinatra wins damages from BBC over programme linking him to Mafia
9 Oct	Andrei Sakharov is refused permission to collect Nobel Peace prize because he is 'familiar with state secrets'
16 Oct	Four western journalists are killed in East Timor village by Indonesian troops
	Italian director Pier Paolo Pasolini murdered by male prostitute in Ostia

1976

14 Feb	Angola's MPLA, backed by 15,000 Cuban troops, repels UNITA
16 Jun	Hector Petersen, 13, dies from a police bullet in student demonstrations against the use of Afrikaans in black schools
23 Sep	Workers' Defence Committee (KOR) sets up *Nowa* to publish banned Polish literature
23 Sep	Four 'long-haired, anti-social elements' of a Czech pop group, Plastic

People of the Universe, are sentenced to nine months for 'jeopardising the education of youth in a socialist spirit'

6 Oct Thai army seizes power

1977

6 Jan 242 prominent persons sign Charter 77, accusing the Soviet government of abusing its commitments under the Helsinki Final Act

13 May 'La Passionara' Dolores Ibarruri returns to Madrid after 38 years in Moscow

19 Jun *Sunday Times* publishes an exposé of the systematic use of torture and coercion by Israeli police

12 Sep Steve Biko dies in police custody

20 Oct Donald Woods, editor of the East London *Daily Dispatch*, is 'banned'

01 Nov Romania bans the use of 'Mr,' 'Mrs' and 'Miss' in the workplace, to be replaced by 'comrade'

21 Nov Anwar Sadat flies to Israel and declares he wants a permanent peace

Novelist Christopher Isherwood comes out as a homosexuality

1978

Schools in Anaheim, California, ban the teaching of George Eliot's *Silas Marner*

14 Mar Israeli army invades Lebanon

1 Sep Exiled Bulgarian writer Georgi Markov is stabbed by a poison-tipped umbrella on London's Waterloo Bridge

4 Sep GDR completes a 635-mile frontier fence from Czech border to the Baltic

29 Oct *People's Daily* denounces Mao's *Little Red Book*. Beginning of 'Democracy Wall' in Beijing

10 Dec Millions march against Shah, forcing him to flee to Egypt

Kenya's Ngugi wa Thiong'o is detained for 12 months for the play I *will marry when I want*

1979

Mar Wei Jeng Sheng is sentenced to 15 years for 'counter-revolutionary propaganda'

2 Apr 2,000 skeletons weighted with stones found in a lake after ouster of Khmer Rouge by Vietnam.

4 Apr Zulfikar Ali Bhutto is hanged

4 May Margaret Thatcher assumes office with a quote from Francis of Assisi

23 Jul Ayatollah Khomeini, Iran's new leader, bans broadcast music

10 Oct *Canard Enchainé* claims 'Emperor Bokassa' gave Giscard D'Estaing diamonds

20 Dec Soviet Union invades Afghanistan

1980

18 Apr Zimbabwe wins independence

22 Apr UK apologises to Riyadh for ITV's *Death of a Princess*

5 May SAS storms Iranian embassy in Knightsbridge

4 Sep — Army seizes power to save Turkish democracy
29 Oct — 20 killed during the funeral for assassinated Archbishop Oscar Romero in El Salvador
19 Nov — The question 'Who shot JR?' is answered as US series *Dallas* ends its run
8 Dec — John Lennon assassinated in New York

1981

27 Jan — Exempted from a monopolies inquiry, Rupert Murdoch buys *The Times* and *The Sunday Times*
24 Feb — Attempted military coup in Madrid
1 May — IRA prisoner Bobby Sands begins a hunger strike till death
Picasso's 'Guernica' is returned to Spain after 40 years in New York.
6 Oct — Anwar Sadat is assassinated

1982

7 Jan — *Bushtrackers*, a film based on a novel by Kenya's Meja Mwangi, is banned on the grounds of violence and lawlessness
Feb — Somali poet Abdul Rage Taraweh is detained for expressing 'anti-government opinions' in his verse
28 Feb — The sale of paper is banned in Warsaw to stem the flow of pro-Solidarity publications
11 Mar — Nobel laureate Wole Soyinka is charged with treason in Nigeria
15 Mar — Michael Bogdanov goes on trial for 'indecency' in the play *Romans in Britain*
2 Apr — Argentina invades Falkland Islands
14 Jul — Iran invades Iraq
19 Jun — Roberto Calvi of Banco Ambrosiano is found hanged in London
7 Sep — Edgar Motuba, editor of the weekly *Ecumenical,* is found murdered in Maseru, Lesotho
18 Sep — Militias massacre refugees at Sabra and Chatila camps in Beirut
3 Dec — Nigerian musician Fela Kuti is charged on seven counts
Diary of a Young Girl by Anne Frank is banned in Alabama because it is 'sexually explicit'

1983

22 Jan — Andrzej Wajda's *Man of Iron* is condemned in Poland as an 'incitement to social anarchy'
4 Mar — Writer Arthur Koestler and his wife commit suicide
25 Apr — *Stern* publishes forged diaries allegedly written by Hitler
29 Sep — President Marcos shuts down newspaper for alleging the army murdered Benigno Aquino
5 Oct — Lech Walesa wins Nobel Prize for peace
10 Dec — End of military rule in Argentina

1984

11 Feb — Clive Ponting acquitted of breaking Official Secrets Act
23 Apr — Discovery of HIV is announced in Washington

Jun	6 Indian troops storm the Golden Temple in Amritsar, killing 800
31 Oct	Indira Gandhi is assassinated

1985

15 Jun	South Africa celebrates its first legal mixed marriage
10 Jul	French agents bomb Greenpeace's *Rainbow Warrior* in Auckland
17 Jul	Live Aid appeal for famine-affected Ethiopia reaches £50m
23 Sep	Murdoch buys 20th Century Fox
2 Oct	Rock Hudson succumbs to AIDS
5 Dec	UK quits UNESCO, citing anti-western bias

1986

31 Jan	Dean Konrad Jaroski of Wroclaw Art School is fired for approving a diploma project on the 1984 murder of Father Jerzy Popieluszko
1 Feb	Gorbachev announces new policy of Glasnost
7 Feb	'Baby Doc' Duvalier chased out of Haiti
16 Feb	5,000 printworkers picket Murdoch's Wapping plant over computerisation
28 Feb	Assassination of Swedish Prime Minister Olof Palme
14 Apr	Simone de Beauvoir dies
20 Apr	Pianist Vladimir Horowitz returns to Russia for first time in 61 years
25 May	30,000 blacks expelled from Crossroads squatter camp
8 Jun	Former Nazi Kurt Waldheim takes office as Austrian president
30 Jun	John Stalker is removed from inquiry into an unofficial 'shoot-to-kill' policy in Northern Ireland
27 Jun	Irish reject legalisation of divorce by 2 to 1
4 Sep	Czech authorities close Jazz Union for advocating freedom of the arts
12 Sep	US imposes economic sanctions on South Africa

1987

2 Jan	Golliwogs replaced by gnomes in Enid Blyton's Noddy books
20 Jan	Terry Waite is kidnapped in Beirut
3 Mar	*Joy of Gay Sex* is ruled to be not obscene in Canada.
May	Surgeon Wilson Carswell is expelled from Uganda for *Guardian* articles about AIDS
26 Feb	Church of England approves ordination of women
3 Jul	Klaus Barbie sentenced to life for wartime atrocities
22 Jul	Palestinian cartoonist who mocked Arafat is shot in Chelsea
23 Sep	UK loses appeal in Sydney against publication of *Spycatcher*
25 Sep	Poet Jack Mapanje is detained indefinitely in Malawi

1988

20 Jan	Palestinian *Intifada* begins
21 Jan	US TV evangelist Jimmy Swaggart admits to consorting with prostitutes
14 Feb	Soviet troops begin withdrawal from Afghanistan
1 Apr	Iran claims Iraq dropped mustard gas on Kurdish villages
30 Jul	Police open fire on Iranian rioters in Mecca
30 Jul	*Kirin B* sails for Italy, filled with toxic waste

8 Aug	10,000 killed in democracy demonstrations in Rangoon
17 Aug	President Zia ul-Haq dies in plane crash
30 Nov	George Orwell's *1984* is published in Poland
8 Dec	Reagan and Gorbachev agree to dismantle all short and medium- range nuclear weapons
14 Dec	Arafat renounces terrorism and recognises Israel

1989

15 Feb	Ayatollah Khomeini declares *fatwah* against Salman Rushdie
28 Feb	Soviet students granted greater latitude in 'interpreting' history
31 Mar	Over 200,000 ethnic Turks flee Bulgaria 'slavicisation' policy
17 May	Playwright Vaclav Havel released from prison
4 Jun	Tiananmen Square massacre
Jul	Aung San Suu Kyi is placed under house arrest
31 Jul	Soviet newspapers announce the publication of accurate maps of Moscow for the first time in 50 years
20 Oct	Guildford Four, wrongly convicted for the 1975 IRA pub bombings, are released
31Oct	Moscow announces it will drop all controls on copying machines.
9 Nov	The Berlin Wall comes down
24 Nov	Dubcek returns to Prague
24 Dec	Manuel Noriega seeks asylum in papal embassy

1990

11 Feb	Mandela freed after 27 years in jail.
28 Feb	Prague's daily *Lidove demokratie* publishes the first accurate casualty list from the 1968 Warsaw Pact invasion.
15 Mar	*Observer* journalist Farzad Barzoft is hanged in Baghdad after 'confessing' to spying.
11 Apr	UK customs seize metal piping en route from Sheffield to Iraq
2 Aug	Iraq invades Kuwait
22 Nov	Margaret Thatcher steps down

1991

1 Feb	President F.W de Klerk abolishes apartheid laws
20 Aug	Estonia proclaims independence, followed by Latvia, Ukraine, Belarus, Moldova, Georgia, Armenia, & Central Asian Republics

1992

2 May	Los Angeles is swept by riots after airing of a video of police beating black motorist, Rodney King
Jun	Canada's Bill C-128 bans depictions of people under 18 engaged in any kind of 'explicit sexual activity', including kissing
22 Dec	Native Title Bill, granting Aboriginals the right to lost land, is adopted into law

1993

9 Jan	Serbian gunmen murder Bosnia's deputy prime minister, Hakija Turajlic
15 Mar	President Walesa bans abortions, allowing prison terms of two years for doctors who perform them
13 Sep	Israel and the PLO sign an accord providing for limited Palestinian autonomy
5 Oct	President Boris Yeltsin orders rule by decree, bans 13 newspapers and re-imposes censorship
	The Bible is challenged as 'obscene' in Fairbanks, Alaska, and Harrisburg, Pennsylvania

1994

	Philippine censor Henrietta Mendez orders three cuts from the film *Schindler's List*. Director Spielberg pulls the film from screening
Apr	Radio-Télévision Libres des Milles Collines embarks on a hate speech campaign encouraging Hutus to eliminate all Tutsis by 5 May
10 Nov	Ken Saro-Wiwa and 8 others are executed for the alleged murder of four Ogoni chiefs
2 Oct	Kenyan politician and rights activist Koigi wa Wamwere is sentenced to four years for allegedly robbing a police station

1995

10 Apr	DNA bank opens in UK to keep genetic records of criminals
21 Apr	100 die in Oklahoma City, bringing the militia movement to the forefront of national consciousness
19 May	Cartoon strip the *World of Lily Wong* is cut from the *South China Morning Post*
Jun	China criticises the *Dying Rooms* TV documentary as 'vicious fabrications'
Jul	Aung San Suu Kyi is released from house arrest
13 Jul	12-14,000 Bosnian Muslim males 'disappear' after Bosnian Serbs capture Srebrenica from UN

1996

8 Jan	A court in Mogadishu jails 30 singers, musicians and comedians for failing to submit their material to prior censorship
3 Feb	Singer Lee Eun-jin and publisher Won Yong-ho are arrested in Seoul for producing a songbook which allegedly 'praises' North Korea
	Leo Nichols is arrested for 'illegal use of a fax machine' in Burma

1997

25 Jan	Photographer José Luís Cabezas of Argentina's *Noticias* is assassinated
29 Aug	Supreme Court rules illegal the Japanese Ministry of Education's deletion of references to germ warfare Unit 731
Oct	Libel charges by Prime Minister Goh Chok Tong against opposition leader Benjamin Jerayetnam are upheld by Singapore court
16 Nov	Wei Jingsheng flies to the US for 'medical treatment'
Dec	Witnesses tell the Truth and Reconciliation Commission how Winnie

Mandela operated a 'reign of terror' in mid-1980s

1998

25 Jan — Pope John Paul II visits Cuba, one year after the opening of a CNN bureau in Havana

25 Feb — President Kim Dae-jung, a former prisoner of conscience, is elected South Korean president

22 Mar — Bill Clinton flies to Ghana, becoming the first sitting president to visit Africa. In Senegal, he later apologises for the slave trade

19 Apr — Dissident Wang Dan is released and flies to the US for 'medical treatment'

20 Apr — Archbishop Trevor Huddlestone, who devoted most of his life to the apartheid struggle, dies. His ashes are scattered near his old church in Sophiatown ❑

*Compiled by **Michael Griffin** from research by **Dolores Cortés, Regina Jere-Malanda, Simon Martin, Emily Mitchell** and **Nicky Winstanley-Torode**.*

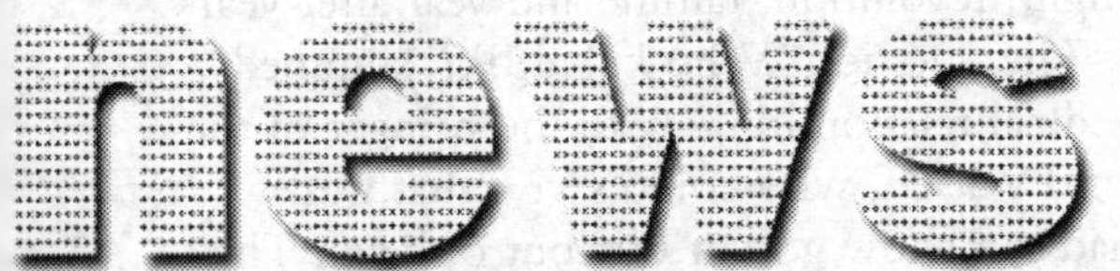

RWANDA

Familiar drums

Michael Griffin

The shadow of *Radio Television Libre des Mille Collines* (RTLM), the station that played a crucial role in inciting the 1994 Tutsi genocide, refuses to go away. The latest in the line of Great Lakes hate media is *Radio Voix du Patriote*, which has been operating intermittently in the Bukavu region of South Kivu. The radio is said to have the backing of ex-*Forces Armées Rwandaises* (FAR), ex-*Forces Armées Zairoises* (FAZ) and the Hutu *Interahamwe* militia that spearheaded the 1994 killings. It was first heard last Novemberin the wake of leaflets distributed throughout Bukavu urging the 'visitors (Tutsis) to go home'.

Voix du Patriote started life as *Radio Kahuzi Biega*, making life difficult for a local evangelical station, *Radio Kahuzi*. Typical broadcasts call on the local population to 'ensure the visitors return to their home'. 'The country has been sold to the Tutsis,' it says. It tells the 'Bantus' to 'rise as one to combat the Tutsis' and describes the Tutsis as 'Ethiopians and Egyptians' who do not belong in the region. The Bantus should 'help their Hutu brothers reconquer Burundi and Rwanda,' another broadcast says. 'We chose arms because the enemy chose them. We shall make them leave with arms.'

INDEX INDEX

The flip side

In the long-gone days, when newspapers were still charting the extraordinary inroads that the newly-introduced medium of TV was making into Britain's social and spiritual life, I would not change into pyjamas until the set was extinguished for fear of being spied on in my nakedness. Aside from the glimpse this gives into the lost woodlands of childhood, it was my first inkling of the power of that unpredictable and monochrome stranger by the fireside, our bringer of fantasy, nightmare and the daily news.

The hearth was soon eclipsed by the white dot: in the fusion of that smouldering eye one discerned Harold Wilson's 'white heat of technology', Kennedy's final ride through Dallas, a Vietnamese Lolita running from a tropical fire fight, revolution, famine and year after year of downright gossip and sell. The question 'Who killed JR?' summed up with Delphic pithy an Oedipal relationship - with the bringer of the pyjamas, the outside world or TV itself, who could say? - that was guilty from the outset, but had somehow gotten way out of hand. The eye turned the boy into the late-night customer in Edward Hopper's painting of a New York diner, a snapshot of the loneliness of the Lutheran soul from which TV, quite as much as free will, is singularly absent.

Successful soap operas mirror precisely the moral contours of contemporary life - with the sole exception that no character, however foul or homely, is ever depicted watching TV, let alone the self-same serials which nightly garner audiences of up to 18 million viewers. But, far from being the mirror of our lives, TV proffers a world without mirrors, a world in which no one switches off but one which, mysteriously, exhibits a staggering ability to replicate and repeat itself. From that, doctrinists of the bigger picture might wonder whether Heaven itself will be wired for TV and if, like soap opera, the flow of information will be restricted on a 'need to know' basis that matches the narrative structure its denizens inhabit.

I'm talking about TV in the late 1950s, before it remodelled our lives and minds along lines that, in retrospect, seem fated. When the Universal Declaration of Human Rights was signed in 1948, TV was still a coltish medium, delving into kitchen-sink drama or putting on dinner jackets to read out the news. It wasn't until 1963, for God's sake, that the BBC lifted its ban on making fun of politicians, the Queen, the Pope or penises.

The Declaration invited us, like characters out of Woody Allen's *Purple Rose of Cairo*, to step out of the Homeric continuum and into a world of promise that, essentially, had been pre-embodied in the Soviet gospel of the apotheosis of man. The Declaration was, initially, an act of thunder-stealing and, like the socialist goals it had plundered, there was no economic room for pay-back.

Watching TV is provided for in the UN Declaration but a large number of the latter's promises, mostly appertaining to our rights as workers and individuals, have vanished in the rapid transition we have made to the role of viewers and consumers. Even in Wao, in southwest Sudan, the rain-forest noises of poor African suburbia fall silent when the introductory notes of an Egyptian serial first sound. Far from spying on my infant nakedness, the television talks to us as a throng.

In the rush for a seat, it's easy to lose sight of the fact that what once were promises are now largely illusions. Perhaps they always were: the Keepers of the Cloth always appreciate the value of the thread. In my nakedness, they speak of things to buy, of the life to be enjoyed if I meet hypothetical and remote criteria. The boulevard of dreams has become littered with the street furniture of commerce, with nary a reminder of the rights of the pedestrian.

This morning, Hopperishly, I awoke with the TV on, like a creature in film perhaps, but more like a creature in life. In the distant Himalayan evenings of childhood, we would bicker about switching over. Now I just flip. ❑

Michael Griffin

A censorship chronicle incorporating information from the American Association for the Advancement of Science Human Rights Action Network (AAASHRAN), Amnesty International (AI), Article 19 (A19), the BBC Monitoring Service Summary of World Broadcasts (SWB), the Committee to Protect Journalists (CPJ), the Canadian Committee to Protect Journalists (CCPJ), the Inter-American Press Association (IAPA), the International Federation of Journalists (IFJ/FIP), the International Federation of Newspaper Publishers (FIEJ), Human Rights Watch (HRW), the Media Institute of Southern Africa (MISA), International PEN (PEN), Open Media Research Institute (OMRI), Reporters Sans Frontières (RSF), the World Association of Community Broadcasters (AMARC), the World Organisation Against Torture (OMCT) and other sources

ALGERIA

Communications Minister Habib-Chawki Hamraoui committed the government to a 'clean break' from its history of censorship and press restrictions when he met with a delegation from the World Association of Newspapers (WAN) on 19 March. Hamraoui guaranteed the five-person delegation that the 'reading committees' that monitored editorial content at printing plants were 'gone for ever and will not return'. He promised that a forthcoming information law would 'guarantee' freedom of the press and access to information; journalists would no longer be arrested, prosecuted or jailed for their reporting activities; no more newspapers would be suspended from publication; and that independent newspapers could set up their own printing facilities as an alternative to the government's printing monopoly. Hamraoui also pledged to end by the end of 1998 the state monopoly on advertising which, critics say, allows the government to favour newspapers that support its policies. On the foreign press, Hamraoui promised that more visas would be available for foreign journalists and that they would soon be allowed to decline the 'protection' of armed guards during their visits. (WAN)

Recent publication: *Neither Among the Living nor the Dead—State-Sponsored Disappearances in Algeria* (HRW, February 1998, 48pp)

ARGENTINA

The offices of Amnesty International and the Association for the Relatives of the Detained and Disappeared were targeted by arsonists on 8 March, with the loss of valuable documents related to the disappearance of Italian and Spanish nationals during the dictatorship from 1976 to 1983. (Equipo Nizkor)

AZERBAIJAN

Salavan Mamedov (*Index* 2/1998), editor of Baku's weekly *Istintag*, was freed from prison on 23 January after his case was raised by a number of newspaper editors with a visiting delegation from the Council of Europe. He still faces trial on criminal libel charges against former district prosecutor Nazim Tagiev. (CPJ)

On 27 February Magerram Aliev, chief of the Baku police, had all remaining copies of the magazine *Monitor* confiscated, justifying his action on the grounds of 'maintaining stability in the city'. (Human Rights Centre of Azerbaijan)

BANGLADESH

In late February concern was expressed for journalist **Mashiur Khan**, who was arrested on 21 November last year, jailed under the Special Powers Act which allows magistrates to incarcerate without trial up for to 90 days anyone suspected of being a 'threat to the country'. The 90-day time period has now expired. (RSF)

The newspaper *Dainik Pratibedan* was banned on 25 February, under the Press and Publication Ordinance of 1994. The paper, published in Brahmanbaria on the border with India, was critical of corruption in the country. (RSF)

Alam Raihan, editor of the weekly *Sugandha Kagoj*, was arrested by detectives on 18 March and charged the next day with publishing 'indecent and defamatory news items that confused and tarnished the image of the present government.' Despite reports that Raihan was tortured in custody, a magistrate sent him back to jail after refusing bail. (RSF, CPJ)

On 18 March **M. Mozammel Hoq** and **Shaukat Mahmood**, editors at the Media Syndicate agency, were questioned by Bureau of Anti-Corruption officials about their sources of information and the agency's assets. The officials reportedly warned the journalists that the government was not happy with their reporting about its lack of transparency. (CPJ)

BELARUS

On 11 February, editor-in-chief of the weekly *Imya*, **Irina Khalip**, was fined 200,000 rubles (US$7) for slapping a senior investigator at a demonstration in August where she claimed she was beaten by police. (RFE/RL).

An estimated 10,000 people marched in Minsk on 22 March to mark the 80th anniversary of an independent state and to protest against President Lukashenka. The crowd began marching towards the presidential palace but was stopped by police. A few dozen protesters, detained after skirmishes with police, were released later that day. (RFE/RL)

On 25 March the government released a document aimed at forbidding state officials from making official documents and comments available for publication in the independent media. The document, addressed to members of the government and state administrators, also forbids institutions from placing advertisements in the independent media, which will severely limit their financial resources. (CPJ)

BOSNIA-HERCEGOVINA

On 27 January a spokesman for the Organisation on Security and Co-operation in Europe (OSCE) said that only 45 of the 136 municipalities had so far respected the results of September's local government elections. The OSCE has threatened to carry out binding arbitration if local leaders are not prepared to convene the new councils. On 19 March the Bosnian Serb Democratic Party and the Serbian Radical Party in Srebrenica said they accepted as 'final and binding' the international ruling on the distribution of posts, meaning the municipal assembly would consist of 20 Serbian and 25 Muslim deputies. However, in accordance with its earlier threat, the OSCE was forced to suspend the authority on 6 April as Serbs had continued to obstruct efforts to convene the council. One attempt to hold a founding session was aborted after Serbs played a nationalistic anthem and Muslim deputies walked out. The OSCE chief of Bosnia, Robert Barry, said an international mediator would be appointed to chair a temporary executive body in the town. The temporary administration will consist of two Serbs and two Muslim with the OSCE appointee as tie-breaker. (B92, RFE/RL)

BOTSWANA

World View Botswana, a locally based non-governmental organisation, was on 27 February, denied a licence to broadcast. The government said there is no need to grant licences to community radio stations because the objectives of community broadcasting are met by the state-controlled Radio Botswana. The licences had been sought to run radio stations in the local community of Basarwa. (MISA)

BRAZIL

Fernando Gabeira, a politician whose life was depicted in the Oscar-nominated film *Four Days in September*, was denied a visa to attend the awards ceremony in Los Angeles. The film of Gabeira's autobiographical account of the 1969 kidnapping of the US ambassador to Brazil was nominated for the trophy of best foreign-language film. A State Department official said that Mr Gabeira was not eligible for a visa, having previously engaged in terrorist activities. (BBC World Service)

BULGARIA

The government was accused of censorship after its 9 February banning of the satirical TV programme *Hashove* (Rebels). A day earlier, the show had poked fun at the decision to appoint President Petar Stoyanov's brother to the board of national television. In the same programme, Prime Minister Ivan Kostov was compared to a petty crook, and Foreign Minister Nadezhda Mihailova to a stripper. Officially, the programme was taken off air 'due to irregularities in its sponsorship contract'. Dimitar Koroudjiev of the National Broadcasting Council said there is 'a limit beyond which democracy must defend itself', accusing the programme of instigating 'chaos and hatred'. (RFE/RL)

BURUNDI

Intelligence agents closed down the Bujumbura news agency Net-press and took its director, **Jean Claude Kavumbagu**, in for questioning on 27 March. He was later released. An employee suggested that authorities had reacted to a Net-Press report on 25 March about the authorities' earlier confiscation of the pro-opposition *L'Aube de la democratie* (The Dawn of Democracy), published by the mostly Hutu FRODEBU party. The paper only reappeared in late March after a two-year suspension. (NDIMA, IRIN)

Concern has been raised for the safety of **Jean Nepomuscene Minani**, who was arrested on 28 November and accused of writing a letter that criticised the government. He has not been seen since. (AI)

Recent publications: *Proxy Targets: Civilians in the Civil War in Burundi*, (HRW, March 1998, 125pp).

CAMEROON

On 14 April 1998 **Pius Njawe**, editor-in-chief of the weekly *Le Messager*, appealed his 13 January conviction for spreading false information (*Index* 2/1998) reduced to one year by the Doula court of appeals. (FXI, RSF, IPI)

CANADA

On 16 February the federal Liberal government asked the Supreme Court to say whether or not the French-speaking province of Quebec had the legal right to secede. The government lawyer,Yves Fortier, said that the case was meant to affirm 'that political choices are made within a legal framework and that political choices have legal repercussions.' The separatist Quebec government sees the case as a scare tactic designed to coerce local businesses into supporting Canadian unity. (Reuters)

On 2 March, the day the Canadian Broadcasting Corporation aired his special report on the Hells Angels, Vancouver-based reporter **Greg Rasmussen** came home to find his house had been broken into and vandalised. His radio, wrapped in a plastic bag, lay submerged in the bath, an echo of the way the gang allegedly disposes of its enemies in larger bodies of water. Police have placed Rasmussen and **Kelly Ryan**, who helped to prepare the report, under protection. In Quebec, where the Angels are waging a bloody war with a rival gang for control of the drug trade, a member shot a Montreal reporter in the leg in 1995. (CCPJ, Reuters)

The Supreme Court said on 9 April that the publication of photographs without the consent of their subject constitutes a breach of privacy. The ruling was made in the case of **Gilbert Duclos**, who was sued by Pascale-Claude Aubry because of a photograph published 10 years ago. Aubry, pictured in the now-defunct magazine *Vice-Versa* relaxing on the steps of a Montreal building, sued 'because her classmates laughed at her'. (Reuters)

CHAD

On 12 February **Yaldet Begoto Oulatar** and **Dieudonné Djonabaye**, director and chief editor of the newspaper *N'Dajmena Hebdo,* were sentenced to two-year suspended prison sentences and fines of CFA100,000 each for defaming President Idriss Deby in a December article entitled 'Deby, a Partisan President'. It was later reported that Djonabaye was flogged with an electric cable in a police cell in N'djamena on 29 March, after being arrested again while visiting the French/Chad military base Epervier. He was freed the same day with serious wounds. (World Association of Newspapers, RSF)

CHINA

On 5 March Tsui Sze-man of the Chinese People's Political Consultative Conference criticised publicly sponsored Radio-Television Hong Kong (RTHK) for adopting a 'confrontational policy' towards the Special Administrative Region's government. Tsui described RTHK as a 'remnant of British rule' and accused the station of hiding its 'true colours' behind the pretext of editorial independence. (Radio-Television Hong Kong)

The US announced on 14 March that it would not sponsor an anti-China resolution at the United Nations Human Rights Commission session in Geneva following the release of selected political prisoners. The US has backed UNHRC anti-Chinese resolutions since the Tiananmen killings in 1989. (Reuters)

A poster by the Body Shop of a flabby doll, which was intended to ridicule the myth of the perfect female body, was banned by MTR, the Hong Kong Railway corporation, it was reported on March 27. (*Independent)*

Dissenting magazine *The Nineties* announced on 30 March that it would end publication in June after 28 years of critical political coverage. Editor **Lee Yee** believes that the influence of political magazines has been reduced because of the information explosion. He denied the decision was linked with political pressure following the handover. The magazine is banned on the mainland. *(South China Morning Post)*

Hong Kong's China-appointed legislature voted by a large margin on 1 April to endorse the editorial independence of government-funded public broadcaster Radio Television Hong Kong, which was attacked by leader Tung Chee-hwa last month for criticising his administration. (Reuters)

The Hong Kong Journalists Association has demanded an apology from Su Xu, first secretary of the Chinese embassy in France, after his comments to reporter **John Liauw Chung-ping** of Hong Hong's TVB news, who was covering Prime Minister Zhu Rongji's visit to Paris on April 6. Liauw had asked Mr Zhu for the premier's response to a protest by members of Reporters Sans Frontières, to which the latter replied that he should not be asking such questions and, if he persisted, any future co-operation would be terminated. (HKJA)

COLOMBIA

On 22 February **Oscar García Calderón**, who covered bullfights for the daily *El Espectador*, was shot death in Bogotá. García was investigating links between bullfighting and organised crime. (CPJ)

Jesús María Valle Jaramillo, president of the Permanent Committee for the Human Rights in Antioquia, was assassinated on 27 February. He had repeatedly denounced the violations of human rights by paramilitaries in the area. (*Derechos Humanos*)

Didier Aristizabal, a radio journalist in the city of Cali, was gunned down by unidentified assailants on 2 March. Aristizabal worked as a political reporter for Radio Todelar in Cali until 1994 before joining the faculty of Santiago University as a professor of journalism. In 1996 he became chief press officer for the Cali Fair, a bullfighting tournament. (CPJ)

Ramiro de la Espriella, **Dario Bautista** and **Fabio Castillo**, columnists for the *El Espectador* for over two decades, were forced to resign following the newspaper's sale to Grupo Bavaria in December. On 8 March, Grupo Bavaria named as new director, Rodrigo Pardo, the former media chief in President's Ernesto Samper's electoral campaign, which was accused of receiving a $6 million contribution from a cocaine cartel. Pardo initially invited the three journalists to continue writing their columns. On 10 March the journalists accepted by letter on condition that *El Espectador*'s editorial independence were guaranteed. The following day, the letter of acceptance was published in the newspaper under the title 'Unfortunate Resignation'. (CPJ)

On 14 March journalist **José Abel Salazar Serna** was found dead in his apartment; he had been stabbed 15 times. Salazar hosted a programme called Youth Action on Radio Todelar in Manizales. (CPJ)

Eight journalists and technicians were kidnapped on 2 April by members of the National Liberation Army (ELN): **Ana Mercedes Ariza** of Radionet and the television magazine *CM&*; **Rocio Chica** of the television magazine *Noti 7*; **Javier Santoyo** of the television magazine *Noticias de la Noche*; and cameramen and technicians **Marcos Quintero, Edgard Osmar Gonzalo Cepeda, Fernando Mogollon, Reynaldo Perez** and **Saul Garcia**. They were abducted following a press conference about a draft peace accord between ELN and the government in February. Two days later, **Sonia Solano** of national television, **Jorge Caicedo** of *Hora Cero* and **Orlando Manzini** of *Uninoticia*, as well as cameraman **Johnny Lopera** and his driver were detained for more than two hours while they tried to to bring their kidnapped colleagues them extra clothing. (RSF)

CZECH REPUBLIC

On 2 February two defamation actions against **Zdenek Zukal** (*Index* 2/98), owner and director of the private TV Studio ZZIP, were redesignated as 'libellous accusations'. The action came on the eve of an amnesty which declared all legal actions for defamation void . (RSF)

Following financial scandals involving the Civic Democratic Party and the Civic Democratic Alliance (ODA), the Social Democratic Party (CSSD) has become embroiled in one of its own. On 9 February, *Respekt* reported that the CSSD had received some 10 million crowns (US$292, 000) from the Communist Party in 1990. The weekly also noted large discrepancies between the financial report submitted by CSSD leadership to the national conference in 1996, and a report given to the Chamber of Deputies two weeks later. (RFE/RL)

CROATIA

On 2 April **Davor Butovic** and **Vlado Vurusic**, the former editor-in-chief and reporter for the independent weekly *Globus*, were convicted on charges of criminal libel and sentenced to suspended jail terms of four and two months, respectively, for defaming the defence ministry (*Index* 2/97). The charges stemmed from an October 1996 article which claimed that Ivica Rajic, an indicted war criminal at large, had been spotted in a Split motel owned by the Defence Ministry . The conditional sentences will only be applied if the journalists are convicted of any other offences in the next year. Butkovic currently has 17 criminal libel cases pending against him, including a suit brought by 23 ministers in connection with a report alleging corruption. The trial on this suit was set to begin on 20 April. (CPJ)

DEMOCRATIC REPUBLIC OF CONGO

Professor Kalele Kabila, an academic and close ally of opposition leader Etienne Tshisekedi, was jailed for two years at the end of January. Professor Kabila, accused of 'propagating false rumours', was tried alongside journalist **Jean-François Kabanda**, who was charged with publishing 'seditious documents'. The Union for Democracy and Social Progress, whose documents were published by Kabanda, described the sentences as 'confirmation of the sham legal proceedings which were organised.' (RSF)

On 20 February copies of the day's edition of private newspaper *Le Soft* were seized at the airport in Kinshasa, shortly after arriving from Belgium. The front page headline was 'Tshisekedi, eternally persecuted', a reference to the country's most prominent opposition leader. (RSF)

Floriber Chebeya Bahizire, president of La Voix des Sans Voix (Voice of the Voiceless), one of country's main human rights organisations, was violently attacked by five men on 20 March. Four of the attackers were said to have worn uniforms from the national army. (AI, Africa News Online)

The UN investigation into human rights violations was suspended on 9 April. The move, ordered by Secretary-General Kofi Annan, follows the detention of a Canadian member of the team at Kinshasa airport and the seizure of some of his documents. The head of the UN mission argued that the authorities' subsequent photocopying of the documents had been a violation of the team's diplomatic immunity, while another said that the confidentiality of the enquiry had been broken and the safety of witnesses could no longer be guaranteed. Forensic experts looking for mass graves also departed in early April after they were forced to leave the north-western town of Mbandaka after facing hostility from the local population for allegedly 'disturbing traditional burial sites'. (AI, HRW)

In early March Pascal Kambale, vice-president of the Zairean Association for the Defence of Human Rights (AZADHO) was summoned to the National Security Council and questioned about an AZADHO report about a civilian massacre allegedly perpetrated by government soldiers in mid-February. On 13 March 1,650 copies of AZADHO's annual report were confiscated by national intelligence agents. On 3 April a complete ban on AZADHO was imposed. (AI, BBC, Africa News Online).

In Kinshasa, **Modeste Mutinga**, editor-in-chief of *Le Potentiel*, was arrested by members of the National Information Agency on 25 February.

His arrest follows an article entitled 'Kabilia's *kassai* [inhabitants] are sulking'. The article concerned the reaction of high individuals on hearing of the return of former prime minister and leading dissident Etienne Tshisekedi to his village. (RSF)

Michel Kadi Luya, editor of the daily *Le Parmarès*, was arrested on 11 April by security agents. No reason was given. On the same day **Mossi Mwassi**, previously a correspondent for the Swahili service of the BBC, was released after being held for four months on charges of spying. **Bossage Yema**, editor-in-chief of newspaper *L'Alarme*, is still in detention following his arrest on 7 February. (IRIN)

DJIBOUTI

On 17 February the publishing director of the private paper *Al Wahda*, **Ahmed Abdi Farah**, and **Kamil Hassan Ali**, one of its correspondents, were arrested and placed in detention. The two journalists appeared in court on 26 February to answer to charges linked to articles that criticised the leadership. *Al Wahda* is an organ of the Djibouti Opposition Front. (RSF)

EGYPT

The independent weekly *al-Osboa* reported on 2 February that the state censor had banned a video featuring former television, film and stage actresses who quit their jobs for religious reasons. Among the women's grievances was that most state-sponsored productions forbade actresses to wear veils. The censor said that by titling their video, *Rightly-Guided Actresses Who Repent*, the women 'defamed other artists by implication'. (*Cairo Times*)

Two Egyptian journalists in Paris to cover the trial of French writer Roger Garaudy were followed as they left court on 27 February and severely beaten. Middle East News Agency reporter **Abdalla Hassan** and **Sayid Hamli**, a Saudi television correspondent, suffered arm, leg and skull fractures after they were beaten with sticks at La Cité metro station, reportedly by members of a Zionist organisation. Garaudy was fined FF120,000 for writings that the court judged anti-Semitic. (Egyptian Organisation for Human Rights)

On 24 February **Magdi Hussein** and **Ahmed Hilal** became the first Egyptian journalists to be jailed for criminal libel when the Bulaq Misdemeanour Appeal Court confirmed the convictions and one-year prison sentences imposed in a case brought by former interior minister Hassan al-Alfi against the opposition daily *al-Sha'ab* (*Index* 2/1997, 5/1997, 6/1997, 1/1998, 2/1998). Hussein, the editor-in-chief, was detained on 8 March as he arrived in Cairo on a flight from Damascus; Hilal, a reporter for the paper, reported to police on 11 March. The libel convictions relate to three minor allegations among a total of 40 in the original article. (Egyptian Organisation for Human Rights, CPJ)

The Publication Censorship Department cancelled *al-Doustour*'s printing licence on 26 February, following the publication a day earlier of an article entitled 'Terrorist Groups Threaten to Assassinate Egypt's Three Most Prominent Coptic Businessmen' which had been approved by the censor. The article alleged the *Jama'at al-Islamiya* had issued a faxed death threat against the three unnamed - but identifiable - businessmen. Though registered in Cyprus, *Al-Doustour* is printed locally and the decision amounts to a ban. A similar article, with names and pictures, had earlier appeared in the state-owned magazine *Rose al-Yusuf* and, on 1 March, the Higher Press Council (HPC) dismissed its editor, **Adel Hamouda**. In a surprise 7 March speech to the HPC, President Hosni Mubarak maligned the two publications as 'yellow media' which harmed Egypt's image by suggesting the state could not protect Christians, and called for a 'rational press'. Since then, three senior employees of *Misr Al Fata* have been charged with libel and **Gamal Fahmy Hassan**, head of *al-Doustour*'s editorial staff was sentenced to six months' hard labour and fined 501 Egyptian pounds at an Appeal Court hearing on 18 March. The case related to a March 1996 article in the Nasserite weekly *al-Arab*. (RSF, CPJ, Egyptian Organisation for Human Rights, *Cairo Times*, *Middle East International*)

On 19 March the Foreign Publications Censor confiscated that day's edition of the bi-weekly *Cairo Times*. Publisher **Hisham Kasim** had received verbal warnings of confiscation after its previous edition which contained an article by the deputy editor-in-chief detailing his arrest and interrogation by the State Security Investigations Office on 17 February. Kasim said he had been given two reasons for the confiscation of the Cyprus-registered, English-language paper. One was an interview with the liberal writer **Khalil Abdel-Kareem** that allegedly 'harmed the reputation' of the al-Azhar seminary, Egypt's highest religious authority. The other, a commentary entitled 'Our Democracy - Yellower than Thou', was highly critical of the state of freedom of expression in Egypt. (Egyptian Organisation for Human Rights)

ETHIOPIA

The government crackdown on freedom of speech plumbed new depths in February and March (*Index* 4/1997, 1/1998, 2/1998).

On 9 February *Agiere* journalist **Abay Hailu** died in prison from pneumonia. He had been unable to pay the 5,000 birs bail, following his sentencing in March 1997 for an article in the weekly *Wolafen* headed 'Addis Ababa is in Danger of Attack by Islamic Fundamentalists'. **Kifle Mulat** (*Index* 3/1997), chairperson of the Ethiopian Free Press Association, and **Goshu Moges**, a journalist with *Ethio-Times,* were also arrested in February. Amnesty International reported that it feared for the safety of arrested *Urji* journalists **Solomon Namara**, **Tesfaye Deressa**, **Garuma Bekele**, **Hundesa Wakwaya**, **Wakshum Bacha** (corrected name) and **Alemu Tolessa**. Fresh arrests included folk-singers **Dawit Mekonnen**, **Abebe Abashu**, **Mohammed Sheka**, **Muktar Usman** and *Barissa* journalist **Alemayehu Umatta**, all members of the Oromo ethnic group. On 4 March **Berhanu Liyew,** a reporter who continued to publish work at the *Keyete* and *Taime Fiqir* papers after his colleagues **Nega Tariku** and **Andualem Muhammed** had fled to Kenya, also escaped across the border. According to the Ethiopian Free Press Journalists' Association, nine journalists from the newspapers *Woncif*, *Zegabi* and *Erotica* were released at the beginning of March after meeting their 10,000 birs bail bonds. Ethiopia held the regional lead for imprisoned journalists, according to an April report by the US-based Committee to Protect Journalists. A total of 16 journalists were newly imprisoned in 1997 and still being held at the end of the year. (RSF, AI, NDIMA, *Addis Tribune,* CPJ)

EUROPEAN UNION

The European Commission announced in early April that it would investigate the claims by News Corporation owner Rupert Murdoch that the subsidies given to the BBC's News 24 television service amounted to unfair competition. Murdoch, whose company holds a majority shareholding in the satellite service BSkyB, raised the issue on 7 April at the Birmingham European Audio-Visual Conference. (*Daily Telegraph, Guardian*)

FRANCE

National Front leader Jean-Marie Le Pen was banned from public office for two years by a Versailles court on 2 April. As well as assaulting socialist politician Annette Plauvast-Bergeal, Le Pen was found guilty of provoking violence at a political meeting. (*European, Guardian*)

GABON

On 2 February the National Communication Council forbade private radio station, Radio Soleil, from further transmissions after a broadcast satirising President Omar Bongo. (RSF)

GAMBIA

On 12 February **Baboucar Gaye,** proprietor of Citizen FM radio, was charged with operating an unlicensed radio station in Banjul. No court date was set, but Citizen FM remains off the air. A week earlier, Gaye and **Ebrima Silla**, the station's news editor, were detained for broadcasting a story about the National Intelligence Agency (*Index* 2/98). Meanwhile, police are denying access to the station's premises, which also house the *New Citizen*. As a result, the paper has not been published for over a month (RSF, CPJ)

GEORGIA

On 19 February **Nodar Grigalashvili**, editor-in-chief of the newspaper *Sakartvelo*, resigned in protest over 'ideological incompatibility' between him and Nodar Natadze, leader of the United Republican Party who, he said, 'wants us to publish in the paper only what he thinks should be published'. The entire staff of the paper walked out in solidarity. Grigalashvili said that he would launch a new twice-weekly, independent paper.

GERMANY

A CD by **Ekkehard Schall**, son-in-law of Bertholt Brecht and a radical left-wing actor, was banned on 16 March on the grounds that it could inspire neo-Nazis. Schall recorded the text of *Mein Kampf* without a critical commentary. Instead sound effects were used to heighten the ironies contained within the notoriously tedious work. The Bavarian state government, which owns the rights to Hitler's banned book, initially gave the project the go-ahead, but then backed down in the face of pressure from Jewish leaders such as Ignatz Bubis. (*Guardian*, *International Herald Tribune*)

GREECE

On 1 April an Athens court confirmed the prison sentence for libel and 'filing a false document' against **Makis Psomiadis,** journalist and owner of the daily *Onoma*, refusing to allow the 50-month sentence to be converted into a fine. The case came to court after Psomiadis accused Minister of the Environment and Public Works Costas Laliotis in an article of having received a commission for awarding the Athens airport construction contract to a German company. (RSF)

GUATEMALA

On 16 February the Association of Journalists asked the government to suspend the implementation of a new Radio Diffusion Law which would sell community radio stations to private business. (Agencial Pulsar)

On 13 March **Eduardo Salermo**, the Argentine lawyer who has taken the October 1995 Xaman massacre to the Interamerican Human Rights Commission in Washington, was followed for 20 minutes by a man in a white vehicle, only days after his car was sabotaged. The incident occurred a day after a press conference in which irregularities in the Xaman case, involving 26 military personnel, were revealed. (*Prensa Libre*)

State agencies have been prevented from advertising in the weekly *Cronica* and the daily *El Periódico*, both of which are openly critical of the two-year-old administration of President Alvaro Arzu Irigoyen. Private sector advertising has fallen by 80 per cent since the government took power and many advertisers claim they have come under pressure to deny revenue to opposition papers. (CPJ)

GUINEA

On 8 March police in Conakry detained **Aboubacar Conde**, editor-in-chief of *L'Indépendant*, for 'purposes of investigation', days after questioning him about an article on the negative public opinion following the temporary closure on 26 December of private newspapers. Two foreign staff journalists were subsequently expelled. **Saliou Samb**, the Senegalese assistant editor-in-chief, was expelled on 16 March accused of 'using forged identity cards'. One day later **Abdoulaye Sankara**, from Burkina Faso, was temporarily arrested and, on his release, immediately escorted to a waiting plane. Two other foreign journalists with the private press have previously been expelled from Guinea (*Index* 2/1998). (RSF)

HAITI

Radio Vwa Peyizan Milo (RVPM), linked to the peasant organisation Mouvman Peyizan Milo (MPM), was attacked on 31 March by police officers just 10 days after members of the movement had occupied several hundred hectares of land which, they claimed, had been sequestered without full payment. (Haiti Info)

HONDURAS

On 10 March the Committee of the Relatives of Detained and Disappeared (COFADEH) denounced a draft law going through the National Congress sponsored by a military representatives and members of the Liberal and National parties. The proposal would halt investigations into disappearances during the last decade and consolidate the immunity of those responsible. (Equipo Nizkor)

General Mario Hung Pacheco asked on 4 April for the detention of **Ramón Custodio**, president of the Committee for the Defence of Human Rights in Honduras. Custodio claims to have proof of Pacheco's involvement in the disappearance and murder of student Roger González in April 1997. (Equipo Nizkor)

INDIA

In the run-up to elections on 16 February, a number of attacks against journalists were reported in the state of Assam. On 12 January police beat **Avirook Sen**, correspondent for *India Today* magazine, and his wife **Suparna Sharma**, a reporter for the *Indian Express* newspaper. Three days later, four Assam-based journalists with the national television network Doordarshan Kendra were arrested for broadcasting an item which allegedly 'heightened communal tensions' in Assam. On 7 February **Prakash Mahanta**, a reporter for the newly founded Assamese-language weekly *Natoon Samoy* (New Times), was assaulted with an iron bar and detained at the Nagaon Sadar police station. Mahanta remains in custody by order of the Judicial Magistrate of Nagaon on charges related to his recent articles about government corruption. He was reportedly denied medical treatment. (CPJ)

On 14 February journalist **Eknath Namdeo Zade** of *Godatir Samachar* was assaulted by Congress (I) supporters during an election event for party nominee Suryakanta Patil in Parhani district of Mararashtra. Patil's supporters were angered by one of Zade's questions. (Press Trust of India)

Painter **M. F. Hussain** was issued a 2,000 rupee bailable warrant in late-February by a magistrate in Indore for painting the goddess Saraswati nude. The complaint was filed by Bharatiya Janata Party leader Lokesh Dhiman. (Press Trust of India)

Fifty armed men attacked the Madurai office of the Tamil-language daily *Dinamalar* on 1 March. Bearing clubs and knives, the armd men assaulted the office watchmen, hurled four molotov cocktails and destroyed press equipment. This action followed the paper's critical coverage of the ruling Dravida Munnetra Kazhagam state government in Tamil Nadu. (CPJ)

On 9 March the Indian Journalists' Association urged the West Bengal government to order an inquiry into the disappearance of **Ankur Barbora**, a special correspondent for the *Asian Age*. Barbora had left his Calcutta office about one month earlier and has not been seen since. (Press Trust of India)

INDONESIA

On 6 March **Margiono**, editor-in-chief of the magazine *Detektif & Romantika,* was suspended from the Association of Indonesian Journalists (PWI) for two years for publishing a front cover depicting President Suharto as the king of spades. Information Minister R. Hartono stated on 4 March that the cover slandered the president in two ways. It could be turned upside down, which in itself was offensive, but in depicting Suharto as a 'king', the picture implied he had achieved power by unconstitutional means. (ISAI)

On 13 March three members of the People's Democratic Party (PRD) were taken from their homes in Jakarta by the military and are now in police custody. They are **Mugianto**, **Nazar Patria** and **Aan Rusdianto.** The police say they were in possession of 'communist literature,' and within days they were charged with subversion,which carries the death sentence. (*South China Morning Post*)

On 3 April, Indonesian anti-riot police beat two Indonesian journalists, **Bambang Soen** of the daily *Republika* and **Dewi Gustiana** of *Suara Pembaruan,* and arrested and seized film from two foreign journalists, **Ahihiro Nonaka** of *Asia Press* and **Anthony Ashley** of the *Western Australian,* while the reporters were covering a crackdown on student protests in Yogyakarta. Scores of other Indonesian journalists were also threatened by the police. (ISAI)

IRAN

In early April the Mayor of Teheran **Gholamhossein Karbaschi**, who also owns a mass circulation daily, was detained by order of the conservative-led judiciary on charges of bribery and fraud (*Index* 6/1997). The arrest was widely perceived as a move to humiliate the moderate government of President Mohammad Khatami, whom Karbaschi supported in the presidential elections. The mayor was released on 16 April but is expected to stand trial within a few weeks. (*Midde East International*).

The former editor-in-chief of *Iran News*, **Morteza Firouzi**, who was sentenced to death for 'spying for a foreign country' in

FARAJ SARKOOHI

Without let or hindrance

What are your plans now that you've been released from prison?

I hope I'll have the opportunity to pursue my cultural and professional activities in the fields of literary criticism and journalism. At the moment, the book *An Imprint of the Times*, a collection of literary articles, is ready for its second edition. Another collection of my articles has been compiled and is ready for publication. A book about contemporary poetry and fiction, and a research work on a number of topics in contemporary culture are nearing completion and I hope these books will be granted printing and publication permits.

What is the situation with your passport and why was this issue raised by foreign media?

I have requested a passport but they haven't given me one. Everyone, nowadays, speaks of the rule of law and civil society but, in some instances, things seem to be much the same as before. On the basis of the court's verdict, I was given the most severe sentence allowed under Article 500; that is, one year in prison. No other punishment was stipulated in the verdict. And the authorities have told me that there is no legal reason why I should not be allowed to travel. I have gone to see the judicial authorities at the Revolutionary Court on several occasions, without any result.

News agencies have reported that you've written a letter to the international writers' association PEN. Why?

While I was in prison, the different branches of PEN, as well as many prominent writers, artists, journalists and intellectuals, did a great deal to defend me and freedom of expression, of which I was unaware. Even now, I don't know the names and addresses of all those people and organisations. PEN has accepted me as a member and I asked PEN to convey my gratitude - by publishing and disseminating my letter - to and everyone who fought for my freedom and for freedom of expression. ❑

Translated by Nilou Mobasser from the Persian original of an edited, exclusive two-part interview with Faraj Sarkoohi by the Tehran daily Jameah *(Society) on 17 and 18 March 1998.*

January (*Index* 2/1998), had his sentence repealed by President Khatami in early March. Firouzi, who remains in detention, is likely to face a retrial. (AI)

On 5 March Iranian journalist **Akbar Gandji** (*Index* 2/1998) was released a few days after a revolutionary court found him guilty of 'spreading lies which disturbed public order'. (RSF)

The coverage of President Clinton's sex scandals, by way of front-page photographs of Monica Lewinsky, Paula Jones and others, led to the prosecution of a magazine director in late March. **Reza Ghanilau** of the *Fakour* weekly was fined one million rials (US$300) and banned from working for six months because the women's clothes did not meet the strict restrictions on 'modesty' under censorship laws. (Reuters).

IRAQ

In the third week of March, the scientist regarded as the father of Baghdad's germ weapons programme, **Nassir Hindwani**, was arrested while trying to flee the country. The arrest is a setback to UN inspectors, who had hoped to talk to the scientist without the interference of the secret police. (*New York Times*)

Radio Free Iraq, dedicated to the overthrow of Saddam Hussein, is set to receive open and official support from the US Congress. (*The Times*)

ISRAEL

Moshe Suissa, a reporter for the daily *Yediot Aharonot*, resigned on 10 March after a story he wrote for the paper in February was revealed to be untrue. Suissa reported that rabbis had forced a man to divorce his wife after she was raped, but later admitted that the piece was based on rumours. (Associated Press)

Ten Palestinian journalists were shot and wounded by rubber-coated metal bullets in two incidents on the evening of 13 March as they covered clashes between Palestinians and the Israeli army in the Old City of Hebron. Eyewitnesses said the army intentionally targeted the first group of journalists. Reuters TV sound technician **Na'el Shuyouki** was hit four times and fell to the ground. Video footage shows him lying, with blood streaming from his forehead, as he is hit by two more shots. Despite pleas to stop shooting, the soldiers continued, wounding Reuters reporter **Mazen Dana**; **Majid al-Tamimi** and **Amer al-Jabari** of ABC News; **Hazem Bader** and **Imad al-Said** of the Associated Press; and **Wael Shuyouki** and **Ayman al-Kurd** of Amal TV. Two more journalists, **Khaled Zighari** and **Farid Arazem**, were shot elsewhere later on 13 March as they photographed paramedics transferring wounded Palestinians. The clashes were sparked by the 10 March fatal shooting of three Palestinians at a checkpoint into Hebron. Al-Said, Dana and al-Jabari were among four journalists shot in similarly deliberate circumstances when covering a demonstration in Hebron on 13 July 1997. (Palestinian Society for the Protection of Human Rights and the Environment, CPJ, *Jerusalem Times*)

On 14 March **Awad Awad**, a Palestinian photo-journalist working for Agence France-Presse, was hit by two rubber-coated metal bullets as he covered a confrontation between protesters and the Israeli army in the West Bank town of Dura. (RSF)

Recent publication: *Demolishing Peace—Israel's Policy of Mass Demolition of Palestinian House in the West Bank* (B'Tselem, September 1997, 35pp)

ITALY

British Prime Minister Tony Blair was alleged by *La Stampa* in early April to have used his personal influence with Prime Minister Romano Prodi to further the business interests in Europe of Rupert Murdoch, owner of *The Times* and the *Sun*, both of which supported the Labour Party election campaign in 1997. Murdoch's offer for a controlling interest in Mediasaet, the group belonging to former prime minister Silvio Berlusconi which runs Italy's three largest private TV channels, was ultimately rejected but not without raising concern about 'cronyism' between the UK premier and Murdoch, a US citizen eager to advance his empire into the EU. (*European, Guardian, Daily Telegraph*,)

Results of a poll published in *La Republicca* on 10 April revealed high levels of public support for far-right politician Gianfranco Fini in his demand that 'declared' homosexuals should not be permitted to teach children on the grounds that they are 'prone to paedophilia'. The statement, made on a television chat show in April, was endorsed by 47 per cent of viewers. (*Guardian*)

JAPAN

Women who served as sex slaves in army brothels during World War II will receive compensation from the government it was reported at the beginning of April. Each of the 155 women registered for compensation will get $25,000. (*Far East Economic Review*)

KAZAKHSTAN

In early April **Medel Ismailov**, a leading opposition activist, was sentenced to a year in prison for insulting President Nursultan Nazerbaev. Ismailov, who heads the leftist Worker's Movement, was convicted over comments he made at a public meeting last November. (BBC World Service, AI)

KENYA

On 11 February a photographer working for the Nation Group of Newspapers, **Stephen Sunguti**, was murdered. The motive for the attack is unknown. (NDIMA)

Two years after applying to the NGO Bureau for registration, Network for the Defence of Independent Media in Africa (NDIMA) was notified that its application had been refused. A letter, dated 15 December 1997, informed NDIMA that it had 60 days to appeal against the board's decision. However, they were not able to do so because the letter was received over two months later, postmarked 25 February 1998, effectively denying NDIMA any opportunity to respond. Failure to register as a NGO means NDIMA has become an illegal operation. (NDIMA, AI)

On 13 March newly-appointed Information and Broadcasting Minister Joseph Nyagah accused an unnamed section of the Kenyan press of 'taking advantage' of the recently repealed law on sedition to conduct a 'vicious campaign' to undermine presidential authority and national stability. On 30 March President Daniel arap Moi ordered a crackdown on 'irresponsible publications', authorising the arrest of editors and closure of papers, specifically naming the *Star*, which had been reporting on matters relating to the armed forces. Employees had to lock themselves in their offices in order to prevent a police search taking place without a warrant one day later. Senior editors of the *Star* have speculated that attempts to silence the paper stem from a story entitled 'How Coup was to be Executed', which allegedly incriminated top leaders in a plot to unseat the president. (NDIMA)

On 20 March the government cancelled a radio and television licence issued to the East Africa Television Network (EATN), a new regional service, two days after the network announced plans to go on air later this year. Information Minister Joseph Nyagah said the cancellation was due to a dispute between EATN chairman Sam Shollei and Nairobi businessman Ahmed Rashid Jibril. But the daily *Nation*, part of the Nation Group that owns EATN, claimed it demonstrated 'a deep-seated fear of truth in public life and the values of free expression.' (IPS)

Assistant Minister Fred Gumo had to be restrained from hitting **Njehu Gatabaki**, parliamentary colleague and owner of *Finance* magazine, after an article entitled 'Gumo, the Politics of Greed, Crime and Violence' was published by the magazine. Gumo accused Gatabaki of waging a 'campaign of hate and false propaganda' on 31 March, attacking him at a reception, minutes before the president arrived for the State Opening of Parliament. (NDIMA)

On 23 March journalists and photographers, including *Kenya Times* photographer **Sammy Kirui**, *Nation* photo-journalist **Rebecca Nduku** and freelancer **Willy Mwangi**, were attacked by rioting Nairobi University students. Students warned journalists against publishing photos showing them burning vehicles. (NDIMA)

Abraham Kipsang Kiptanui, former controller of State House, was awarded over $250,000 in damages on 31 March for libel caused by an article published in *Target* magazine. Kiptanui sued over an article entitled 'Three Billion Shilling Deal Off'. (NDIMA)

KUWAIT

In the second week of March,

the government resigned over the political storm raised by the display of 'un-Islamic' books at a book fair. The Islamists were threatening to bring down the government through a no-confidence vote against the information minister, a member of the royal family, who had allowed the fair to continue. (*Economist*)

KYRGYZSTAN

In the last half of February the National Agency on Communications (NAC) closed the radio station *Almaz* and shut down the media company *VOSST* for 36 hours. NAC said *Almaz* had been closed 'on technical grounds', but **Rustam Koshmuratov**, station director, said that the agency was testing its power with a mind to taking more actions against independent media. On 6 March the NAC issued *Almaz* with a temporary permit to broadcast that requires it to re-register for a licence. (Bureau on Human Rights and Rule of Law)

On 26 February the independent radio station *Piramida* said that **Mayram Akaeva**, wife of President Askar Akaev, had approached parliament to request that it pass legislation banning pornography and violence in the media and advertising. (Bureau on Human Rights and Rule of Law)

LATVIA

On 10 February, three Russian-language newspapers strongly criticised an amendment to the labour code whereby an employee can be fired for 'insufficient knowledge of the Latvian language'. *Biznes & Baltija*, *SM* and *Panorama Latvii* urged President Guntis Ulmanis to veto the amendment. Having deemed the reaction of the Russian language press 'excessively dramatic', the president nevertheless rejected the amendment the following day. (RFE/RL)

The SS Legion held a memorial day rally for its 55th anniversary on 16 March, with the 'voluntary' participation of some army units. Some 300 Russian-speaking demonstrators staged a simultaneous protest with banners demanding citizenship for 700,000 Russian-speaking residents. The press service of President Guntis Ulmanis issued a statement that, as in any democratic state, everyone has a right to express his or her opinion openly - but that they should refrain from 'comments insulting to human honour and extremist evaluations'. Russia's foreign ministry expressed indignation at the Legionaries' celebration, saying that the legion 'gave an oath of allegiance to Hitler and ... destroyed thousands of Jews, Russians and Belarusians'. (SWB)

LIBERIA

On 27 December **Al-Jerome Chede**, producer and announcer of privately owned Radio Monrovia's phone-in shows, *Issues in the Press* and *Press Fire*, fled the country with his wife after an attempted kidnapping by agents of the former National Patriotic Front (NPFL). Chede, who has been a target of press freedom violations before, is seeking refugee status in a neighbouring country. On several occassions in the past year he has received anonymous death threats. (CPJ)

MALAYSIA

Reports broadcast on 26 March throughout Asia of riots by Indonesians at a local detention centre were blacked out across Malaysia, according to a 1 April report. At least nine people died in the violence. (*International Herald Tribune*)

The government is to repeal the Film Act of 1952 and enact a new Censorship Act to deal with developments in the film industry, Deputy Home Minister Datuk Ong Ka Ting announced on 3 April. The new bill would provide for stiff fines and/or jail terms of three years for people found to be distributing, selling, renting or reproducing pornographic materials. Enforcement officers will be given greater powers to seize reproduction equipment. Studies to amend the Printing Presses and Publications Act of 1984 are also in their final stages. (Reuters)

MAURITANIA

Three journalists and human rights activists, **Professor Cheihk Saad Bouh Kamara**, **Boubacar Ould Messaoud** and **Brahim Ould Ebetty**, arrested in January (*Index* 2/1998) in connection with a documentary on slavery, were each sentenced to 13 months imprisonment and fined 30,000 ouguiya. **Fatima Mbaye**, a lawyer, was also arrested on 5 February and given the same sentence. **Abdel Nasser Ould**

Ethmane, Secretary for Foreign Relations for SOS Slavery, was convicted *in absentia*. On 24 March the president announced that all four would be able to return home that day, and would not serve their sentences. (*Observatory*, AI)

MOLDOVA

At the end of March, the director of the Committee for Radio and Television of Transdniestria asked the minister responsible for security in the 'self-proclaimed Republic of Trandniestria' to shut down the TVK television chain, which broadcasts from Tiraspol. He also asked for the station's director, **Ernest Abildaiev**, to be brought before a criminal court on charges of 'illegal activities and defamation', which carry a potential prison sentence. (RSF)

LEBANON

On 23 February three journalists from the newspaper *al-Diyar* were charged by Judge Said Mirzaa with defaming President Elias Hrawi. The charges against the paper's owner, **Charles Ayyoub**, its director **Youssef Howayyek** and cartoonist **Elie Saliba** relate to a 15 October column in which Ayyoub claimed that 'violations of the constitution have become normal' and were 'tolerated by President Hrawi'. All three face up to two years in jail and fines of up to $66,000 if convicted. (CPJ)

LIBYA

The daily *al-Zahf al-Akhdar* was banned indefinitely on 19 March for printing 'articles attacking fraternal Arab states and friendly countries' and 'deviating from the revolutionary organisation that governs the media'. All staff were suspended without explanation. (RSF)

MEXICO

The French Catholic priest **Michel Henri Jean Chanteau** was detained and expelled on 26 February. Chanteau, a priest in Chiapas for 32 years, was a frequent witness to human rights violations. (Equipo Nizkor)

On 11 March Brigadier General **José Francisco Gallardo Rodríguez** was sentenced to 14 years and eight months imprisonment for 'misappropriation of government property and destruction of military activities'. He has been detained since 9 November 1993 and both military and civil courts have filed 15 preliminary investigations and nine criminal proceedings against him, all of which were either dropped for lack of evidence or cleared on appeal. In October 1993 Gallardo wrote an article accusing the army of carrying out human rights violations. (PEN)

Journalists **Oriana Ericabe** from *France Press* and **Pascual Gorris** from the agency *AP* were detained and beaten by police on 13 April. (Equipo Nizkor)

NICARAGUA

On 4 March **Zoilamerica Narvaez** publicly accused her stepfather, former president Daniel Ortega, of having sexually abused her from the time she was 11 years old. Rosario Murrillo, Zoilameirca's mother, says that she has received death threats since the accusation was published in a weekly Managua magazine. There is speculation as to why Narvaez, 30, admitted this so soon before the next Sandinista National Liberation Front party congress in May and at a time when there are political differences within the party. (*La Prensa*)

NAMIBIA

Hannes Smith, jailed editor of the weekly *Windhoek Observer*, was released on bail on 19 February pending the outcome of an appeal against his contempt of court conviction (*Index* 2/98). (MISA)

NIGERIA

On 16 February **Christine Anyanwu**, jailed editor-in-chief and publisher of the *Sunday Magazine*, was awarded the 1998 UNESCO/Guillerno Cano World Press Freedom prize. Anyanwu was imprisoned in July 1995 for exposing a government round-up of political opponents (*Index* 3/1995, 6/1997). (IJC)

Tokunbo Fakeye, defence correspondent for the *News* and *Tempo* magazines, collapsed in military detention on 18 February and was rushed to hospital in Ikoyi, Lagos, where he received treatment for three days. He was returned to detention in the military detention camp at Park Lane on 20 February. (IJC)

On 22 February armed soldiers invaded the Ondo state television station, ransacked the editorial offices and took away the evening bulletins which included accounts of the assault two days earlier of the station's two media managers. The two men, **Dunni Fagbayiyo** and **Tunde Yusuff**, have since been suspended. ('IPR')

Unidentified gunmen killed **Tunde Oladepo**, a senior editor of the *Guardian*, on 27 February, after breaking into his Ogun State home. He was shot to death in front of his wife and children. The murderers stayed in the house for another 30 minutes after shooting him to make sure the journalist was dead. The motive for his killing has not been established. (CPJ)

Ten journalists from different organisations were beaten up and detained by police at a pro-democracy rally in Lagos on 3 March. They were released later the same day. One of them, **Monday Emoni**, picture editor from the *News*, had his camera smashed. ('IPR')

On 3 March **Olisa Agbakoba**, a human rights lawyer, was detained after being beaten and pistol-whipped by police as he was trying to negotiate a pro-democracy march in Lagos. He was charged with public order offences and released after two days in detention.(AI)

Joshua Ogbonna, publisher of the *Rising Sun*, was arrested on 9 March by officers of the Criminal Investigation Unit in Lagos. The police did not give reasons for his arrest, but colleagues said it might be related to a series of articles critical of an Abuja hotelier said to be involved in the continuing campaign to have General Sani Abacha transformed into a civilian president later this year. ('IPR')

On 10 March **Abdul Rahma Maliki**, a journalist with Kwara State Television, was beaten by police in Ilorin as he covered a protest march by students of Kwara State Polytechnic over the increasing shortage of fuel. ('IPR')

On 12 March **Joe Ajaero**, labour correspondant for the *Vanguard*, was arrested by State Security Service agents while attending a seminar to review Nigeria's labour law at a hotel in Ilorin. He was held for six days. (CPJ)

Morgan Omodu, general manager of state-owned Radio Rivers, was fired on 12 March after the station reported that the United Nigeria Congress Party senatorial primaries had been cancelled and one of its candidates Ombo Isokariari, disqualified. The party had earlier denied the report. ('IPR')

On 26 March two in-house newsletters of the Osun State chapter of the National Union of Local Government Employees (NULGE) were banned on the orders of the state's military administrator, Anthony Obi. The government said the continued existence of the NULGE *News* and the *True NULGE News* was 'threatening effective local government administration'. ('IPR')

On 2 April two government journalists in Akwa Ibom state were suspended without pay in connection with reports considered to be distasteful by the government. **Sam Akpe**, a reporter with the state-owned newspaper *Pioneer*, had analysed a crisis in an oil company operating in the state. **Roland Esin**, of the state radio station, was punished for broadcasting a contributor's commentary which criticised the delay in the payment of workers' salaries because of the government's computerisation exercise. ('IPR')

Isaac Agbo, correpondent for the *Diet*, was severely beaten on 6 April and subjected to physical drills by security officers with the Special Military Tribunal responsible for the trial of the 26 coup suspects in Jos. The officers said Agbo, who was on his way to cover the trial, was guilty of 'driving on the same road used by vehicles carrying the suspects to court'. He was charged with speeding. ('IPR')

Niran Malaolu, editor of the *Diet* newspaper, is to face trial for allegedly plotting a coup. On 14 February he was among 27 suspects paraded at the inaugural sitting of the special military tribunal, which is trying persons accused of plotting to overthrow the military government in December. Malaolu was arrested, along with three of his colleagues at the *Diet*, on 28 December (*Index* 2/1998). The other three were later released. The military authorities have given no details of Malaolu's offence. ('IPR')

PAKISTAN

In mid-February the government of Punjab announced that it would be mandatory for all girl students from Class 6 upwards to wear a veil from 23 March. Girl students are required to swear to observe *purdah* outside their school or college premises, as are all women teachers. The restriction, however, does not define *purdah*. (*Asian Age*)

On 20 February it was reported that the Chief Accountability (*Ehtesab*) Commissioner, retired Justice Ghulam Mujadid Mirza, found that more than a dozen references in the government case against former Prime Minister Benazir Bhutto were legally flawed, with little or no chance of their success in any court of law. (*Asian Age*)

In early March the Lahore High Court told Prime Minister Nawaz Sharif's government to alter a provision in last year's anti-terrorism law which allows the police to convict on the basis of a confession alone. The court said that confessions must be taken in the presence of a magistrate or high-ranking police officer, and insisted that the accused be given the right to challenge evidence presented as confessional. (BBC World Service)

On 19 March the Urdu-language daily *Public of Karachi* was banned by the local magistrate. **Anwer Senroy**, the paper's editor, said in a statement that the order was a restriction on freedom of expression and that it would be appealed against. (Pakistan Press Foundation)

In a 317-page judgement the Supreme Court decided on 3 April to dismiss contempt of court cases against Prime Minister Nawaz Sharif and other politicians and officials. The cases date back to a constitutional crisis late last year which led to the resignation of the president, and a confrontation between the government and the Supreme Court over the independence of the judiciary (*Index* 1/98). The chief justice said that the prime minister, who faced possible dismissal from office if found guilty, and others were guilty of contempt, but the cases had been dropped because of what he called 'special circumstances'. (BBC World Service)

PALESTINE (AUTONOMOUS AREAS)

Police entered the studios of Shepherd Television in Bethlehem on 16 February, ordered staff to stop all broadcasts and told them to leave. The station's closure followed several programmes in which viewers were invited to express solidarity with the Iraqi people during the weapons-inspection crisis. On 15 February the Palestinian Authority invoked 'national security' in ordering all Palestinian media to censor comments that supported Iraq in conflict with the authority's official position. (RSF)

PANAMA

On 5 March Ombudsman **Italo Antinori** denounced the government to the Interamerican Commission for Human Rights (CIDH) for preventing him doing his job. Antinori said that, since assuming his post, he has been intimidated for his defence of freedom of expression, particularly in the cases of the journalist **Gustavo Gorriti** (*Index* 5/1997, 6/1997, 1/1998, 2/1998), and the lawyers **Miguel Antonio Bernal** and **Sydney Sittón**. (*La Prensa*, *El Siglo*)

PAPUA NEW GUINEA

Prime Minister Bill Skate stated in February that he would no longer speak English to foreign journalists as he said he had been treated unfairly by the Australian media. Skate said he will speak only in Tok Pisin (Pidgin) and Motu, inconvenient for Australian journalists who speak neither. Skate's main aim is to prevent the reporting of corruption allegations against him. (PINA)

On 2 March Prime Minister Skate proposed constitutional reforms that, he said were designed to bring stability and investment to the nation. Skate wants to change the existing rules, whereby a vote of 'no-confidence' can unseat a prime minister, and instead create a government caucus, chaired by the prime minister,that could recommend the prime minister be removed at any time. Opposition leader Barnard Narokobi said that the changes favoured solidifying Skate's hold on power. (PINA)

PERU

On 3 March the District Office for the Supervision of Magistrates in Cuzco ordered disciplinary proceedings against three judges in Madre de Dios: Fausto Cornejo Alvarez, Marina Tagle de Revatta and Jorge del Caprio Pacheco. Earlier this year the judges sentenced **Ruben Zurita**, co-owner of a radio station in Madre de Dios, to one year in prison for 'illegally practising journalism', contempt and other charges. The judges are suspected of abusing their authority and failing to properly conduct their functions. (Institute for Press and Society)

The Interamerican Commission for Human Rights of the American States Organisation accepted on 10 March the case presented by **Baruch Ivcher Bronstein** against the government. Ivcher (*Index* 4/1997, 5/1997, 6/1997, 2/1998), the former main shareholder of *Frecuencia Latina* of Channel 2, has accused the authorities of unconstitutionally depriving him of his citizenship in 1993. (*Derechos Humanos*)

On 19 March the Second Criminal Court of Lima rejected accusations presented by public prosecutor Alejandro Espino Méndez against journalist **José Arrieta Mattos** for lack of evidence. On 3 March Espino Méndez had requested legal proceedings against Arrieta for obstructing justice and general contempt. Arrieta was obliged to leave the country on 7 January after being informed that there were plans to have him arrested (*Index* 2/98). (Institute for Press and Society)

On 3 April the secretary of journalist **Miguel Bravo Quispe**, Olga Lena Campos, was sentenced to 10 years in prison for his assassination on 7 January 1997 (*Index* 2/1997). (Institute for Press and Society)

Isabel Chumpitaz, presenter of the phone-in programme *People's Voice*, in which villagers voiced complaints against the government, was shot to death with her husband at her home on 6 April. (Reuters, Institute for Press and Society)

PHILIPPINES

On 30 March **Reynaldo Bancayrin**, crusading anchorman for Radio DXLL, was murdered in the southern city of Zamboanga. Bancayrin was in the middle of broadcasting his show *Bale Todo* when two men came into his booth and shot him in the head at point-blank range. The assailants then left the station on a motorbike. Police said that they were 'looking into all angles, including the possibility that this may be the result of his commentaries against corruption in some government agencies.' (RSF)

RUSSIA

On 9 February it was reported that Moscow-based private radio station Russkoe Radio, which broadcasts to more than 200 hundred cities, had been unable to broadcast in Belgorod for nearly two months. The Belgorod authorities have denied the station a licence citing 'the special mentality of residents of the *oblast*', and programme content which contradicted 'the moral and ethical foundations of Belgorod'. (RFE/RL)

On 12 February the Prosecutor-General's office charged retired Colonel Yakov Popovskikh, who formerly served in military intelligence, with planning and taking part in the murder of **Dimitry Kholodov**, in October 1994. Kholodov, a reporter for *Moskovskii komsomolets*, was investigating military corruption when he was killed opening a booby-trapped briefcase. (RFE/RL)

The State Anti-Monopoly Committee's demand that NTV pay commercial tax rates (*Index* 2/1998) was overturned by the Moscow Arbitration court on 11 February, which upheld the station's claim that it was unconstitutional. (RFE/RL)

On 2 March Prosecutor General Yuri Skuratov announced that investigators had made significant progress in the investigation into the murder of high-profile journalist **Vladimir Listyev**, shot to death outside his apartment building on 1 March 1995. Skuratov said new evidence had been found abroad linking the murder of Listyev to his business activities, rather than his journalism. At the time, his death was widely believed to be connected to his decision, as executive director of Russian Public Television (ORT), to re-evaluate the company's policies on advertising, an industry with links to organised crime. (RFE/RL)

On 13 March **Timur Kukuyev** and **Yuri Safronov**, members of a Russian film crew for local M-5 television station and ORT stringers in Daghestan, were beaten by men in paramilitary uniforms. The journalists, who had been attempting to film at the Chechen border, had their equipment stolen despite border guards who witnessed the incident, but failed to intervene. Three days later, Kukuyev was again beaten in central Makhachkala by men who warned him against 'filming anything else on foreign territory in the future'. He was admitted to hospital with broken ribs, concussion and a badly disfigured face. (RFE/RL)

On 13 March a Tomsk district court found that newspaper *Tomskaya nedelya* guilty of libelling the city's mayor, Aleksandr Makarov. The court awarded Makarov damages of 91,000 rubles (US$$15,000) and ordered the paper to pay another 30,000 rubles to co-plaintiff Nina Igorenkova, a local official in charge of combating economic crime. The lawsuit concerned an article on the business practices of Makarov's relatives and another accusing him of carrying out attacks on the property of his political opponents. The editor of *Tomskaya nedelya*, **Oleg Pletnov**, is an outspoken critic of Makarov. (RFE/RL)

Marina Kalashnikova was told on 17 March it was likely she would lose her job as a journalist for *Kommersant-Daily* after she had written a number of articles portraying the Slovak Premier Vladimir Meciar in an unfavourable light. According to the Czech daily *Lidove noviny*, one of **Kalshnikova's** articles quoted Meciar as saying the Russian presidential spokesman Sergei Yastrzhembskii was 'Slovakia's ambassador to Russia'. In *Lidove noviny* Kalashnikova quoted Yastrzhembskii as saying that 'Russia's interests are closely tied to our support for the current government of Meciar.'

On 25 March members of the tax police searched the flats of two St Petersburg journalists, television reporter **Liubov Amromina** and **Ruslan Linkov**, a correspondent of Russian and foreign newspapers. Both work as assistants to deputies of the lower chamber of Parliament. According to Linkov, the police officers were looking for some documents about two politicians and the search had been authorised by the Governor of St Petersburg, Vladimir Yakovlev, after the release of information against him. (RFE/RL)

On 31 March **Ivan Feduyin**, a reporter with the *Bryanskie Izvestia* local newspaper, was stabbed to death in his apartment. His body was found by police on 2 April. (CPJ)

RWANDA

On 23 February Jean Bosco Barayagwiza, a senior administrator with RTLM, pleaded not guilty to six counts of genocide, complicity to genocide, conspiracy to commit genocide, direct and public incitement to commit genocide and crimes against humanity. (RSF, African News Online)

Ex-defence minister Paul Quiles, who is heading the parliamentary probe into France's role during the 1994 genocide, has asked to see the secret defence accords between Paris and its African allies. The accords allegedly contain articles concerning the maintenance of law and order. The request follows an article by the daily *Le Figaro*, which reported that the crew of a plane which crashed in 1994, killing the Rwandan and Burundian presidents, were covertly working for the French government. A top gendarme, Paul Barril, has denied the allegations but the Belgian expert Filip Reyntjens, who has testified before the enquiry, stated that France knew who was responsible for downing the plane. (Agence France Press, IRIN)

Andre Sibomana, priest, journalist and former editor-in-chief of the newspaper *Kinyamateka*, died on 7 March following an illness. A long-time grassroots militant, Sibomana was awarded the Reporters Sans Frontières prize in 1994 for defending freedom of information. (RSF)

SERBIA-MONTENEGRO

On 25 February, FEMAN Television in Jagodina was closed down by government inspectors who arrived with police but without proper warrants. (B92)

On 2 March, Albanian journalist **Ibrahim Osmani**, working in Kosovo for Agence France Presse, was severely beaten by police while covering demonstrations in Prishtina. After checking his press identification card, police apprehended Osmani and beat him with their rifle butts. On the same day, **Vetan Surroi**, editor of the

SAVEA SANO MALIFA

The devil in the branches of the guava

'I write to let you know what has happened to the criminal defamatory libel filed by Prime Minister Tofilau Eti Alesana against the *Samoa Observer*.

The matter was heard in the Court of Appeal on 5 March. On 6 March, the court in its ruling ordered the removal of the charge to the Supreme Court for the determination of certain constitutional issues. The court was asked to decide if the letter complained of was 'capable of being criminally libellous' and it said 'yes'. But, since constitutional matters in the claim had not been determined, it ordered removal to the Supreme Court for this to be done.

But the ruling means that the hearing has no been heard five times - three in the Magistrate's Court, once in the Supreme Court and once in the Court of Appeal. The next hearing will be in the Supreme Court and it is not clear when this will be but the cost of defending this case has become very expensive.

So far, we have paid out some NZ$104,000 in legal fees, travel and accommodation for Queen's Counsel Lyn Stevens from New Zealand who helped with the hearings. This does not include the fees of our local solicitor, Patrick Fepuela'i, who has not yet sent his bill.

Then there is also the civil defamation claim for $500,000 by Prime Minister Tofilau coming up in the Supreme Court next month. For that case, we've had to engage the services of another New Zealand lawyer, Rodney Harrison QC. It is not clear what his fees will be.

Needless to say, we would welcome any financial help we can get to help defend the cases. ❑

Publisher/editor Savea Sano Malifa and his wife Jean built the Samoa Observer *from a hand-typed weekly in the 1980s to the island's only independent daily which, in 1994 won the International Freedom Award from the Pacific Islands News Association. On 6 June, it published a letter from a 'Mistauveve Joe Hollywood' in the Samoan language which Prime Minister*

*Tofilau considered defamatory, excerpts of which are printed below. Malifa and his Samoan-language editor Fuimaono Fereti Tupua face six months in prison if convicted (*Index *4/1997, 5/1997, 6/1997, 1/1998). Malifa can be contacted by fax at (00685) 21195*

'...Then it was sent for me one who was becoming in his attire and spoke to me. Then I asked the gentleman, 'who is he, whereabouts is the old man, who is hardly seen now on Televise Samoa or his crying heard on Radio 2AP, especially his photo in the newspaper, the *Savali.*?'

'I then sat upright and continued to talk to myself: "Why did he want to be Prime Minister, instead of making Prime Minister his supporter who is now spokesman for the government?" Then I sneeringly laughed all by myself, because it seems he is now shaken and debilitated, his skin is beginning to tire out by the actions of this newspaper, the *Samoa Observer.* And then I said: "Go *Samoa Observer*! Go *Samoa Observer!* Hit him! Hit him! Hit him hard, he'll soon crumble to pieces."'

'However, like the rumble of thunder, the roaring voice of Tulisapelu ("armed with machete"), the Queen of Hell spoke, and I could see the devil taunting from behind her saying "Behold! Be Prepared! Be prepared now as he does not have many more days on earth before we will be together over here, because he is extremely senile now, and very soon he will die suddenly from being hit by a mosquito or a fly."'

'Then I saw the devil swinging on the branches of the guava tree in the Garden of Eden, tauntingly poking out his tongue as if saying, 'He is the one who is not only dead in the soul, dead in the body but, likewise, he will die from the earth where his body will lie, it will be severely accursed and will no longer cultivate a Samoan tobacco."'

'The living thing said: "If this is the one who looks after transport and civilian airlines, there is a special job right now for him in my Kingdom. He will be in charge of the handing out of pairs of wings for the angels of Hell, and not of Heaven."'

Albanian-language daily *Koha Ditore*, **Agron Bajrani**, a journalist with the paper, and **Sherif Konjufca**, a freelance radio and television journalist, were also beaten up. *Koha Ditore*'s offices were also raided and journalist **Fatos Berissahen** was forced to jump from a second-floor window, breaking his leg in the process. (RFE/RL)

While covering the mass demonstrations in Prishtina on 19 March, at least two television cameramen were beaten by plain clothes police officers. **Taras Protsyuk**, a Ukrainian working for Reuters TV, was attacked from behind as he shot footage of a weeping Albanian woman, who also claimed to have been struck by police. **Michel Rouserez**, a cameraman for Belgian Radio-Television, was beaten unconscious after he had been prevented from continuing to film at the University. Since the beginning of March at least five other journalists have been attacked by the Serbian police force. (CPJ, B92)

On 23 March the government agreed to the normalisation of education in the Kosovo region. Under the agreement the keys of Kosovo high school in Podujevo were handed over to the Albanian community on 3 April. (CPJ)

Recent publication: *Kosovo: A short history by Norman Malcolm (Macmillan)*

SIERRA LEONE

At least 22 newspapers have been banned by the restored government of President Ahmad Tejan Kabbah, including the *Express, New Pioneer, Rolyc, Independent Observer, New Times, Morning Post, Watch, Triumph, Financial Times, Reporter* and *New Nation*. The reason given was the papers' non-registration but no newspapers are currently registered and, therefore, the ban appears to be discriminatory. (A19)

Teun Voeten, a Dutch freelancer, escaped to safety on 8 March after two weeks in hiding from soldiers of the Revolutionary United Front soldiers (RUF). He went into hiding on 13 February. (Journalists Safety Service)

Sorie Fofana, editor of the *Vision*, was detained by police on 26 March in connection with an article saying President Kabbah's military advisor, Sheka Mansaray, had refused to allow the police to search his car at a checkpoint in Freetown. He was released the following day. (CPJ)

Four journalists, formerly with the Sierra Leone Broadcasting Services, are being detained at Pademba Road Prison in Freetown on undisclosed charges. **Denis Smith, Gipu, Felix George**, **Olivia Mensah** and **Maada Maka Swaray** appeared before a magistrates court in Freetown on 31 March. Also appearing was **William Smith**, a reporter with the *We Yone* newspaper. Their case was postponed to 6 April. (CPJ)

SLOVAKIA

Concern was expressed on 19 March for the safety of **Eugen Korda**, a correspondent for Prague-based Nova Television after another incident of harassment. On this occasion, his car was seriously damaged by unidentified persons who slashed the tyres, damaged the bodywork and smashed the windows with an iron bar. (CPJ)

SOMALIA

On 4 March **Hassan Said Yussuf**, editor of *Jamhuria*, and **Yassin Mohammed Ismail**, editor of *Republican*, were arrested by order of Prosecutor General Hassan Hersi Ali of the self-declared Republic of Somaliland. Yussuf was charged with defamation, primarily over an article focusing on press freedom. Ismail has not been charged, but the *Republican* has been banned for not being officially registered. Ali also warned the National Printing Press (NPP) to close down its operations or face legal actions. On 19 February **Mohamed Abdi Shida**, publisher of both newspapers and owner of the NPP, was sentenced to a six-month prison term for printing government revenue receipts without authorisation. (CPJ)

SOUTH AFRICA

The public will not be allowed access to the findings of the Mohamed Commission's report of its inquiry into the now-discredited intelligence report in early February which alleged the existence of a military plot to assassinate Nelson Mandela and overthrow his government. The report was found by the judicial commission of inquiry to be 'procedurally flawed'. National Defence Forces Chief General George Meiring, who had handed the handed the report to President Mandela on 5 February, admitted to an 'error of judgement' and resigned on 6 April. (BBC News, Beeld News)

On 20 March Zimbabwean journalist **Newton Kanhema**, currently facing deportation (*Index* 2/1998), was prevented from delivering his acceptance speech for a CNN-African Journalist Foundation award honouring his exposure of a multi-billion rand arms deal with Saudi Arabia. Kanhema had planned to speak about threats to press freedom in South Africa, but was bundled off the stage in Johannesburg by CNN anchorman Riz Khan. CNN's holding company, Time Warner, is part of a consortium known as Midi-TV bidding for the country's first commercial 'free-to-air' TV licence. (*Southern Africa Report*)

In early April, the Independent Broadcasting Authority (IBA) awarded the first free-to-air broadcasting licence to Midi-TV. Midi argued that its identity would be controlled by 'historically disadvantaged' people through partnerships with trade union investment vehicles Mineworkers Social and Benefit Investment Co. (Pty) Ltd., Sactwu Investment Group (Pty) Ltd, together with Hosken Consolidated Investments Ltd and the Disabled Employment Concerns Trust. Midi chairperson is Nomazizi Mtshotshisa, former wife of former trade unionist and National Congress secretary Cyril Ramaphosa. Midi will be operational in February 1999. (*Southern Africa Report*)

Three former IBA councillors have been found by the auditor-general to have misappropriated nearly R204,000 (US$41,375) of public funds and to have abused the use of corporate credit cards nearly two years ago. (*Southern Africa Report*)

Recent Publications: *Negotiating the Past: The Making of Memory in South Africa* (Oxford 1998); *A Long Night's Damage: Working for the Apartheid State* (Contra Press 1998).

SOUTH KOREA

The Seoul newspaper *Dong-a Ilbo* published on 19 February secret documents from the former Central Intelligence Agency which lent credence to a claim that the newly elected President Kim Dae-jung was abducted in Tokyo in 1973 by government agents. (Associated Press)

On 25 February President Kim freed 2,304 prisoners as part of a general amnesty celebrating his inauguration on 25 February. **Yoon Yong Ki**, the country's longest-serving prisoner of conscience, was released on 13 March along with 74 other political prisoners. On leaving prison he said: 'Just because I'm free doesn't mean I'm free to talk about whatever goes on inside.' (AI, *International Herald Tribune*)

SPAIN

On 9 March ABC and *El Mundo* published letters written from prison by ETA members **Jose Angel Anguirre** and **Inaki de Juana Chaos** which expressed approval of recent terrorist acts directed against the Popular Party in the Basque region. (*European*)

SRI LANKA

Six days after **Pradeep Dharmaratne** had a piece about an alcohol- trafficking gang published in the Sinhala-language daily *Dinamina* on 10 February, police officers from Aranayake broke into his home and beat and arrested him. On 18 February, the officers took Dharmaratne to a clandestine distillery where he was forced to leave his fingerprints. The following day he was charged with having ties with traffickers and was released on bail. On 4 March Dharmaratne's house was burned down. (RSF, Free Media Movement)

On 19 February the government announced a ban on the publication of photographs of bombs or bomb victims. (Reuters)

Foreign Minister Lakshman Kadigamar announced on 4 April that the government would pass an amendment to exclude journalists from being prosecuted under the law banning contact with the Liberation Tigers of Tamil Eelam (LTTE). The ban had raised fears amongst journalists, who regularly receive LTTE press statements from its international headquarters in London and include them in their reports, that they would be prosecuted. (Reuters)

Recent publication: *Implementa-*

tion of the Recommendations of the UN Working Group on Enforced or Involuntary Disappearances following their visits to Sri Lanka in 1991 and 1992 (AI, February 1998, 19 pp)

SUDAN

In March, Sudanet, the country's only Internet provider, was the focus of Islamic clerics, who claim the Internet is 'pollutive' and represents a threat to youth. (IPS)

On 27 March armed men abducted **Alim Ismail Atabani**, publisher and chairman of the private newspaper *Al-Rai al-Aam* and warned they would burn down his newspaper's offices if any more articles on 'mafia' usury were printed. This followed the publication of articles reporting that farmers and businessmen had been jailed for not paying back loans given to them by high interest money-lenders. (NDIMA)

SWAZILAND

Two journalists working for state-controlled Swazi Television were threatened with dismissal on 12 March for leaving a road construction site during a visit by Prime Minister Sibusiso Dlamini before the tour was over. The prime minister accused **Mbuso Matsenjwa** and **Xolile Ginindza** of frustrating his work by not giving him full coverage. The journalists said they had, in their judgement, insufficiently covered all the relevant parts of the prime minister tour. (MISA)

SYRIA

Rifaat Asad's ex-press officer **Zubayda Muqabel** (*Index* 5/1997) was released from jail in mid-February as an apparent result of the political realignments that followed the dismissal of her former boss as vice president on 8 February. Muqabel's crime was reportedly to film a 1997 meeting between Rifaat and Saudi Arabia's Crown Prince Abdullah, who are related by marriage. She was jailed in July after the meeting was broadcast on the Arab News Network, the London-based satellite TV station owned by Sawmar al-Asad, Rifaat's son. (*Middle East International*)

TIBET

China's most senior Tibetan official, **Ngabo Ngawang Jigme**, has responded to the publication of the Secret Report of the 10th Panchen Lama's Petition with a strong denial of its accuracy, it was reported on April 6 (*Index* 2/1998). *(Tibet Information Network)*

TOGO

In March, the Berlin-based Association des Togolaises (ATBB) circulated a complaint against the regime of General Gnassingbe Eyadema listing a number of human rights infractions carried out against members of the press. The list includes: the total suspension of *Lettre de Tchaoudjo* and a prison sentence of five years and a fine of US$10,000 for its director **Moudassirou Katakpaou-Touré**; and a six-month suspension for *La Tribune des Démocrates* and the sentencing of its director, **Eric Lawson**, to five years in prison and a fine of US$6,000. (ATBB)

TONGA

The Pro-Democracy Movement parliamentarian and publisher **Akilisi Pohiva** was cleared of the charge of criminal libel which grew out of an interview he gave to the *Wall Street Journal* in 1994. Pohiva had called King Taufa'ahau Tupou a 'dictator' and accused him of corruption over the sale of passports to foreigners. In the ruling handed down on 5 March, Justice Daniel Finnigan said Pohiva's claim seemed to be legally or factually correct. Finnigan said he believed Pohiva was simply seeking greater accountability from the King and government. (PINA)

TUNISIA

Khemais Ksila, vice-president of the Tunisian Human Rights League, was sentenced on 11 February to three years' imprisonment on charges including 'outraging public order'. Ksila was arrested on 29 September 1997 after declaring a hunger strike in protest at his harassment by the authorities. (AI)

TURKEY

On 3 March **Namik Durukan** of the daily *Milliyet*, and a contributor to the BBC's Turkish service, went on trial in Diyarbakir's security court, accused of aiding and abetting the Kurdistan Workers Party (PKK). The indictment claims that the journalist took orders from a PKK commander to report that Turkish troops forcibly evacuated villages to

SANAR YURDATAPAN

Throwing the book at the State

'The Freedom of Thought movement started when Yasar Kemal was called to the State Security Court in January 1995 to be questioned about an article he wrote for *Der Spiegel*. We decided to participate in his so-called 'crime' by becoming co-responsible for the publication of those writings. We collected the signatures of people willing to be prosecuted for the 'crime' of free speech and, when we got to over 1,000 signatures, we published a book of articles by banned writers like Ismail Besikci, Yasar Kemal, Haluk Gerger, Leyla Zana and others.'

'According to Article 162 of the Turkish Penal code re-publishing an article that is a crime becomes a new crime and the publisher is liable for the same sentence as the writer. So we used this law in a positive way. We took a copy to the State Security Court in Istanbul and submitted it as a crime and said: "Now. do your duty." During the next six weeks, 185 people were interrogated and the trial lasted 21/2 years. It was a very funny trial – usually the Court chases you and you run away! This time we were pursuing and the State was avoiding and taking its time.'

One of the publishers, Mahir Gunsiray, is a theatre actor. During his court hearing, he began to read an extract from Franz Kafka's book *The Trial* and the State Prosecutor became furious, he said "He is insulting us!" He was sentenced to six months in prison, which was converted a fine of 900,000 Turkish lire, about US$4, and that was also suspended. Gunsiray said that, if Kafka were alive, he would write to him and bemoan the fact that the freedom of a Turkish intellectual was only worth US$4.'

Film composer and freedom of expression activist Sanar Yurdatapan is one of the 1,000 intellectuals who signed as responsible editors of Freedom of Expression in Turkey, *a book of articles which had been banned or whose authors were in prison. Some 184 'publishers' are currently on trial for 'disseminating separatist propaganda', including Yurdatapan, who was recently sentenced to 10 months. He was interviewed by Gill Newsham.*

deny shelter and supplies to the guerrillas. The charge carries a penalty of at least five years. (Reuters)

Every Wednesday in Istanbul the campaign to remove obstacles to freedom of expression continues with writers and intellectuals going to court to demand their own prosecution. On 4 March, poet **Suna Aras,** writer **Cengiz Gundogan**, poet **Berrin Tas** and **Tomris Ozden** signed the 'Freedom Of Thought' booklet number 4, thereby ensuring their own prosecution as joint publishers. (Med-TV)

Aydin Koral, journalist for the pro-Islamist newspaper *Selam*, was sentenced on 5 March to nearly two years in prison for an article criticising Ankara's growing relations with Israel. The court ruled that the piece was a threat to national security and the paper was closed down for two weeks. (Associated Press)

On 8 March journalists **Faruk Aktas** and **Bulent Acar** of the Kurdish *Ulkede Gundem* newspaper were detained with 50 others at an International Women's Day demonstration in Istanbul. The two were held for four days. (RSF)

Ten police officers were acquitted on 10 March of torturing 16 teenagers at Manisa headquarters between 26 December 1995 and 5 January 1996. The youths described being sexually and physically tortured. The appeal court will re-examine the case against the policemen. (AI)

Ozgur Celik, a reporter for left-wing weekly *Halkin Gunlugu*, was detained on 13 March. Previously he had been arrested and sentenced *in absentia* following obscure accusations. (RSF)

On 19 March **Tahir Filimci** and **Veysel Dagdas**, the owner and editor-in-chief of *Ozgur Halk* newspaper in Istanbul, were arrested in police raids of several premises, including the offices of *Ulkede Gundem* where the editor-in-chief, **Hayrettin Demircioglu**, was also picked up and detained. (RSF)

On 20 March journalists **Mehmet Ali Birand** of *Sabah*, **Yalcin Dogan** of *Milliyet* and **Muharrem Sarikaya** of *Hurriyet* were banned by the military from covering any events organised by the army, including press conferences, visits to military sites or interviews with members of the armed forces. After complaints from international press organisations, the ban was lifted. (RSF)

On 19 March five of the 11 police officers accused of having beaten **Metin Goktepe** to death (*Index* 2/1996, 1/1997, 6/1997, 1/1998, 2/1998) were sentenced to seven and a half years in prison for involuntary homicide by the Court of Assizes in Ayfon, western Turkey. Six officers were acquitted. (RSF)

On 30 March the Islamist mayor of Istanbul, Recep Tayip Erdogan, rejected charges that he tried to incite enmity and hatred in a speech he made in 1997. 'The minarets are our bayonets, the domes helmets, the mosques our barracks, the believers our soldiers,' Anatolian news agency quoted Erdogan as saying. (Reuters)

UKRAINE

On 26 March *Vseukraineskiye Vedemosti* published its last issue after losing a controversial libel case to a government-tied sports organisation for 3.5 million hrynyas ($US1.8 million) in 'moral damages'. Editor-in-chief **Volodynyr Rudan** said the case, filed by Hryhoriy Surkis, president of the Dinamo Kiev and head of the national soccer foundation, was illegal since it was filed in a court with no jurisdiction in defamation cases. Given the 'arbitrary and harsh' decision, it was widely felt that the court's intention was to silence the paper prior to the 29 March parliamentary elections. (RFE/RL)

UNITED KINGDOM

Stuart Proffitt resigned as editor-in-chief of Harper Collins in late February after proprietor Rupert Murdoch pressured him to drop a book by former governor of Hong Kong Chris Patten. News Corporation, Murdoch's company, stated that Murdoch had 'expressed dissatisfaction' with Patten's book *East and West*,which was expected to be damaging to the media owner's business interests in China. (*Guardian, Independent, Times*)

In early March police appeared to be involved in a crackdown on 'pornography'. The University of Central England, Birmingham, was raided and a book by photographer **Robert Mapplethorpe** was seized. The university has subsequently been ordered to destroy the work. Police are considering whether to press charges against the publisher. Greater Manchester's obscene publications squad then confiscated 535 video tapes from David Flint, an author commissioned by Creation press to write a history of pornographic film. Flint publishes a magazine called *Sexadelic* and stated: 'I have been told by the British Film Institute that no one is cataloguing these films and I think it's an important study...'. (*Guardian*)

Artist **Ralph Steadman** alleged in early March that comedian Tony Hancock was dropped from a series of stamps honouring British comic talent because the Royal Mail did not want 'the Queen's head on a stamp with a man who died a suicidal alcoholic'. Steadman was paid $2,000 for his portrayal of Hancock before the plan to include it in the issue was abandoned. (*Guardian*)

On 17 March the Court of Appeal ruled that 'considerations of national security can justify a departure from the principle of open justice.' The Court was dealing with a case that involved the right of MI5 officers to give evidence anonymously during trials. (*Guardian, Independent*)

An uncut version of a new film of the novel *Lolita* was passed by the British Board of Film Classification in late March. Andreas Whittam Smith, the new president of the BBFC, declared himself 'satisfied it cannot be seen as corrupting or encouraging of paedophilia' (*Index* 1/1998). (*Guardian, Independent*)

In early April publisher Random House announced the imminent publication of a paperback edition of Salman Rushdie's *Satanic Verses* through its Vintage subsidiary. The novel, a long term target for Islamic extremists, has sold more than a quarter of a million copies in hardback since its publication in 1988. Viking-Penguin abandonded the rights to publish a paperback edition of Rushdie's work in 1992 following a series of terrorist attacks throughout the world. (*Guardian*)

Saxon Wood, **Noel Molland** and **Steve Booth**, three 'anarchist' journalists imprisoned under conspiracy laws in November, were freed on bail on 27 March (*Index* 1/1998). They await confirmation of a date for their appeals against their three-year jail terms. (*SchNews*)

USA

On 23 February the Supreme Court refused to hear the government's appeal of a constitutional ban on television advertising for private casinos. The original ruling in 1934 was challenged in 1992 by Valley Broadcasting and Sierra Broadcasting, two television companies in Las Vegas and Reno. (Reuters)

Independent counsel Kenneth Starr violated international law in forcing **Sidney Blumenthal**, an advisor to President Clinton, to tell a grand jury the names of journalists and contents of the discussions he had with them on 27 February. Starr said he needed the testimony for his investigation of a possible obstruction of justice but, in questioning Blumenthal, he has broken the confidential relationship between journalists and their sources. (A19, Reuters)

The number of hate groups grew by 20 per cent in 1997, according to the annual report released on 3 March by the Southern Poverty Law Center's Intelligence Project. Among the 474 groups counted in 1997 report were 127 Ku Klux Klan, 100 neo-Nazi and 42 skinhead groups, 81 groups linked to the Christian Identity movement and 12 black separatist groups. The report also found 163 websites dedicated to the doctrines of US hate groups. (Reuters)

California's Supreme Court has ruled that Boy Scout organizations can exclude homosexuals and atheists, saying scout troops are voluntary clubs not covered by state civil rights laws (*Index* 2/1998). (Reuters)

A Pentagon report on 7 April said that the Navy's 'Don't Ask, Don't Tell' policy on homosexuality (*Index* 2/1998) has seen more people discharged from the military than ever before. There were 997 discharges based on homosexuality in 1997, up 67 per cent from 597 in 1994, the report said. (Reuters)

The Mississippi Department of Archives and History opened some 124,000 documents from the files of its now defunct Sovereignty Commission (SC) to the public on 17 March, ending a 21-year legal battle between Mississippi and the

American Civil Liberties Union, as well as several individual plaintiffs. From 1956 to 1977, the SC was responsible for spying and plotting against civil rights individuals thought to be supportive of desegregation. (*Economist*)

A San Francisco school board proposal in March states that at least half the books assigned to school students must be by 'authors of colour'. The board argued that the change would better reflect the district's diverse student population as almost nine of every 10 students are black, Asian or Hispanic. To accommodate the proposal to form a list of 10 approved works, texts such as *Canterbury Tales* and *Huckleberry Finn* may be ousted. (*Daily Telegraph*)

In the first trial under the new California anti-smoking law, which bans smoking in more than 35,000 bars and casinos (*Index* 2/1998), a bar owner in Auburn California has been convicted of two infractions for allowing patrons to light up in violation of the new state anti-smoking law. The bar owner, **Bill Ostrander**, who said he could not force his customers to stop smoking, stated: 'It's not my job'. Ostrander was fined $300. (*International Herald Tribune*)

A Santa Ana federal jury found **Richard Machado** guilty of civil rights violations for threatening 59 Asian students at a college on the west coast via electronic mail on 10 February. Machado, who signed his electronic mail messages 'Asian hater', faces a maximum of one year in jail, which he has already served. The decision is the first conviction for a hate crime perpetrated over the internet. (Associated Free Press)

URUGUAY

The Ministry of Defence presented on 15 March a proposal that would punish with up to four years in prison the use of radio frequencies without authorisation. Radio stations that 'loan' wavelengths to unlicensed broadcasters will be similarly penalised. (AMARC)

UZBEKISTAN

In early April eight female students were expelled from university in Tashkent for wearing traditional veils. While the country is secular, and wearing the veil is not illegal, the authorities are worried that the wearing of Iranian-style *hejab* denotes a rise in Islamic extremism. (BBC World Service)

VANUATU

Remarks by Ombudswoman **Marie Noelle Ferrieux Patterson** concerning political corruption were aired on Radio Vanuatu, the island's sole broadcaster. She expressed alarm at threats against Radio Vanuatu journalists, one allegedly from a former minister, Willie Jimmy, and urged them to lodge formal complaints to the police. Patterson has previously complained that the Bislama-language news of Radio Vanuatu ignores her office's public reports. (PINA)

VATICAN

The Vatican issued a statement in mid-March expressing 'deep sorrow' at the involvement of some Roman Catholics in the Holocaust. However both Jewish religious leaders and Holocaust historians have criticised the statement on the grounds that it does not implicate the church itself in Nazi extermination programmes. (*European*, *Guardian*)

YEMEN

Writer and poet **Mansur Rajih**, arrested in June 1983 and charged with murder, has been recently been released. In March 1984 the Court of First Instance in Ta'iz sentenced Rajih to death, though it was widely believed that he had been victimised for his non-violent opposition to the government and his political views (AI)

ZAMBIA

Frederick Mwanza (*Index* 2/1998), writer and member of the opposition United National Independence Party, was released on 25 February having spent three months in detention for suspected involvement in the failed 28 October coup against President Frederick Chiluba. Mwanza is a frequent contributor of critical articles to both the state-owned *Times of Zambia* and the *Post*. (MISA)

On 20 March President Chiluba lifted the state of emergency imposed after the abortive October coup. Under the legislation, at least 90 people were arrested or detained and some were severely tortured (*Index*

1/1998). President Chiluba warned that he would not hesitate to reimpose the emergency if 'the need arose'. (*Southern Africa Report*)

The house of former president **Kenneth Kaunda** has been turned into a prison. On 4 April the government of President Chiluba gazetted Kaunda's plush Lusaka home into a unit falling under the prisons department. Visits to Kaunda, who is charged with 'failing to inform the authorities of an impending coup', will be restricted and normal prison rules will apply. (*Times of Zambia*)

Dickson Jere, a reporter with the independent *Post*, was detained on 9 April and interrogated in connection with an interview he made with former president Kenneth Kaunda shortly before the October attempt (*Index* 2/1998). Jere, who is also a journalism student at a Lusaka college, had been in hiding since Kaunda's arrest on Christmas Day. Police cornered him when he tried to sneak into the college to find out about his studies. He was released after four hours. (MISA)

Masauso Phiri (*Index* 5/1997), former projects editor for the *Post* newspaper, appeared before a magistrates court in the central town of Kabwe charged with conduct likely to cause breach of the peace. He denied the charge. Phiri was arrested on 23 August while covering a rally at which former president Kenneth Kaunda was shot and wounded. (MISA)

Recent publication: *Misrule of Law: Human rights in a State of Emergency* (AI, March 1998, 52pp)

ZIMBABWE

On 12 March the Zimbabwe Congress of Trade Unions (ZCTU) called for a workers' boycott of the *Herald*, to run every Thursday and Friday, in protest at what it sees as biased reporting. The ZCTU accused the paper of being a government propaganda tool 'embarking on a a public disinformation campaign of all activities seen to be critical of president Robert Mugabe's government.' In retaliation, Information Minister Chen Chimutenfwende announced on 14 March that all state-controlled media should boycott coverage of all ZCTU activities. (MISA)

Compiled by: Lucy Hillier, Regina Jere-Malanda (Africa); Peter Beveridge, Andrew Kendle, Jennie Roberts, Nicky Winstanley-Torode (Asia); Simon Martin, Vera Rich (eastern Europe and CIS); Dolores Cortes (south and central America); Rupert Clayton, Gill Newsham, M. Siraj Sait (Middle East); Andrew Elkin, Suzanne Fisher (north America and Pacific); Andrew Blick (UK and western Europe).

Freedom of expression organisations

The growth of free expression organisations worldwide has been one of the more encouraging trends in the past decade. Many are grouped in the International Free Expression Exchange (IFEX) and share information and action alerts via e-mail. Current members are:

Accuracy in Media (AIM), 4455 Connecticut Avenue, NW, Suite 330, Washington DC 20005 Tel: 202 364 4401, Fax: 202 364 4098

Article 19: International Centre against Censorship, 33 Islington High Street, London N1 9LH, Tel: +44 171 278 9292, Fax: +44 171 713 1356

Canadian Committee to Protect Journalists (CCPJ), 489 College Street, Suite 403, Toronto, Ontario M6G 1A5, Canada, Tel: +1 416 515 9622, Fax: + 1 416 515 7879, Email: ccpj@ccpj.ca

Californians against Censorship Together (ACT), 1800 Market Street, Suite 1000, San Francisco, A 94103 USA, Tel: 510 548 3695

Committee on International Freedom to Publish, c/o Association of American Publishers 71 5th Avenue, New York, NY 10003, Tel: 212 255 0200, Fax: 212 255 7007

Committee to Protect Journalists, 330 Seventh Avenue, 12th Flr, New York, NY 10001 Tel: 212 465 1004, Fax: 212 465 9568

Feminists for Free Expression, 2525 Times Square Station, New York, NY 10108, Tel: 212 702 6292, Fax: 212 702 6277

Freedom of Information Clearinghouse, PO Box 19367, Washington, DC 20036 USA Tel: 202 588 7790

Freedom Forum, First Amendment Center, 1207 18th Avenue South, Nashville, TN 37212 Tel: 615 321

Egyptian Organization for Human Rights (EOHR), 8/10 Matahaf El-Manial St, 10th Floor, Manial El-Roda, Cairo, Egypt, Tel: +20 2 363 6811/362 04647, Fax: +20 2 362 1613 Email: eohr@link.com.eg

Free Expression Ghana, PO Box 207, The Human Rights Centre, Ghana International Press Centre, Nkrumah Circle, Accra, Ghana, Tel: +233 21 229875, Fax: +233 21 237004 Email: freedom@africaonline.com.gh

Free Media Movement (FMM), Lucien Rajakarunanayake, 73/28 Sri Raranankara Place, Dehiwala, Sri Lanka, Tel/Fax: +941 735 182, Email: lucien@eureka.lk

Freedom House, 120 Wall Street, New York, New York, 10005, USA, Tel: +1 212 514 8040 Fax: +1 212 514 8050, Email: kguida@freedomhouse.org

Freedom of Expression Institute (FXI), PO B0X 30668, Braamfontein 20178, Johannesburg South Africa, Tel: +27 11 403 8403/4, Fax: +27 11 403 8309, Email: fxi@wn.apc.org

Hong Kong Journalists Association (HKJA), Flat A, 15/F Henta Commercial Building 348-350 Lockhart Road, Wanchai, Hong Kong, Tel: + 852 2591 0692, Fax: +852 2572 7329 Email: hkja@hk.super.net

Human Rights Watch (HRW), Empire State Building, 34th Floor, New York, NY 10118-3299 USA, Tel: 212 290 4700, Fax: 212 736 1300, Email: hrwnyc@hrw.org

Independent Journalism Centre, Tejumola House (1st Floor), 24, Omole Layout, New Isheri Road, PO Box 7808 Ojudu, Ikeja, Lagos, Nigeria, Tel/Fax: + 234 1 4924998/4924314, Email: ijc@linkserve.com.ng

Index on Censorship 33 Islington High Street, London N1 9LH, UK. Tel: +44 171 278 2313; Fax:

+44 171 278 1878; Email contact@indexoncensorship.org *or namedindividual*@indexoncensorship.org

Institute for Studies on the Free Flow of Information (ISAI), Jalan Utan Kayu 68-H Jakarta 13120, Indonesia, Tel: + 62 21 857 3388, Fax: +62 21 857 3387 Email: harsono@nation.nationgroup.com

Instituto Prensa y Sociedad (IPYS), Miguel Dasso 153, oficina 7 "M", San Isidro, Lima 27 Peru, Tel/Fax: +511 2 211523, Email: postmaster@ipyspe.pe

Inter American Press Association (IAPA), Melba Jimenez, 2911 NW 39th Street Miami, Florida 33142, USA, Tel: +1 305 634 2465, Fax: +1 305 635 2272

International Federation of Journalists (IFJ), Rue Royale, 266 B-121-, Brussels, Belgium Tel: +322 223 2265, Fax: +322 219 2976, Email: ifj.safety@pophost.eunet.be

IFJ Affiliates, Federacion Internactional de Periodistas (FIP), IFJ Latin American Regional Office Calle Santos Erminy, Edificio Beatriz, Piso 7, Oficina 74, Sabana Grande, Caracas, Venezuala Tel: + 582 763 1971, Fax: + 582 763 3778, Email: fip@eldish.net

IFJ Algerian Centre, Maison de la Presse Tahar Djaout, 1 rue Bachir Attar Algiers, Algeria, Tel: +2132 659470, Tel/Fax: +213 265 9479

IFJ Palestinian Media Monitoring Centre, Ruba Hussairi, Jerusalem, Email: ifjruba@trendline.co.il

IFJ/WAN Co-ordinating Centre for Balkan Media, Vosnjakova 8 , 6100 Ljublana Slovenia, Tel/Fax: + 38661 323 170, Email: ifj.fiej@k2.net,

International Press Institute (IPI), Spiegelgasse 2, A-1010, Vienna, Austria, Tel: +43 1 512 90 11, Fax: +43 1 512 90 14, Email: ipi.vienna@xpoint.at

Journalist Safety Service (JSS), Joh. Vermeerstraat 22, 1071 DR Amsterdam The Netherlands, Tel: +31 20 676 6771, Fax: +31 20 662 4901, Email: jss@euronet.nl

Media Institute of Southern Africa (MISA), Private Bag 13386, Windhoek Namibia, Tel: +264 61 232975, Fax: +264 61 248016, Email: research@ingrid.misa.org.na

Network for the Defence of Independent Media in Africa (NDIMA), PO Box 70147, Nairobi, Kenya, Tel: +254 154 41403, Fax: +254 154 51118, Email: ndima@arcc.or.ke

Norwegian Forum for Freedom of Expression (NFFE), Menneskerettighetshuset Urtegata 50, N-0187 Oslo, Norway, Tel: +47 22 67 79 64, Fax: +47 22 57 00 88, Email: nffe@online.no

Oficina de Derechos Humanos del Periodista (OFIP), Roberto Mejia, Jr. Huancavelic 320 Of.204, Lima, Peru, Tel: +5114 270 687, Fax: +5114 27 84 93, Email: anp@amauta.rcp.net.pe

Pacific Islands News Association (PINA), Pina Freedom of Information Network, Mailing Address: PINA Private Mail Bag, Street Address: 46 Gordon Street, Level II, Damador Centre Suva, Fiji Islands, Tel: +679 303623, Fax: +679 303943/302101, Email: pina@is.com.fj *or* plomas@ibi.com.fj

Pakistan Press Foundation (PPF), Press Centre, Shahrah Kamal Ataturk, Karachi Pakistan, Tel: + 92 21 263 3215, Fax: +92 21 263 7754, Email: owais.ali@ibm.net

Periodistas, Argentine Association for the Protection of Independent Journalism, Sarmiento 1334, Buenos Aires, Argentina, Tel/Fax: +54 1 372 6201, Email: periodis@mail.netizen.com.ar

Reporters sans frontières (RSF), 5, rue Geoffrey Marie, Paris 75009, France Tel: +33 144 83 84 84, Fax: +33 145 23 11 51, Email: rsf@calva.net

West African Journalists Association (WAJA), Mailing Address: PO Box 4031, Accra, Ghana, Tel: +233 21 234692, Fax: +233 21 234694, Email: waja@africaonline.com.gh

World Association of Community Radio Broadcasters (AMARC), 3575 St Laurent, 611 Montreal, Quebec H2X 2TJ, Canada, Tel: +1 514 9482 0351, Fax: +1 514 849 7129 Email: amarc@web.net

AMARC Latin American Regional Office, Oficina regional para America Latina Av.Atahualpa 333 y Ulloa, Casilla 17-08-84, Quito, Ecuador, Tel/Fax: +593 2 501 180/551 6474 Email: ignacio@pulsar.org.ec

AMARC European Regional Office, The Media Centre, 15 Paternoster Row Sheffield S1 2BX, Tel: +44 1142 795219, Email: amarc@gn.apc.org

World Association of Newspapers (WAN), 25, rue d'Astorg, 75008 Paris, France Tel: +33 14 742 8500, Fax: +33 14 742 4948, Email: fiej.nemo@nemo.geis.com

World Press Freedom Committee (WPFC), 11690-C Sunrise Valley Drive, Reston, Virginia

20191, USA, Tel: +1 703 715 9811, Fax: +1 703 620 6790, Email: freepress@wpfc.org

Writers in Prison Committee (WiPC), International PEN, 9/10 Charterhouse Buildings Goswell Road, London EC1M 7AT, UK, Tel: +44 171 253 3226, Fax: +44 171 253 5711 Email: intpen@gn.apc.org

PEN Canada, 24 Ryerson Avenue, Suite 309, Toronto, Ontario M5T 2P3, Canada Tel: +1 416 703 8448, Fax: +1 416 703 3870, Email: pencan@web.net

PEN American Center, 568 Broadway, Suite 401, New York, NY 10012 USA, Tel: +1 212 334 1660 Fax: +1 212 334 2181, Email: diana@pen.org

IFEX Clearing House, 489 College St, Suite 403,Toronto, Ontario M6G IA5, Canada Tel: +1 416 515 9622; Fax: +1 416 515 7879; Email: ifex@ifex.org

Among other organisation regularly supplying Index with information on the state of media freedom and attacks on journalists:

Action Committee For Media Freedom, 445/1 Prince Of Wales Avenue, Colombo 14, Sri Lanka, Tel: 00 941 393 4069, Fax: 00 941 44 95 93

Alliance of Independent Journalists, RSTA Blok 39 Lt. II No 4, Jl. KH Mas Mansyur 25-Jakarta 10240, Indonesia Tel/Fax: 62 21 315 5918

Asociación de Periodistas de Guatemala, Comisión de Libertad de Prensa,14 Calle 3-29, Zona 1, Ciudad de Guatemala, Guatemala, Tel: 00502 232 1813 (tel), Email: cerigua@guate.net

Australian Centre for Independent Journalism, PO Box 123, Broadway NSW 2007, Australia

Sierra Leone Association of Journalists, PMB 724 Freetown, Sierra Leone Tel: 00 232 22 228

Bahrain Freedom Movement, Fax: 0171 278 9089, Email: 100542.1623@compuserve.com

B'Tselem,The Israeli Information Center for Human Rights in the Occupied Territories, 43 Emek Refaim Street, 2nd Floor, Jerusalem 93141, Israel Tel: 972 2 617271, Fax: 972 2 610756

Centre Haïtien de Défense des Libertés, Boite Postal 2408, Port-au-Prince, Haiti, Tel: 5 5103

CERIGUA news agency, 9a, Calle 'A' 3-49, Zona 1, Ciudad Guatemala Fax: 00 502 232 4419 Fax: 00 502 253 6670, Email: cerigua@guate.net

Iranian PEN Centre in Exile, c/o The Rationalist Press Association, 47 Theobald's Road, London WC1X 8SP, Fax: 0171 430 1271

Frente Nacional de Abogados Democráticos, Nezahualcoyotl 51, Despacho 21, Centro México 06090, DF Mexico, Tel: 761 9457

Glasnost Defense Foundation, 119021 Moscow, 4 Zubovsky bulv, room 432, Russia Fax: 007 095 201 4947, Directors fax: 007 095 194 4848, Email: eoznobki@iphras.irex.ru

Havana Libre Tel: 53 7 33 31 52, Fax: 53 7 33 87 92

Co-ordinating Centre for Independent Media of the Balkan Region, Cufarjeva 15, 61000, Ljubljana, Slovenia, Tel: 00386 61 131 72 39 Fax: 00386 61 132 70 34 Email: Balkan_media@Zamir-LJ.ztn.zer.de

independent belarus.net site, Tel: 00375 17 239 04 75 Fax: 00375 17 276 83 71 Email: admin@jornal.minsk.by

Media Watch, GPO Box 3521, Dhaka, Bangladesh Tel: 00880 2 956 7070, Fax: 00880 2 956 2882 (attn Media Watch)

Free Information Institute, kv. Sv. Troica, bl. 297, Sofia 1309, Bulgaria Tel/Fax: 0059 2 203 622, Email: cts.0487@main.infotel.bg

NDIMA, PO Box 70147, Nairobi, Kenya Tel: 00254 154 41403, Fax: 00254 154 51118, Email: ndima@users.africaonline.co.ke

OSCE Mission to Bosnia, Sarajevo Head Office, PO Box CH 4410, Liestal, Switzerland Email: tanyad@oscebih.org

The Media Institute, Tumaini House, Nairobi, Kenya, Email: GOwor@ken.healthnet.org

Pacific Media Watch, PO Box 273, University Post Office, NCD, Papua New Guinea Tel/Fax: 00675 326 7191, Email: niusedita@pactok.net.au, journupng@pactok.peg.apc.org

CUPAZ, Linea 556, esq D, Vedado 4, Havana, Cuba, Tel: 32 05 06, Fax: 32 04 90 Email: cupaz@tinored.cu

NEIL MIDDLETON

Poverty goes global

Poverty is the worst and most widespread of all human rights abuses. The main offenders are the world's trading and financial institutions in pursuit of more and faster returns on capital

An estimated 1.6 billion people live on incomes at, or below, the level of what the World Bank calls 'absolute poverty' and the number is rising. 'Life expectancy', 'maternal mortality', 'infant mortality' and 'malnutrition', somehow sanitise the reality that women, children and men are dying in huge numbers from being too poor. According to UNICEF's 1998 The State of the World's Children, even in years without notable droughts or famines, 12 million children under five die in families in the developing world too poor to afford basic sanitation, adequate diets and minimal health care. Like their elders, they generally die of the preventable diseases of poverty rather than of absolute inanition. This is a litany of woes so often repeated that we no longer hear it.

And almost without exception, poor people are getting poorer. One example, Mexico, will serve for many. The decade 1984-94 was one in which the 'benefits' of the North American Free Trade Association (NAFTA) were supposedly accruing to Mexico. To no-one's surprise, it was its wealthiest 10 per cent whose incomes increased by 20.8 per cent. Everyone else followed a lengthy trend in losing both relatively and absolutely, but the poorest 10 per cent were hit hardest with an absolute income loss of 23.2 per cent.

For a variety of reasons, income poverty is only one guide to deprivation. In its 1997 report, the UNDP (United Nations Development Programme) attempts the creation of a Human Poverty Index based on three main criteria: longevity, literacy and 'a decent standard of living'. The first criterion uses a life expectancy of 40 years as an indicator, the third is based on access to clean water, sanitation and health services and on the number of malnourished children. It lists 78 developing countries for which 'adequate data' are available. Of these, 47 have at least a quarter of their populations living in absolute poverty; in eight of them the proportion is half or more. Over 25 per cent of them will die before they reach 40 years of age; 30 per cent of them have no access to safe water or health services; 49 per cent are illiterate; 38 per cent of their children will die before they are five years old; almost 85 million people have been killed or affected by disasters; 6.6 million are refugees; and further untold numbers are displaced.

Enormous numbers of people do not have adequate diets, and malnutrition in its many forms, commonly associated in the public mind with disasters or famines is chronic. Those suffering from it are acutely vulnerable to disease and commonly without even the simplest health care. Many children who do not actually die as a consequence are exposed to numerous other subsequent hazards.

This sketchy and obviously selective recitation of figures is necessary because most of us rarely encounter the physical reality of extreme poverty nor do we easily grasp its scale. Even more important, we tend to give little more than a passing thought to its causes. Susan George has written extensively and impressively about the issue of Third World debt and even the World Bank acknowledges that there is an overall net return of financial resources from the poorest countries to the richest. Despite endless promises, little has been done by the world's banking system to resolve the issue; even when proposals for debt cancellation are advanced their prosecution is at best dilatory and, of course, they are modest – they rarely, if ever amount to more than small percentages of the total. Most important, debt cancellation seems never to be considered in regional, but only in national terms – banks, including the multilaterals, deal piecemeal. As George points out, it is easier to keep individual states in thrall, and it makes the bribery of ruling elites simpler. George also comments that debt cancellation, by itself, may do little to assist the poor, serving only to line, yet further, the pockets of corrupt rulers. Nonetheless, one of the most obvious consequences of

Child dressing in a North London squat – Credit: Donovan Wylie/Magnum

the incubus of overwhelming external debt is economic stasis in the countries afflicted by it. Severely indebted countries are compelled, if they want their debts rescheduled or to borrow further, to open their markets to cheap imports, particularly food, from the industrialised world, thus drastically undermining indigenous production and further impoverishing their own workers.

When, a decade or so ago, 'globalisation' was widely discussed, it was equally widely misunderstood; commentators referred to the frightening ability of trans-national corporations (TNCs) to move themselves and their production to wherever it suited them. In practice, TNCs usually stay in their countries, or regions, of origin – the overwhelming majority of them are to be found in the US, Europe and Japan. Produc-

tion, on the other hand, moved, and still does, in pursuit of low wages and minimal environmental regulation. Notorious examples are to be found in the exploitation of impoverished Mexicans in US *maquiladora* industries, further encouraged by NAFTA; but this process is not new, Marx, for instance, refers to an early version of it in the first volume of *Capital.*

Globalisation consists of two principal elements: the elimination of protectionism of all kinds and the reduction of regulations governing the movement of investment capital. Barriers to 'free' trade were progressively to be dismantled, direct subsidies to production were to be stopped and everyone was thus to trade on supposedly equal terms. All national borders were to be as porous as possible in order to facilitate trade. There was much nauseating rhetoric from supporters of the Bretton Woods triplets (the World bank, the International Monetary Fund and the World Trade Organisation) about the creation of 'level playing fields' which completely ignored, among many other things, the advantages of scale enjoyed by TNCs and the hidden infrastructural subsidies given to producers in the industrialised world. The OECD estimates that every farmer in the USA is indirectly subsidised to the tune of US$29,000, thus creating a 'playing field' in which few, if any, farmers in the Third World are able to compete. The World Trade Organisation (WTO) is an organisation for dumpers with ludicrously minimal safeguards for vulnerable economies.

The second element in globalisation, the reduction of governmental interference in foreign investment, is being negotiated in great secrecy by the industrialised countries within the OECD in the form of an agreement called the Multilateral Agreement on Investment (MAI) that will reduce to almost nothing the power of national governments to regulate investment in the public interest. Oxfam ascribes the origin of this agreement to pressure from business, the EC, the USA and other industrialised nations. Since it will render illegal any national agreements designed to protect workers, the environment or other essential interests which TNCs define as obstacles to investment, it is a devastatingly undemocratic proposal for everyone, but here we are concerned with its effect on the acutely poor. The MAI will achieve for investment capital what the WTO's porous borders achieved for trade. If the MAI becomes, as the OECD expects, the model for a worldwide agreement administered by the Bretton Woods triplets, then it will be illegal for any country to erect protective barriers, including worker and environmental protection, against foreign predatory investment in its resources.

Globalisation is the macro-economic condition within which poverty flourishes. Uncritical worship of free markets – 'free', of course, only to those rich enough to benefit from them – the relentless demand for modernisation in production, the facilitation of the power of TNCs which already control 70 per cent of the world's trade, all conspire to render the poor yet more powerless.

Examples are legion and we need only consider one, the destruction of nomadic pastoralism throughout the Greater Horn of Africa. The final collapse of the Somalian state followed an extensive and bloody campaign by its military ruler, Siad Barre, which, among other things, had the sequestration of productive farmland as its object. Sedentary farmers, holding land by ancient customary laws, and nomadic pastoralists, with whom they had coexisted relatively peacefully, were driven from their land and ranges to make way for plantations controlled by Barre's satraps. These plantations were devoted to the production of crops designed for the international food commodity trade, were environmentally destructive of extremely fragile ecosystems and were financed by international capital. Farmers and pastoralists became refugees and died in appalling numbers in the disaster of 1991-3. That disaster continues, like so many other chronic disasters, and is related to others in the Greater Horn.

In Kenya, President Daniel arap Moi's continued assault on the Kikuyu, together with his less well-known attacks on the vast numbers of refugees along the Somali border, includes similar objectives. The process, aptly described by the campaigning researchers of African Rights as 'land-looting' (they coined the term for Somalia), is part of an overall attempt to incorporate Kenyan agriculture into the world market. Since Kenya, unlike Somalia, still has a government of sorts, it is backed heavily in this programme by the IMF. Similar ambitions drive the racialist government of Sudan in its genocidal wars against the Nubans and the South.

In each of these cases, and in so many more about the world, international 'humanitarian' aid can be relied upon to provide temporary welfare states for the dispossessed for as long as the particular 'emergency' remains in the industrialised world's public consciousness. Indigenous venal governments are often partly responsible for the plight of many of their people, but even relatively honest and progressive governments in the developing world are caught in the toils of the international free market and the global reach of its financial and trading institutions. We must recognise the extent to which globalisation is creating a new geography of poverty. The world's most fundamental abuse of human rights is perpetrated not so much by despotic states, even though they play a part, but by the world's trading and financial institutions. Even Shell's involvement in the exploitation of the Ogoni pales beside the universal and deadly abandonment of the world's poor by all such institutions in their preposterous pursuit of faster and faster returns on capital. ❑

***Neil Middleton** is a consultant with ETC resident in the Irish Republic. He is co-author, with Phil O'Keefe, of* Disaster and Development, *Pluto Press, 1998.*

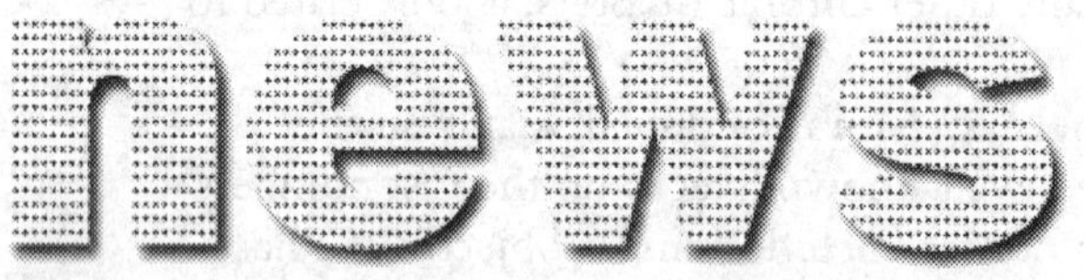

SOMALIA

Panic attack

Andrew Kendle

'He cut loose with the M60 and his rounds tore through the crowd like a scythe. A Little Bird (gunship) swooped in and threw down a flaming wall of lead. Those who didn't fall fled. One moment there was a crowd and the next instant there was just a bleeding heap of dead and injured.'

On 22 March, the day President Clinton began his historic trip to Africa, the London Observer reported that Mark Bowden of the Philadelphia Inquirer had revealed that on 3 October 1993, trapped US troops, in Mogadishu as part of the UN humanitarian mission, abandoned their rules of engagement and shot down every Somali they saw, including women and children, killing over 1,000. The figure was five times the 'official' death toll. Shocking though this revelation is, the Boston-based Z Magazine, citing CIA figures quoted in Foreign Policy, revealed in the summer of 1995 that between 7,000 and 10,000 Somalis were killed by US soldiers in the 16 months – December 1992 to March 1994 – they were in Somalia. No single member of the mission has ever been held to account.

ALEX DE WAAL

Return to fundamentals

The prevention and punishment of genocide requires an intellectual and moral honesty that can only exist where there is complete freedom of information and expression

Writing in the *New Yorker* last year, Philip Gourevitch commented that if the cataclysms of central Africa had occurred in Europe, they would have been called a 'world war'. Fifty years after the writing of the Genocide Convention, the comparison is apt. Africa today is a continent emerging from genocide, total war and economic disaster; and a continent in which political extremism and continuing economic problems such as unemployment and painfully slow reconstruction pose a threat to democratic aspirations.

The parallels go further. Just as World War II in Europe discredited the League of Nations and its failed instruments, and instituted instead a new world order comprising both the United Nations and new humanitarian laws, the disasters in Africa have led to a collapse in the credibility of much of the current international order. But this time the answer is not to start from scratch but to return to the fundamentals established half a century ago.

The fundamental human rights and humanitarian legislation of this century was drawn up in the years after World War II by men and women who had seen the horrors of war and genocide themselves. In the space of just a few years, they drew up the Universal Declaration of Human Rights (1948), the Genocide Convention (1948), the Geneva Conventions (1949) and the Refugee Convention (1951). These documents are at once a product of their times – which is one of the reasons why they speak so strongly to the contemporary African experience – and have the most powerful claim to universal validity of any international treaties drawn up before or since. Time, relevance and universal acceptance have given them a stature as the 'hard' law of nations and international obligations that no succeeding treaties – often much more aspirational and 'softer' – can claim.

The Declarations and Conventions themselves are remarkable balancing acts: the privileges of sovereignty paired with the rights of citizens, civil and political liberties interwoven with social and economic rights. Above all, there is pragmatism conjoined to idealism, found most clearly in the twins of the Genocide Convention and the Geneva Conventions, the foundation of international humanitarianism.

The laws of war are an older tradition than human rights. Every society has a concept of humanity and restraint in warfare: 'the warrior's honour', as Michael Ignatieff has recently encapsulated it. War involves the systematic violation of human rights – killing. The laws of war are a means of legitimising this while regulating it. They come into force when a sovereign state will not or cannot fulfil its basic human rights obligations to its citizens or the citizens of another country, because of war. Hence the traditional barrier between the laws of war (now generally known as 'international humanitarian law' or IHL) and human rights law. Important human rights provisions are found in IHL (notably the right to a trial), but it is clear that human rights law cannot be applied wholesale in conflict. There is an equally firm traditional barrier between it and international law: the distinction between the laws of war and the right to wage war. IHL makes no comment on the latter.

It may come as a surprise to some contemporary humanitarians to discover that the foundation of modern humanitarianism is intense pragmatism. The central doctrines of IHL are that there is legitimate military necessity but that, conversely, the means of combat are not unlimited. The central concept is 'proportionality': the military means used and the damage inflicted should be proportional to the military advantage to be gained or threat faced. In black and white, the basic law of humanitarianism says: 'The presence of a protected person may not be used to render certain points or areas immune from military operations.' (Convention IV Article 28.) In humanitarian law, the term 'protected' is a legal term of art: it refers not to physical protection or immunity but to the fact that combatants should do all they can to avoid harming such people. But both in practice and in a reading of the laws, 'military necessity' can override this rather insubstantial 'protection'. In fact, IHL places an implicit obligation on civilians to get out of the way of combat.

Similarly, what might be called the 'humanitarians' constitution' gives little solace to relief workers. Their access and work is conditional on the consent of both sides, who are entitled to object if their security concerns are jeopardised or if they have serious reason to believe that aid to civilians under enemy control is not properly supervised, may be diverted, or may even bring indirect military advantage to the adversary – by freeing economic resources for the war effort, for example. Where these conditions are not met, humanitarian assistance can be terminated by a belligerent. Of course, 'subject to consent' is also a legal term of art: many belligerents cannot stop relief in their adversaries' territories. But the legal implications are clear: if consent is withdrawn by one party, a relief operation loses its neutrality and 'protected' status, for what it is worth. Famously, the International Committee of the Red Cross suspended its operations in Biafra in response to a Nigerian government objection; other agencies forfeited their neutrality but carried on.

It is a commonplace to claim that contemporary war is somehow different from the supposedly Clausewitzean war that went before. But all the horrors of Bosnia or Angola were prefigured in 1940s' Europe: ethnic cleansing, the destruction of cities, irregular armies and the use of starvation were all part of the conduct of World War II. There is nothing so novel in the 1990s that could justify a claim that IHL has lost its relevance.

Perhaps the greatest weakness of IHL is enforcement. It is up to the belligerent forces themselves to do it voluntarily. They can be exposed and shamed, perhaps bullied a bit, but between the war crimes trials of the 1940s and the current tribunals in The Hague and Arusha – the record of which has yet to be proven – there have been virtually no enforceable criminal sanctions.

The weaknesses of IHL do not invalidate it. On the contrary, it is their pragmatism that is their strength. The negotiating teams at the 1949 Diplomatic Conference included many soldiers who simply said no to any provisions that would, they believed, have prevented them from fighting in the ways they needed.

By contrast, the Genocide Convention is the simplest and starkest of all international instruments. Without any qualification or ambiguity it demands that states prevent and punish the crime of genocide. Killing in war might be acceptable – including killing civilians in certain (in fact rather many) circumstances – but genocide was completely beyond the pale. War and genocide were less than four years past when these Conventions were drawn up: the men and women who wrote this legislation knew what they were dealing with.

The post-Geneva shift in terminology to 'international humanitarian law' is more than an abandonment of blunt monosyllables: it is the embrace of a somewhat slippery euphemism. The 1977 Additional Protocols to the Geneva Convention and subsequent innovations in IHL were pioneered by professional humanitarians and lawyers; the soldiers and diplomats who had negotiated the 'laws of war' in 1949 were much less prominent. (The USA, at the insistence of its generals, has long objected to ratifying the 1977 Protocols.) In fact, the new doctrines of IHL that have emerged in the 1990s and been applied in Africa have not been negotiated with a single African chief of staff.

The 1977 Protocols plugged some gaps in the 1949 Conventions but also created some problems. The definition of 'civilian' was hardened to apply with equal force to a guerrilla out of uniform, a munitions engineer and an infant and her mother. Challenging the common sense of military commanders' judgement in this way is not a sensible path. Already, some of the most experienced and humane commentators, such as the historian Geoffrey Best, were reluctantly considering that IHL was becoming 'over-inflated': that it was unrealistic and impracticable.

This advice has not been heeded. On the contrary, relief agencies, human rights organisations and international bureaucrats and lawyers have been busily puffing more and more air into IHL in the last decade. Some have assiduously broken down the old wall between IHL and human rights law, so that commanders are expected to observe a raft of human rights requirements when fighting wars. This will not concern the US armed forces, who will cite 'justifiable exception' every time, and bring on their own highly paid lawyers to argue the case. But for the chief of staff of, say, Tanzania, the moral contest with, say, the New York-based Lawyers' Committee for Human Rights, will be an unequal one.

The United Nations Security Council, assiduously abetted by a number of humanitarian agencies, has developed doctrines of humanitarian intervention and the use of foreign troops to provide physical protection to foreign relief workers and their supplies. This new doctrine in IHL has privileged aid providers, arguably at the cost of neglecting civilians who may become merely consumers of aid rather than subjects of legal protection. And the humanitarian agencies themselves have drawn up their own codes of conduct and 'humanitarian principles'. Though an inherently worthy exercise, these are perhaps rather misguided. Concepts such as 'humanitarian space', which have neither any legal colour nor practical application, have come to replace the precise requirements for safe zones, protected sites (such as hospitals) and impartial relief assistance under the Geneva Conventions. In the hands of ardent laymen, legal 'protection', physical 'protection' and 'immunity' have become conflated.

Principled aspirations are wonderful. But IHL is not the right repository for them. A mass campaign can succeed in prohibiting the manufacture of land mines, but the Red Cross 'Code of Conduct' cannot succeed in immunising relief aid from attack, when commanders see their military imperatives jeopardised. In a recent Adelphi Paper, published by the International Institute for Strategic Studies, Professor Adam Roberts commented:

> 'Not one of the 10 points [in the 1994 Red Cross Code of Conduct] addressed in any way the critical issue of how to protect vulnerable populations and aid activities, nor how impartial relief work could be combined with human-rights advocacy, sanctions or other coercive measures. [Donor] governments and NGOs appeared to be addressing humanitarian issues in a pious and abstract manner far removed from the harsh dilemmas resulting from wars.'

Counterposing abstract statements about the aims of humanitarian relief with far-reaching concrete demands from host governments and belligerents to respect and privilege relief agencies is not sensible. It risks bringing the entire edifice of IHL into disrepute. If it is not realistic, it will be ignored. The bubble will just burst. And this is more or less what has happened.

The moral failure of most sovereign governments and international institutions to prevent the genocide of the Rwandan Tutsis in 1994 is well accepted. The Organisation of African Unity is currently setting up a Panel of Eminent Persons to investigate the genocide and surrounding events. Its mandate is to examine whether states and

international institutions met their obligations under the Genocide Convention. This will be the first ever such inquiry. It may be a model for Bosnia. It has echoes in the negotiations among the World War II Allies that led to the creation of the United Nations. It has already drawn apologies from the US government that they did not do all they could, and an admission from the UN Secretary General that he was warned of the planned genocide some months in advance, but did not act.

The requirement of the Genocide Convention is simple and overriding. The means for implementing it were left unspecified. Exceptional crimes call for exceptional measures: to legislate for them in advance would be an impossibility. Law can only spell out the obligation, it is for human morality and ingenuity to do the rest.

Arguably, the proliferation and 'over-inflation' of human rights instruments and institutions and 'humanitarian principles' have stood in the way of addressing the problems thrown up by the genocide in Rwanda. Watching their galaxies of little stars through their sophisticated human rights telescopes, the specialist humanitarian astronomers failed to see that the sun had risen. Genocide: the reason why they were all there in the first place. But almost all missed it.

It was partly an institutional failing, but partly also a failing of misdirected idealism. And those failings have become clearer as subsequent events unfolded. Unlike the Nazis in Germany, the genocidal killers fled with their forces largely intact and a hostage civilian population and sought refuge in a neighbouring country. Mobutu Sese Seko was happy to host them in Zaire: ethics had never been a concern for him.

This posed enormous dilemmas for humanitarian agencies: how to provide for a million-strong displaced population controlled by mass murderers intent on completing their unfinished business. Reading the Geneva Conventions, the Genocide Convention and the Refugee Convention would have stood them in good stead. Sadly, they chose not to do so – even the staff of the UN High Commission for Refugees (or 'UN Refugee Agency' as it revealingly prefers to call itself in the 1990s). Instead the humanitarian institutions turned to 'humanitarian principles', which they were busily drawing up. In pursuing these, they violated humanitarian law in four main respects.

One, they insisted on awarding refugee status to people who were fugitives from justice, namely the armed *Interahamwe* and the former

Rwandan army, and their hostage civilian population. They also failed to maintain the exclusively civilian and humanitarian nature of the camps. Guy Goodwin Gill, an authority on refugee law, has said that UNHCR's presence in these camps was 'probably unlawful'.

Two, as explained, IHL has rigorous preconditions on humanitarian assistance if it is to be considered neutral and impartial, These conditions were not met, yet the relief agencies who did not meet them still claimed protected status under IHL. There are honourable precedents for forfeiting neutrality in favour of providing solidarity assistance (such as aid to the Eritrean Relief Association during the Eritrean war for independence from Ethiopia, and arguably some of the aid to the Biafrans). Where IHL fails, moral choices remain. The moral choice to assist the Eritreans was commendable. Where the beneficiaries include genocidal criminals, the moral choice has a different colour.

Three, while UNHCR, relief NGOs and their governmental donors may not have felt legally bound by the Genocide Convention, they were acting in violation of its spirit. Unlike the men and women who wrote the 1948 and 1949 Conventions, they appear to have held genocide to be a negotiable difficulty – a responsibility for others to pursue – but physical protection of relief agencies to be an absolute.

Four, the agencies interpreted IHL – or rather 'humanitarian principles' – to mean that it was not legitimate for one belligerent (the Rwandan Patriotic Army and its allied Zairean rebel forces) to attack another (the *Interahamwe* and former Rwandan army) simply because the former were based in a populated area receiving relief aid. This is simply absurd. These forces were merely exercising their rights under the Geneva Conventions to take on their adversaries. The agencies compounded their error by calling for an international military intervention to protect their aid programmes and, by extension, not only the civilian population but the *Interahamwe* too. In the final days of the genocide, the French army's 'Operation Turquoise' had, in the name of 'humanitarian intervention', saved the *Interahamwe* from complete defeat by the RPA, and the outcome was entirely predictable.

In short, some humanitarian agencies tried to abolish the foundations of IHL, namely the concepts of proportionality in use of military force and the legitimate military objective, and to immunise themselves from any obligations under IHL. The entire structure of IHL is jeopardised by these actions, which turn IHL from a practicable reality into a naive and unrealisable aim. One immediate consequence was that the Rwandan government/Zairean rebel alliance provided no 'humanitarian space' for relief organisations during its advance through Zaire, with predictable results.

Africa has suffered – and continues to witness – great evil. Many individuals and some governments are trying to cope with the enormity of what has happened and what needs to be done. The need for justice is paramount; the needs for civic and economic reconstruction are immense. The OAU Panel to investigate the genocide is an enormously important initiative that could help bring a new legal and moral order to the continent. Or, to be more accurate, it can help rescue humanitarian values from the institutions that have inadvertently subverted them by over-inflating some aspects of the laws of war and ignoring others.

The hard basics of humanitarianism are still there in the great Conventions of 1948 and 1949. They are as valid as ever: an inspired and enduringly relevant combination of pragmatism and principle. It is important for Africans – and indeed the wider 'international community' – to retrieve them before it is too late. ❑

***Alex de Waal** is a member of the Inter Africa Group based in Addis Ababa*

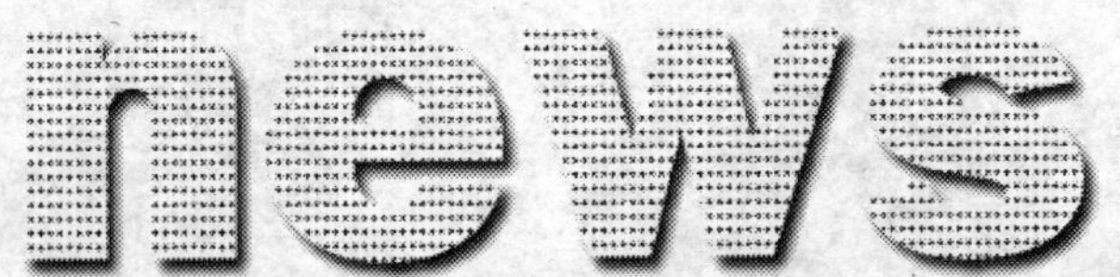

HUNGARY

Death of a magnate

Irena Maryniak

Hungary's leading print media tycoon, Janos Fenyo (44), was shot dead in his car on 11 February while caught at traffic lights in Budapest's evening rush hour. The gunman discharged over 20 bullets through Fenyo's side window, deposited his weapon under a parked car and left the scene on foot.

Prime Minister Gyula Horn blamed the killing on the presence of too many foreigners in the country, claiming that 80 percent of crimes were committed by non-Hungarians. The government subsequently apologised for his 'outburst'. Although the media treated the murder as a gangland vendetta, journalists privately admit that the assassination was almost certainly commissioned either by the criminal underground or by someone in authority. At the time of his death Fenyo is said to have been facing about 30 court cases.

Fenyo began his career as a photographer in the US and returned to Hungary in the late 1980s to create the network of video-rental businesses that grew into his media empire, VICO Rt. The company is currently the biggest print media-owner in Hungary, controlling the popular, middle-of-the-road daily *Nepszava*, along with three weeklies.

'Children shall enjoy social protection'

Article 25 (2) Motherhood and childhood are entitled to special care and assistance. All children, whether born in or out of wedlock, shall enjoy the same social protection'

Child scavenging, Manilla, Philippines – Credit: Stuart Franklin/Magnum

Child prostitutes, Pattaya, Thailand – Credit: Patrick Zachmann/Magnum

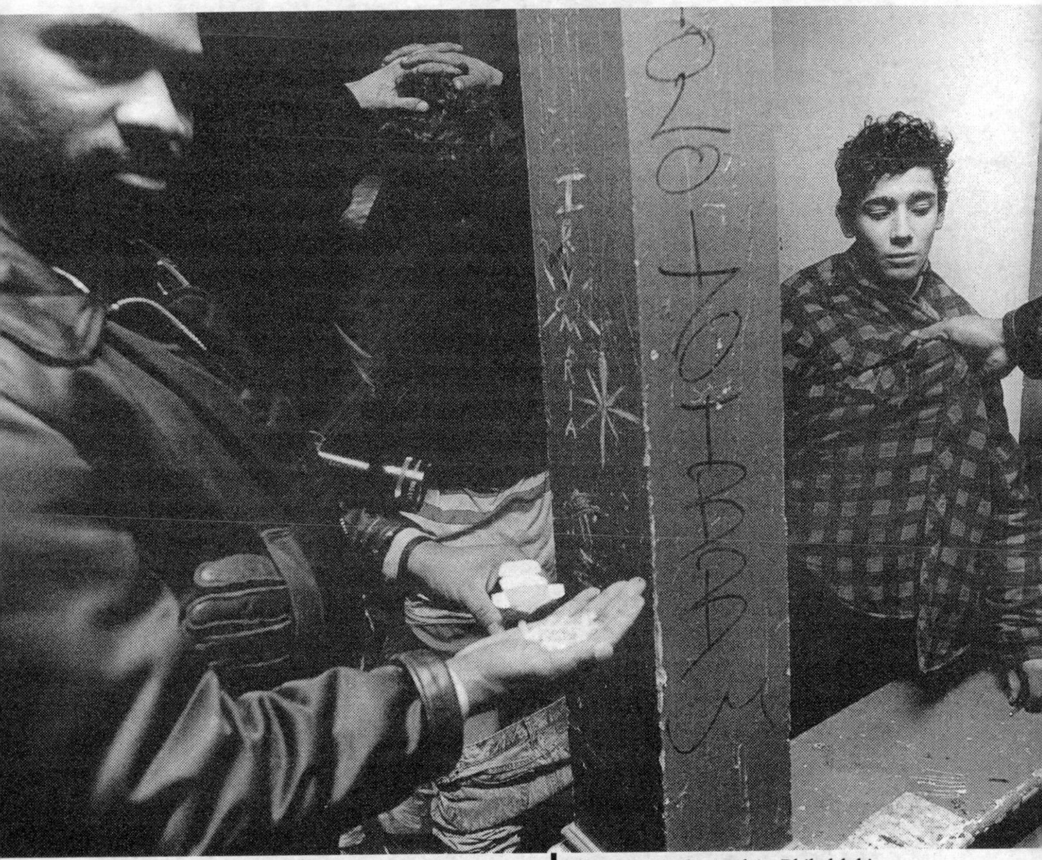

'Shorty', 13, detained in Philadelphia crackhouse – Credit: Eugene Richards/Magnum

Children gathering firewood, Cusco, Peru – Credit: Eli Reed/Magnum

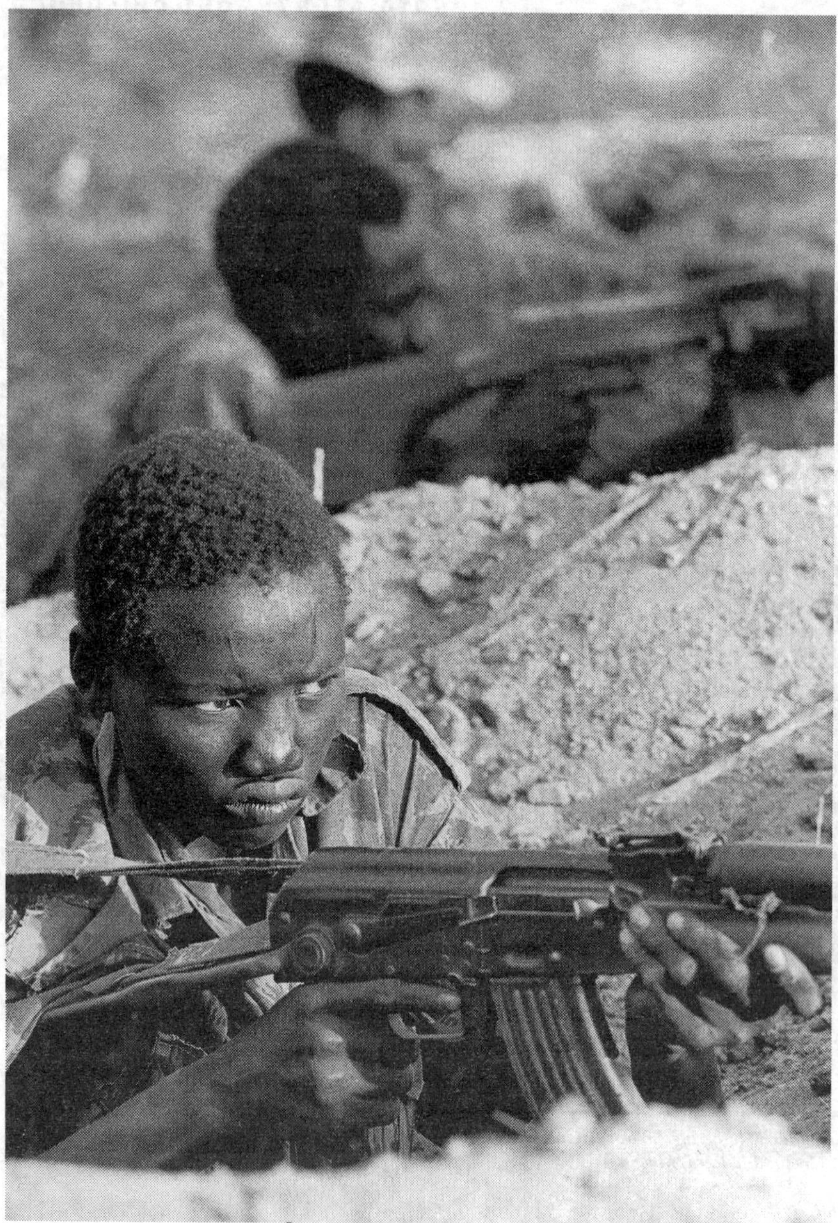

Boy soldier, Buno, Sudan – Credit: Martin Adler/Panos

Michaela, Strabane, Northern Ireland – Credit: Martine Franck/Magnum

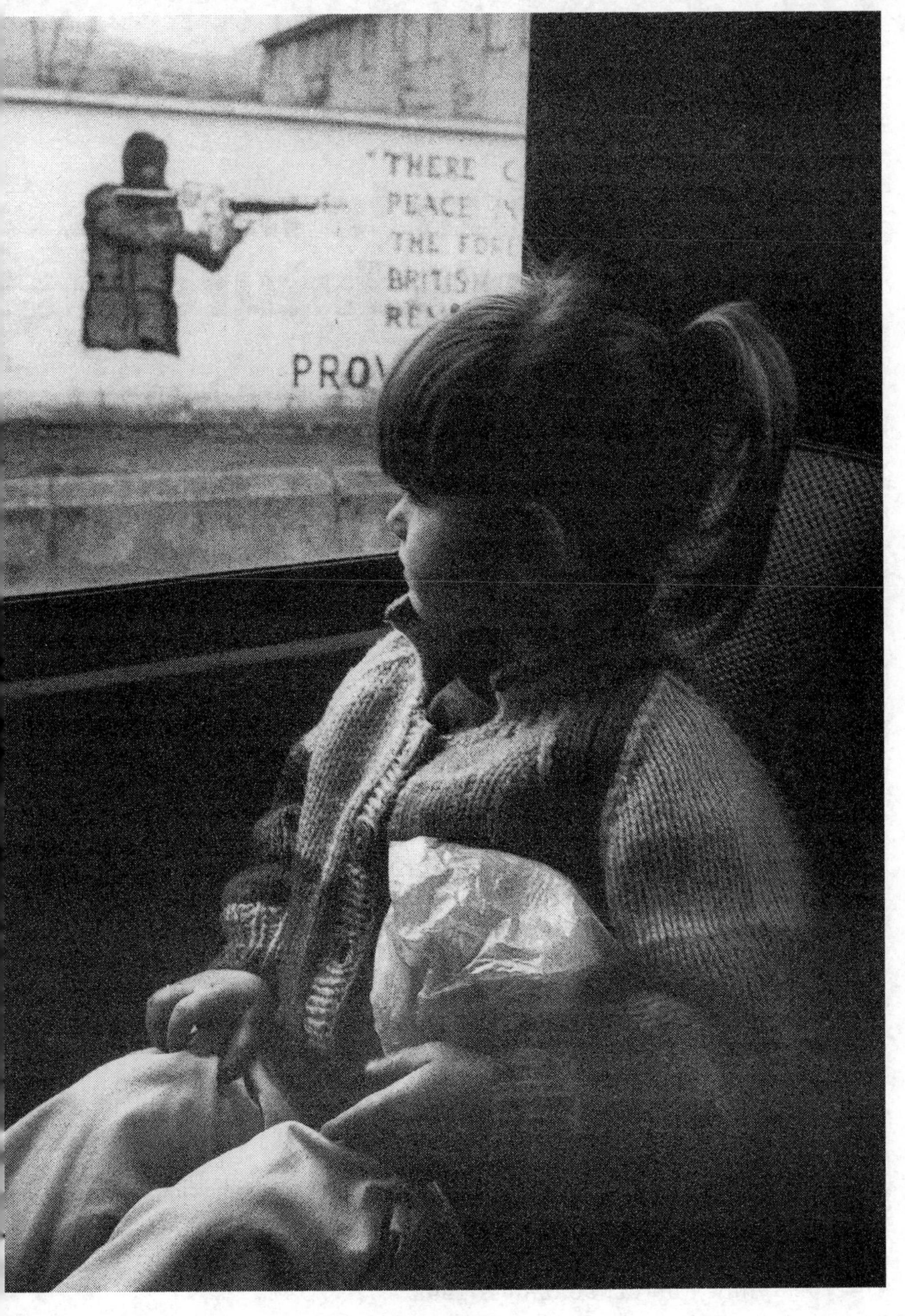
THERE
PEACE
THE FOR
BRITIS
PROV

Article 26 'Everyone has the right to education. Education shall be free, at least in the elementary and fundamental stages. Elementary education shall be compulsory'

NAILA KABEER

'Education is my daughter's future'

Bangladeshi women, denied education themselves, have seen its value as the way to a better future for their daughters. In their own words, they tell of their dreams and aspirations, their insecurities and constraints and of their hopes for the next generation

Gender inequality in education is very much the pattern throughout much of the Indian subcontinent and the story behind it now well-established. There is a strong culture of son-preference in much of this region. Boys are much more active in the labour force and they are expected to look after their parents in old age; investment in sons' education makes economic sense. Girls, on the other hand, are not active in the labour market. They are meant to observe *purdah* and remain modestly within the confines of the home. They go to live with their husbands' families after marriage and provide little support to their parents. They are regarded as economic liabilities and, with the spread of the practice of dowry, even to parts of the subcontinent where it was previously unknown, the costs of marrying off daughters have become prohibitive.

Given women's economic dependence on men, sons are even more critical to them as a source of support in their old age than they are to men. There is no economic nor social incentive to educate girls.

All this has been true of Bangladesh. However, as the *Human Development Report, 1995* points out, girls are now being sent to school in such large numbers that the gender gap in education appears to be closing more rapidly than in better-off neighbouring countries such as India and Pakistan.

The case for investing in girls' education has powerful advocates in the public domain. Mainstream development agencies see it as the most significant route for maximising social welfare since female education has been associated with, among other things, higher contraceptive use, lower fertility rates, reduction of infant mortality, better nutrition and family welfare. NGOs and feminist groups see education, properly used, as a tool for women's empowerment, enabling them to fight social injustice in their lives. The government of Bangladesh has also made a public commitment to women's education part of its development goals.

However, parents, particularly poor parents, are unlikely to be moved by public pronouncements on the value of education, unless they perceive this value for themselves. One reason why the perceived value of girls' education in Bangladesh may have changed is the increase in women's economic activity. Women are no longer seen as quite the economic liabilities they were.

And there is another factor at work. Economic resources in the hands of women appear to be more significant in closing the gender gap in education than economic resources in the hands of men. My own research supports this finding. In 1988, I carried out interviews with women who had joined the newly established export-oriented garment industry. Nearly a decade later, in early 1997, I carried out interviews with a number of rural men and women who had received loans from local development organisations. While the value of education was widely affirmed, on both occasions women appeared to have a special stake in the education of daughters.

Their testimonies on the importance of female education make an important point: there is no single reason that leads women to value education for their daughters or for themselves. Rather, the reasons they gave were bound up with the circumstances of their lives and with the values of their communities. The discourse around education as a human right sometimes overlooks an important factor: what it means to be human in any society differs for women and men. Consequently, the value given to female education by women in a society that has traditionally denied it to them tells us something important about what it means to be a woman in Bangladesh today. It tells us about their dreams and aspirations, about their insecurities and constraints; it also tells us about the changing nature of gender relations in the country.

For some women, the reason to educate their daughters was associated with marital prospects – getting a good husband, making a good wife or mother, paying less dowry:

> 'Why do I want to educate my daughter? The era it is now, you need to educate a girl to make a good marriage. Even if her education does not lead to a reduction in dowry demands, it is still an advantage for her… An uneducated girl will only attract an uneducated boy. Before, you could still get an educated husband… now they want educated girls because they conduct themselves well, it is good for the family, when she has children, she can bring them up properly. If only the husband is educated, he can't pass on these advantages.'
>
> **Razia Sultana,** widowed garment worker

> 'If my daughters keep their eyes on the ground and don't go looking at men, I will educate them as far as they want. If I educate them, they might make a good marriage, we won't have to give 10 or 20 thousand takas in dowry. We are poor people, we can't afford that. (Average agricultural wage in 1997: 40 takas daily.) Even if one spent Tk50,000 on a girl's education, then we might need to pay only Tk5000 in dowry. An educated boy will think, this girl is educated, I will marry her for less dowry. If he is also educated, they can both get jobs, they can put their heads together and do some business. That is why men want to marry educated girls.'
>
> **Romesa Khatoon**, married rural loanee

For some, education simply has a value in itself:

> 'Society says that it is enough for girls to be able to read and write but I think the more education the better, whether for boys or girls. The more they study, the more valuable it will be. If I had a child, I would want them to become a doctor or an engineer, whatever their sex. Educated people have one value and illiterate another. For example, if I don't have education, I won't know how to conduct myself with other people. A job is not the

main incentive for education. Even illiterate people work while not everyone studies just to get a job. They want to know how to behave with others.'

A number of women who had only daughters hoped that investing in their education might give them the economic security in their old age previously only expected from sons:

'I have a lot of hope for my child but I cannot always do what I want for her. I need money and I don't have it. I will put her in school in the new year. But I want her to pass her MA. She will do it if she is lucky. Then when she is educated, she will know what her mother has done for her. She will know she has given her life for her. Then maybe she will give me some respect. If I am lucky, she will look after me. She will realise that, even though her father has not given anything. If she is educated, she can work for the country. If she is a doctor, she will understand the hardship of the poor and realise that she was like that once.'

Momota, divorced garment worker.

'I have only one child, a daughter. She is 7-years-old and in Class 1. I want her to study as far as possible. Now girls study, those with education can earn. This girl can stand on her own feet and she will bring me peace in my old age. If she gets a job, she will survive and we will survive. She will think, my parents have spent so much money on educating me, I will look after them.'

Nurjahan, married loanee.

Some believed education gave their daughters a better future, the opportunities they had never had themselves:

'I have not studied, I can just write my name. In the village, they do not educate girls. But though I have no education, we must still educate our daughters. They have a future, they might be able to work. The girls say they want to work, they would like jobs like you. We can have hope, because these days in Bangladesh, prime ministers are women.'

Sufia Begum, married loanee

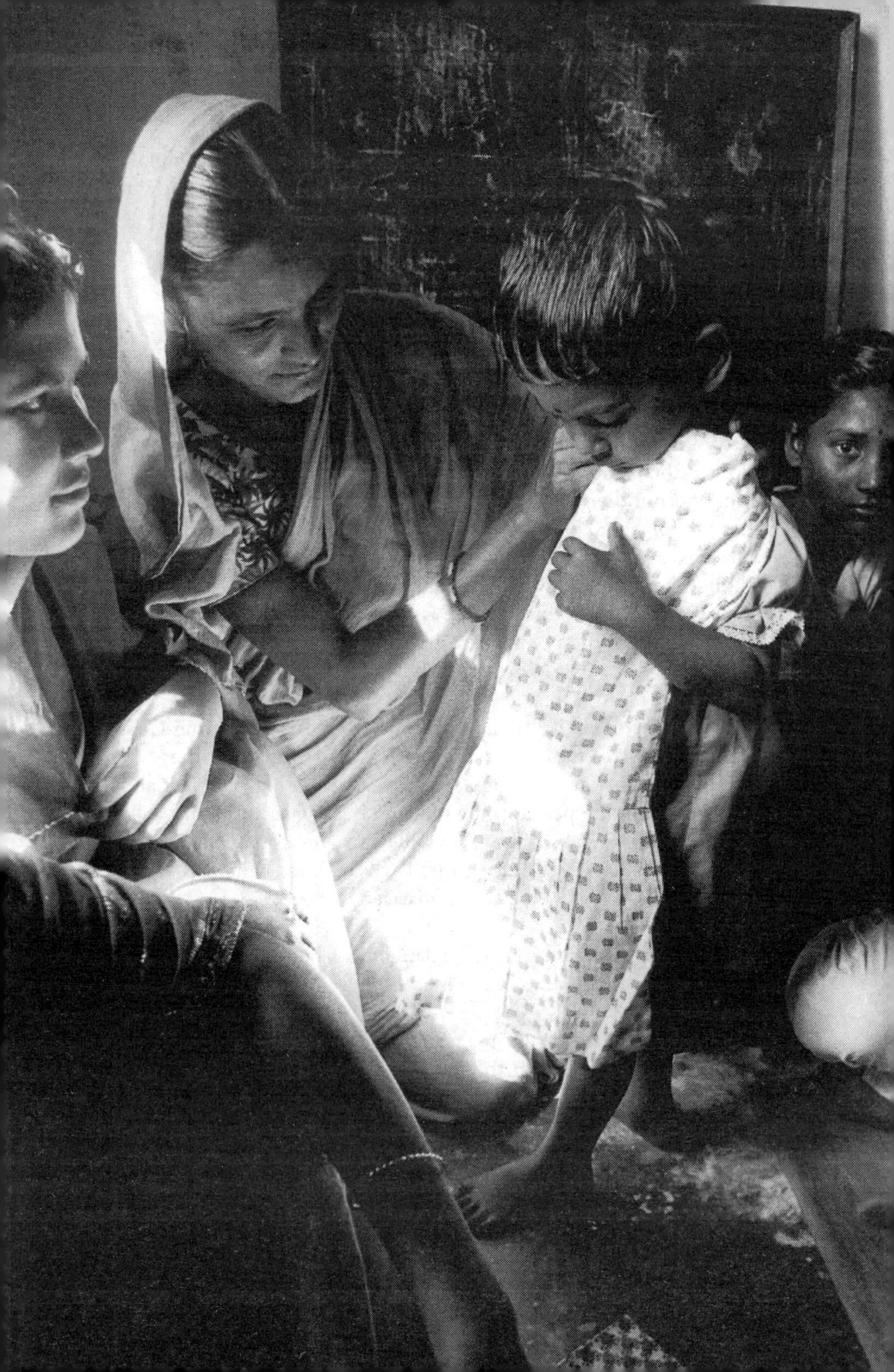

Sewing class, Bangladesh – Credit: Chris Steele-Perkins/Magnum

> 'I want my daughters to study a lot, but my husband thinks up to primary eduation is fine. He thinks girls don't need too much education, just educate them a little and marry them off. My own opinion is with more education she will be able to get a job; we'll see what happens. If they study up to Matric, they will be able to work, to feed themselves. I don't want my daughters to be like me, uneducated. When I went to get the loan, I could not sign my name. I was so ashamed in front of so many people ... That is why I would like to educate them so that they need never feel ashamed.'
>
> **Zahera Khatoon**, married loanee

One theme surfaced again and again in the women's testimonies: mothers did not want their daughters to suffer in the way they had. They spoke repeatedly of the everyday humiliations of economic dependency: of knowing that they had to ask their husbands for every paisa they needed; of having to put up with abuse and violence in their marriages; of living with the fear of being widowed, divorced or abandoned. What education symbolised for these women was the ability to 'stand on your own feet', to make your own way in life if necessary. To be independent:

> 'I don't think it's a good idea to marry off your daughter too young. The thing is to marry them off after they have received an education and can stand on their own feet. All men are not the same...So many girls end up getting married off and then their husbands don't keep them. If they have an education, they can get a job. They can feed themselves. If their husbands won't support them, they can look after themselves. Just because I am uneducated doesn't mean I will allow my daughters to be the same.'
>
> **Asma**, widow, garment worker

> 'I don't have any children yet but I think it is good to educate your children. And girls should be educated highly because that will be good for them in the future. And do you know why it will be good? Because if their husbands die, then they will be able to get a job without any trouble. And even if their husbands

don't die, it may still be good for them. With a little effort, they can remember what they learnt in school and then at some later point, they may be able to put that knowledge to good use.'

Hawa, divorced, garment worker.

'My first child died of hunger but I will educate the others. I would like my daughter to study till BA at least. I want her to stand on her own feet, I don't want her to suffer as I have done. If I had known how much suffering was involved, I would not have agreed to get married. I would have stood on my own feet. I would have worked and fed myself. The mistakes I have made, I will never let her make them, as long as I am alive. It is because of my children I have stood on my own feet now, I have improved my situation, I have given them a future.'

Begum, abandoned loanee

'If they have education, women have independence, they can feed themselves with their own earnings. And if I don't educate my daughter, she will say, "my parents did not educate me, they married me off to some no-good man". The husband will come home from the field, he will abuse her, beat her up, she will have to come back to her father's house. Then she will have to kill herself or go her own way. But if I educate her, she will say to her husband, 'Take care, I can stand on my own feet, I will work to feed myself, you can't say anything to me'. It was not like this when I was young, otherwise my life would never have turned out this way.'

Rizia Begum, loanee married to violent husband. ❑

***Naila Kabeer** is a fellow at the Institute of Development Studies at Sussex University. Her latest publication is* Can buy me love *(IDS discussion paper);* The power to chose *(Verso) will appear later this year*

RICHARD GOLDSTONE

Truth, trials and tribunals

Judge Richard Goldstone,the former chief prosecutor of the International Criminal Tribunal at The Hague, discusses the establishment of an International Criminal Court and its relationship to Truth Commissions such as that in South Africa

Machteld Boot & Richard van Elst: *What did you feel when you were asked to become chief prosecutor for the International Criminal Tribunal for the former Yugoslavia at The Hague?*

Richard Goldstone: I was surprised: I'd never been a prosecutor. I was a judge in what was then South Africa's highest court, in the appellate division, and I had been appointed to the Constitutional Court the same week. I discussed it with President Mandela,the Minister of Justice and the president of the Constitutional Court. It was the first really international position offered to a South African after the new government's inauguration.

What was your first experience working as a prosecutor at the Tribunal?

Fortunately, I was able to get expert prosecutors to assist. Graham Blewitt, the deputy prosecutor, had had tremendous experience in the Australian Nazi war crimes prosecution. My position was not only prosecuting, it was also diplomatic, dealing with governments and with the media. I spent maybe 30-40 percent of my time prosecuting, the rest getting money from the UN, from governments and NGOs. I had also had some experience in the Commission of Inquiry regarding Public Violence and Intimidation in South Africa. Twenty thousand people were killed between 1984 and 1994 in political, violence-related incidents. It was jeopardising the whole negotiation process between the ANC and the National government. A lot of the political violence was instigated as a means of stopping the negotiating process from succeeding. Without the Commission's work, there would not have been a settlement.

You said in December 1997 that Nuremberg-like trials would have been impossible in South Africa.

I did not say they would have been impossible, I said there would have been no negotiated settlement on the basis that, after the settlement, there would be Nuremberg-style trials against the leaders of the former government. But there could still be trials against people who have not been granted amnesty.

If there were a permanent International Criminal Court would it still be possible to try the leaders of the apartheid regime?

If we have a permanent court it will be forward-looking, not backward-looking. Nobody will agree to jurisdiction going backwards. And quite rightly so. Unfortunately, we shall have enough to look forward to without going backwards. No country will agree on a treaty knowing that its own actions 30-40 years ago are going to be examined.

South Africa started by investigating criminal acts; later it decided to hold a Truth and Reconciliation Commission. Wouldn't the same approach have been possible in former Yugoslavia?

It is difficult to transplant from one country to another. South Africa was lucky in a number of respects. First, there was no religious divide. In Yugoslavia, that is the heart of the difficulty. All the south Slavs come from the same ethnic stock; they all speak the same language. The difference between them is religious. Second, there are centuries of distrust between the three groups. I do not believe you can impose a Truth Commission from the outside; it has to come from within. Also, I think it's really difficult to have a Truth Commission when serious crimes against humanity have been committed. I do not underestimate what happened in South Africa, but we did not have genocide. It is bad enough granting amnesties to people who have killed four, five, maybe 10 people, but not tens of thousands.

And what about a Truth Commission in Rwanda?

The Rwandan people are just not going to accept it. I think you could have a Truth Commission for people at the bottom. But how do you grant amnesty to people who organised the murder of hundreds of thousands and expect people to accept it? They want executions.

During the discussions on setting up a permanent tribunal, was there any mention of alternative ways of dealing with the situation?

I have not heard any serious suggestions. In Rwanda, the government sent high-level delegations to South Africa to review the Truth Commission. Rwanda is very interested because it has to find a way of getting over 100,000 people out of their prisons and they are not going to do that by criminal trials. At the rate they are going, it will take about 300 years. They are looking at the prospect of a Truth Commission, at least at the lower levels. It is not one or the other; one has to be flexible. And Yugoslavia? Maybe at some point it will be possible, but it seems to me you cannot have a Truth Commission during a war. But you can have an International Criminal Tribunal.

Will it prevent crimes?

It depends how seriously the leaders take the tribunal. Unfortunately, people like Karadzic and Mladic have always been confident they would not be handed over, so there is no deterrence at all. I have never accepted the argument that you cannot have an international tribunal during a war. How long must you wait? How do you know when the war is finished anyway? Let's hope it's finished; it could be just a lull. It could start again.

Suppose a country decided to establish a Truth and Reconciliation Commission when there was already a permanent International Criminal Court – South Africa for instance?

If there were a permanent court, the prosecutor would have had to consider bringing charges against South Africans for grave breaches of the Geneva Conventions. There were cross-border raids into neighbouring countries which, clearly in my view, constitute grave breaches. The prosecutor would have to say to herself or himself: 'Is there something that I should investigate, or do we leave it to the South African Truth Commission?' I think the international community has been sensible to leave it in the case of South Africa. The South Africans are handling the case in a moral way, which is conducive to respect for human rights in the future. Really it is both a party political and a legal solution that has to be taken.

Does the establishment of a Truth and Reconciliation Commission exclude the functioning of an International Criminal court?

I don't think so. In South Africa, prosecutions have been continuing and are going to continue.

But only of those who did not apply for amnesty. Suppose one of those who had been granted amnesty were indicted by an International Criminal Court?

It would be a political decision. Obviously, if there is an International Criminal Court, it must have primacy. If we have an International Court it will be by treaty. South Africa would have known before appointing a Truth Commission that there is an International Court. That would have to have been taken into account during the legislation setting up the Truth Commission. It would have been built in.

Presumably, had there been an International Tribunal already in existence, there would be some sort of principle that, before matters come before the Commission, the prosecutor of the International Court would have to say: 'I am interested in the following people.' There would be some sort of negotiation. We had similar negotiations with the Rwandan government, when it objected to Karamira being sent from Cameroon to the International Tribune in Arusha. I really did think that, as the most important known war criminal in the Rwandan situation, Karamira must come to the Tribunal. I insisted on taking Karamira and I said we are interested in the 'following people' and there was some discussion. He is now awaiting trial in Arusha.

The Apartheid Convention provides for universal jurisdiction and so do the Geneva Conventions. When a suspect is in a state which is party to one of the Conventions, the state may want to try him, while the suspect claims that, since he was granted amnesty, he cannot be prosecuted.

Amnesty has no extra-territorial effect. There is no universal right to grant amnesty. People who have been granted amnesty by the Truth Commission could be arrested outside South Africa.

Hasn't the South African Commission turned into a court with interrogations not hearings in, for example, the case of Winnie Mandela?

This is what the Commission has been doing since the beginning. The only difference is the media attention that was paid to Mrs Mandela. There is nothing new. The other applications have been on exactly the same basis. It is not a trial. There is going to be no finding of guilt or innocence.

But all the evidence produced in front of the Commission could be used in a criminal case?

Yes, it could be used in a criminal case, but not her evidence.

Why is it unlikely that leaders like Karadzic and Mladic, who keep a low profile, will stand trial?

Karadzic is not keeping a low profile. He is becoming more and more actively involved in the country. Whether Karadzic is arrested or not is a political decision. It seems to me that there is unlikely to be peace so long as he is free. The heat is off Mladic and more on Karadzic; Mladic has kept a low profile. Ultimately, if the Bosnian Serbs want to be accepted by the international community, they are going to have to play by the rules. And the rules require that they be handed over. So I think it will be in their interest to hand them over, and this is what counts. ❑

*Excerpted from an interview by **Machteld Boot** of Tilburg University and **Richard van Elst** of Erasmus University, Rotterdam published in the December 1997 issue of the* Newsletter *of the Research School on Human Rights*

Article 27 'Everyone has the right freely to participate in the cultural life of the community, to enjoy the arts and to share in scientific advancement and its benefits.'

IRENA MARYNIAK

Return of mother hero

For 70 years, Soviet film audiences viewed to order. Then came the market and freedom of choice. And Russian audiences were quick to tell it what they wanted: good old-style heroes and villains and more than a touch of the Soviet ethic

Vladimir Sorokin was, until very recently, Russia's most radical and innovative post-modernist writer. He spent the 1980s deconstructing canons of socialist realism and examining symbols and hierarchies of meaning. He was both monster and idol of the new Russian literature.

Last year, with film director Aleksandr Zeldovich, Sorokin composed a screenplay for a film entitled *Moskva* (Chekhovian trio – Olga, Masha and Irina – are transported to contemporary Moscow and make their way as night-club hostesses) which has had critics issuing warnings of another turnabout in literary history and a revival of Soviet-style culture. Had Sorokin written a new novel it would have mattered a lot less. Books are pricey and no-one reads much any more. Literature, as Sorokin says, has ceased to be a viable communication medium. His co-writer, Zeldovich, considers cinema 'the only way to convey the way a nation sees itself: the Russian woman as a "type", for instance, or the Russian man portrayed so successfully in Stalin's time and in the 60s.'

Moskva is to be an authentically 'Russian' film. 'We're trying to identify a new, post-Soviet way of living,' says Sorokin 'It's already discernible as a cultural phenomenon. This is a film not just about Moscow but about a style of being. Russia is experiencing the birth of a morality radically different from the West's. It's the morality of people who are trying not just to survive, but to survive with style.'

The Russian depression of the 1990s has prompted comparisons with 1930s America; there is widespread support for film as the escapist medium that entertains and diverts attention from the misery inflicted by market reform. It enables audiences to recover pride in their past and take a more optimistic look at the future. If the early years of *perestroika* had Russian directors looking to western film festivals, Andrei Tarkovsky, the radical and the avant-garde (Abuladze's *Pokayanie* [Repentance] is remembered as the archetypal picture of the time), an aesthetic and political conservatism has now set in. 'People's cinema' is back.

In Russian cinemas today, the appearance of the *Mosfilm* logo with its beefy urban worker and sturdy *kolkhoz* woman is a regular cue for applause. Screen heroes are either well-heeled new Russians, mafia killers or street-wise survivors moving in a world populated by shadows from Dostoyevsky, Chekhov or Gorky. Valery Todorovsky's recent *Strana glukhikh* (Land of the Deaf) – a window on Moscow's deaf mafia, said to shoot faster and more erratically even than their hearing counterparts – features a prostitute in the vein of Sonia Marmeladova from *Crime and Punishment*. Gorky's revolutionary heroine from that prototype of the socialist realist novel *Mat* (Mother) is back in Denis Evstigneev's forthcoming film *Mama* in which the heroine incites her five children to hijack a plane.

The most widely debated film of the season – already hugely successful on video – is Aleksey Balabanov's *Brat* (Brother) the tale of a conscript back from the Chechen war who sets about putting St Petersburg to rights and, as the film concludes, turns his attention to Moscow. It stars Sergei Bodrov whose meteoric success followed his performance as a Chechen hostage in *Kavkazsky plennik* (Prisoner of the Mountains). Here he is a swashbuckling young killer, chivalrous, invincible, protector of the weak, defender of justice, ruthless with scoundrels, honourable with women - and a cult figure among Russia's urban teenagers: Russia's answer to Arnold Schwarzenegger.

'Cinema for the ideal audience,' the film journal *Iskusstvo kino* called it, 'a "pioneer cinema" audience to be precise, one that knows all about *us* and *them* and falls into transports of delight when *they* go tumbling to the ground with that funny wriggle, singly or in dozens. And even if our hero is despatched, *they* will never escape just punishment; so it doesn't really matter. Because there's "no such thing as death, lads".'

Which brings to mind that account of the chat Stalin and Pasternak had following the poet Osip Mandelstam's first arrest. Stalin had telephoned Pasternak and as conversation wound up, Pasternak requested a meeting to discuss a matter of importance. And what was that, Stalin asked? 'Life and death,' Pasternak said. Stalin put the phone down.

The language of Stalin's Soviet Union excluded notions of personal life and death, just as it denied individual rights and free speech. It recognised affirmations, imperatives, answers and groups: Russians, Germans, Jews, 'us' and 'them'. When *Brat* was shown in Cannes, Russian critics were concerned that its undeniably racist lexicon might reflect badly on the national image. They have also been at pains to emphasise that in the Russian context, this was not a far-right syndrome. 'Balabanov's hero is a product of the far-left,' critic Andrei Plakhov wrote, 'the protest of the lumpen masses against a cruel and indifferent system.' ('I'm no brother of yours, black arsed git'.)

The socialist realist aesthetic has been inverted: a backcloth of clean-cut soldiers/workers with gleaming kalashnikovs/tractors has been replaced by a tapestry depicting the drunk and the violent in squalid communal apartments, dealing in stolen money. The revolutionary fighter has become the market's avenger. All of which is agreeably piquant for audiences who remember the stars of the 1960s and '70s – Vyacheslav Tikhonov, Mikhail Ulyanov, Nonna Mordyukova – all back on the big screen once more.

In May 1986, as *perestroika* got under-way, reformers were convinced that film audiences would freely choose to deny themselves lightweight neo-Hollywood entertainment in favour of Tarkovsky and Bergman. But curiosity and the fascination with political revelation were short lived; it came as a complete surprise to the new men when the time-honoured fascination of free-market cinema with sex and guts reasserted its hold on audiences.

Nearly 400 full-length features appeared in 1992, most of them cheap productions from new private film houses. Audiences were initially curious, but interest cooled rapidly. With economic 'shock therapy' a daily problem, people had little time for more mafiosi, prostitutes and addicts on the screen. Western films were flooding cinemas, but US companies chary of piracy would not risk their box office hits on the Russian market. Auditoriums were uncomfortable, technically shambolic and increasingly expensive. With street crime on the up, nights out at the movies were also potentially dangerous, and audiences voted with their feet. It became more fashionable and prestigious to stay in with a pirated video.

'an edifying night out, she claims, can reduce pill-popping and alcohol consumption'

By 1996 the Russian film industry was almost bankrupt. The state funder, *Goskino*, shelved most of its projects and dropped some altogether. Just 20 films were released – a figure redolent of the years shortly before Stalin's death when every film project came under his personal control. The distribution system which had operated in the Soviet years collapsed. Ticket costs in 1995 were the equivalent of 25 cents in the country and just over US$2 in cities; but only 3-8 per cent of seats were filled. Most films shown were foreign and second rate; just one tenth were Russian and only 5 per cent were new. Given the choice, managers turned cinemas into showrooms for furniture or cars.

The Yeltsin government has now added 'culture' to its list of rallying cries and culture minister Natalya Dementyeva talks of 'feeding the emotional life of the people'. An edifying night out, she claims, can reduce pill-popping and alcohol consumption. Last year, 53 new films appeared and the trend is up. If in the early '90s, before the crisis, a third of films produced were co-productions with western companies, now most are financed locally by the state or private sources.

This year the state will pay an estimated US$30 million in film subsidies. New cinemas have opened and a ticket at the US-style *Kodak-kinomir* in Moscow costs US$20, around 10 per cent of an average monthly salary; prices doubled for the premier of *Titanic*. But the auditorium fills up and the ticket touts are kept busy outside. Hollywood hits are shown on Russian screens almost simultaneously, but its the old-style domestic product that most people really want.

Television has helped by continuing to show those unambiguous, reassuring Soviet classics for which viewers have an insatiable appetite. It is also investing in film production and the development of private studios. Lost stars of the Soviet screen are making appearances in documentaries and public-information films.

But directors have moved on. Nikita Mikhalkov of the Oscar winning *Utomlennye solntsem* (Burned by the Sun) and about to complete his new US$30 million *Sibirsky tsiryulnik* (The Barber of Siberia) is now the only successful director over 50. The new generation are grouped around Moscow's Gorky Studio which has initiated a series of 'low budget' projects designed to help increase the number of films produced. Many harp back to Hitchcock, Lynch or Tarantino, but the best also give insights into the ways of the Russian provinces, for example, or the underground sub-cultures of St Petersburg.

Mainstream material comes mostly from *Mosfilm* productions (which, like the Gorky Studio, is to all intents and purposes in state hands) and from the studio NTV-PROFIT financed by the private television company NTV. Kira Muratova, who began working during Khrushchev's thaw, recently filmed her satirical crime comedy *Tri istorii* (Three stories) there. But PROFIT is generally more concerned with

making films for a mass audience: Zeldovich's *Moskva* is likely be one.

The studio's most successful venture to date is Pavel Chukhray's *Vor* (Thief). It won an Oscar nomination for its portrayal of the relationship between an engaging burglar, who masquerades as a Soviet officer, and his two accomplices – a woman and her son – whose mixture of adoration and hate for him is being seen as yet another allegorical portrayal of the relationship of Russia's population with Stalin.

The new awareness of the market, that it really is a matter of supply and demand, has made the survival of experimental work in the Tarkovsky tradition much tougher. Aleksandr Sokurov's Russian-German co-production *Mat i syn* (Mother and Son), much acclaimed at last year's Berlin Film Festival, is likely to leave Russian audiences unmoved. Sokurov was a cult figure in the late 1980s when admirers regarded his work as the flagship of perestroika in cinema. Adversaries accused him of ignoring his viewers.

Mat i syn is an intimate and savage exploration of the relationship between a dying woman and her son, portrayed in static two-dimensional screen images. Against a backdrop of autumnal void, the son performs minor domestic duties, leafs through old postcards and books, waits for the end. It is an intensely private ritual, starkly different from the frozen formality of the customary Soviet marriage rite in the last scene of Zeldovich and Sorokin's *Moskva*, where a wedding party drives up to the walls of the Kremlin and pays its respects. On the surface, it's an unconventional arrangement – one husband, four rings, two wives, four passports – but petrified as ever in its unquestioning acknowledgement of where real authority lies. And, with success in sight, how *could* there be any hint of a Mayakovskian 'slap in the face of the public' where the survival of an industry is at stake? ❑

Irena Maryniak

GRANVILLE WILLIAMS

When more is less

Cost cutting, market forces, ratings and vertical concentration of ownership are undermining the media's coverage of anything that doesn't look like entertainment

In January 1997, a group of human rights experts from five continents met at the United Nations High Commissioner/Centre for Human Rights in Geneva. Their deliberations resulted in *More than 50 ideas for commemorating the 50th Anniversary for the Universal Declaration of Human Rights*. Under the section on the Media and the Internet, suggestion 56 reads: 'Establish a regular time on radio and television for human rights programming ... and human rights education themes.'

Now we know that criticising regimes with terrible human rights records can cause problems for global media corporations. The most dramatic, and best publicised, recent example in the UK was the intervention by Rupert Murdoch to prevent HarperCollins publishing former Hong Kong governor Chris Patten's book *East and West*. But other persistent pressures are at work in our media to downgrade and displace human rights reporting and programmes with a critical edge.

The *Oxford Dictionary of New Words* (1997) identifies one of the first uses of 'infotainment' in 1992 with a quote from the UK *Independent*, 6 January: 'We've got tabloid television shows (news as infotainment), we've got trash television (talk shows as confessionals), and now we've got reality TV, cop and crime shows,' and comments: 'the word is sometimes applied pejoratively to news bulletins which overemphasise entertainment at the expense of information.' Since then we've had 'infomercials', 'docusoaps' and other words to describe the new types of programmes that are moving centre stage in television schedules. These words are pointers to the pressures that are driving out certain types of programmes and replacing them with other, quite different, products.

Let's take a relevant example from Danny Schecter's intriguingly titled book *The More You Watch, The Less You Know* (Seven Stories Press). The author has been a journalist in the US media for many years, including an eight-year stint as producer on ABC's *20/20*, but as an independent producer he sought to get programmes with a human rights emphasis on the myriad TV and cable channels in the USA. 'We created *Rights and Wrongs* because we believed that human rights was *the* post-cold war challenge, and that neither network news nor public television were paying enough attention to it,' he explained. 'The networks were shutting down overseas bureaus and moving down-market with tabloid-style journalism.'

But the networks and cable channels (with the exception of Faith and Values, a channel reflecting the concerns of mainstream religious denominations and reaching only a small percentageof cable viewers) weren't interested. The Public Broadcasting Service (PBS), created in 1967 as an alternative to commercial broadcasting, didn't even want to see a pilot, dismissing the idea because they considered human rights 'an insufficient organizing principle for a TV series'. Fortunately, despite the PBS hierarchy dismissing the idea, 140 local PBS stations carried *Rights and Wrongs,* and, despite constant financial difficulty, a series of 62 half-hour programmes went out between 1993 and 1996. The series was finally silenced by the paucity of funding.

Schecter learned that only a certain type of content was acceptable, and quotes one cable executive turned sales agent describing what programmers needed: 'Avoid philosophy – just show it. All the execs I know are terrified of taking a stand – whether of the liberal or conservative variety. They want you to keep it entertaining and energetic.'

Further evidence from the UK supports this drift away from subjects which may be controversial or unlikely to attract high audiences. In January 1998, the Campaign for Quality Television published *Serious Documentaries on ITV.* This highlighted the decline in the transmission of major documentary films, usually aired at 10.40pm on Tuesday evenings in the Network First slot, from 34 hours in 1994 to 18 hours in 1997. The subject matter was also narrowed, with a greater focus on crime, domestic reports, and a dilution of the previous commitment to providing a 'window on the world' which had been at the heart of the ITV documentary tradition. Finally, from the middle of 1997, ITV ceased to commission new Network First documentaries, and as a result of *Neighbours from Hell*, a repackaging of a series of stories about feuding neighbours which attracted 11 million viewers, a follow-up series was commissioned to repeat the success.

ITV was also responding to the success of a series of so-called 'documentary soaps' on the BBC, such as *Airport*, *Driving School*, *Hotel* and several other vet- or hospital-based programmes, which attracted high audiences and undermined ITV audience shares.

The decline of hard-hitting current affairs programmes in ITV is also startling. *World in Action* is the last of an important group of programmes (*This Week*, *First Tuesday*) that exposed corruption, righted wrongs and debated issues. The fate of the programme is now uncertain. The talk is that the ITV network want a more reactive, 'consumer' type programme. Jeff Anderson, the new *World in Action* editor, has said, 'It's not enough to be doing marginal subjects. We have to go for mainstream targets, things that the average viewer is concerned about: health, crime, money, social issues - the standard fare of any popular newspaper.'

It's an uninspiring prospect, and a narrowing down of the vision that won ITV current affairs programmes innumerable awards. It seems that,, the prime-time slot that *World in Action* occupies can be used more profitably, and the programme relegated to a later time.

It's not enough to dismiss all these examples of the fate of programmes that seek to explore difficult topics, often in faraway countries, with the convenient phrase – 'dumbing down'. The term obscures rather than illuminates; if we want explanations and answers to what's going on in the media we have to look closely at the real structures and processes that shape what we see, hear and listen to.

In his book on the subject, *On Television and Journalism* (Pluto), Pierre Bourdieu points out: 'In editorial rooms and publishing houses, a "ratings mindset" reigns ... the market is accepted more and more as a legitimate means of legitimation.' It generates a 'vicious information circle' and represents an invisible censorship that ignores or marginalises issues and works that may not meet audience expectations.

The present and emerging shape of the media is far different from anything envisaged by the drafters of the 1948 Universal Declaration. Then the concern was to establish in countries like West Germany new patterns of media organisation and ownership that would ensure diversity; and to use the media as instruments of democracy, in contrast to the Nazi regime's use of film and radio as propaganda.

At the end of the century, we are witnessing massive changes in the range and variety of media we consume. Ben Bagdikian alerted us to one important change in his book *The Media Monopoly* where he identifies the accelerating pace of media concentration. In the preface to the fifth edition he points out: 'At the time of the first edition of this book, in 1983, the biggest media merger in history was a US$340 million matter, when the Gannet Company, a newspaper chain, bought Combined Communications Corporation, an owner of billboards, newspapers, and broadcast stations. In 1996, when Disney merged with ABC/Cap Cities, it was a US$19 billion deal – 56 times larger.'

Such mega-mergers raise concerns about the powerful influence these corporations have on democratic processes by shaping countries' political and economic agendas and espousing the values of corporatism. Bagdikian asserts: 'To give citizens a choice in ideas and information is

to give them a choice in politics; if a nation has narrowly controlled information, it will soon have narrowly controlled politics.' And, as the Tom Tomorrow cartoon amusingly highlights, information that helps to shape our thinking and responses is going to be filtered through precisely these media.

But counterposed to this gloomy analysis, a positively up-beat vision of our media future is being heavily promoted. It's one based primarily on technology – we've got the Internet to give us alternative information sources, and digital television will soon be the electronic equivalent of a bookshop or well-stocked news and magazine store with literally hundreds of channels to choose from. It's difficult to buy into this vision. History points to the fact that while new media technologies can have enormous impact, their development is vitally related to who owns and operates them. The reality, both in the USA and elsewhere, is that there isn't much space for new entrants: existing telecommunications, computer and media companies are involved in mergers, alliances and joint ventures to ensure that this remains so in the future. The range, quality and choice we get from the new media will continue to be determined by ratings-driven criteria. And human rights gets a low score in this scheme of things.

Article 19 of the UDHR is most clearly and publicly challenged by despotic governments able to manipulate and control both their own national media and global media companies that want to do business with them. But in industrialised countries, where television has become such an extraordinarily powerful instrument of communication, the people living in Asia, Africa and Latin America – 80 per cent of the planet's population – remain largely invisible on the small screen. The competition between the proliferating new channels will mean that the already limited coverage becomes even more scarce and superficial. It's that omission, and the largely unpublicised processes that produce it, that needs attention. ❑

{In* Index 4/98 *Granville Williams will continue his examination of changing news values with an in-depth look at the likely impact of digitalisation of broadcast media}

Granville Williams *teaches Media Policy and Journalism at the University of Huddersfield. He also edits* Free Press, *the journal of the Campaign for Press and Broadcasting Freedom*

SIRAJ SAIT

Time for dialogue

Human rights might be better enforced if their 'universality' were more widely regarded

The idea of universal and individual human rights has been long in the making. After the heady rhetoric of the American Declaration of Independence in 1776 and the French Declaration of the Rights of Man in 1789, Thomas Paine, in his *Rights of Man* (1791/2) sought to put a more formal construct on the concept, basing his theory on natural law and religion. Since the individual is in no position to enforce his inherent rights, Paine argues, these must be transformed into civil rights. In the century that followed, despite strong opposition, the concept of individual rights granted and enforceable by the state continued to gain momentum.

The UDHR is a continuum of the same western liberal tradition, an 'exceptional' reference point in the evolution of the human rights system. While it does not appeal directly to God, reason or religion, it assumes a natural order in which those rights outlined are universally applicable regardless of a particular social or cultural context. For those who see the UD as essentially a product of the *Realpolitik* of the time, it is much more 'the starting point for the development of a new thinking on modern human rights'.

When the first Chairman of the United Nations Human Rights Commission, Eleanor Roosevelt, set about drafting an international bill of rights, on 27 January 1947, she had neither direction nor mandate. The three-member drafting team of Eleanor Roosevelt, P C Chang of China and Charles Malik of Lebanon met only once – over afternoon tea at the Roosevelt's Washington Square apartment – and without even a consensus over where to start, gave up the unequal

acts violating the fundamental rights granted him by the constitution or by law' struggle.

These were the times when the UN made up its rules as it went along. Mrs Roosevelt made her first unauthorised decision: to accommodate a hostile Soviet Union threatening to stay out of the human rights project. She expanded the drafting committee to include representatives from Australia, Chile, China, France, the Lebanon, the United States, the United Kingdom and the Soviet Union. Even then, it was scarcely representative of the 58 member states. No African or Islamic states were included; even China failed adequately to reflect the views of its regional constituency.

The best-kept secret of the drafting process has been the source of the blueprint for the UDHR. Mrs Roosevelt asked for and received an in-house UN Secretariat draft outline drawn almost exclusively from US and UK sources. It was this that formed the basis of the drafting Committee's discussions at Lake Success from 9-25 June 1947.

When the UDHR draft came to be debated by the UN member nations in 1948, many states were clearly unaware of its implications. Some representatives were on unfamiliar ground; others were unable to take a position independent from the West. Had they done so, they would have been stonewalled. Despite 168 resolutions proposing amendments, and 81 lengthy sessions, the final UDHR still bore the imprint of the UN Secretariat outline.

Even at the time, the vote on the UDHR was not unanimous. The Soviet Union and the socialist countries did not vote for the UD on the grounds that it neglected certain rights and did not allow prevailing economic, social and national conditions to be taken into account. Saudi Arabia also abstained saying that while they had no problem with human rights initiated by Islam, the declaration was a western model applicable only in a very different social and cultural context. In the final vote, 48 states supported the UD, eight abstained.

Lacking the rhetorical passion of the French or the lofty idealism of the American Declaration, the UDHR opts for a simpler phraseology capable of translation into the many languages of its member states. In places, it is clear that its provisions have been left deliberately vague or open-ended in the interests of the widest possible consensus: just what is 'a social and international order in which the rights and freedoms set forth in the Declaration can be fully realised' (Article 28); or 'duties to the community, in which alone the free and full development of his personality is possible' (Article 29).

'The Declaration is not and does not purport to be a statement of law or legal obligation,' Mrs Roosevelt categorically asserted; and international lawyers such as Sir Hersch Lauterpacht immediately discounted its relevance. Unlike the other two parts of the human rights trilogy - the twin 1966 International Covenants which are binding treaties - the UDHR did not pretend to be anything more than 'a common standard of achievement'. But far from sinking out of sight or remaining a dead letter like so many other UN resolutions, the UD not only acquired a status comparable to that of the UN Charter itself, it became the inspiration for all subsequent statements on human rights.

While it never achieved the status of customary international law – as some at the time and again now argued it should – in 1968, the first International Conference on Human Rights in Teheran proclaimed that the UDHR 'constitutes an obligation for the members of the international community', establishing its status as one of the key international documents of the century.

As the sole reference point for all human rights discourse, the UDHR offends several constituencies. The rights of minorities and indigenous people were totally left out; gender is not part of its discourse; it has not show the same concern for economic and social rights as for civil and political rights; there is absolutely no mechanism for enforcement nor for the sanction of offenders; nor does it lend itself to the expanded horizons of the discourse demanded by, for instance, Muslim and Asian constituencies. Across the board, its legitimacy has been dented by selective application, double standards, and politicisation.

When the 1981 African Charter on Human and People's rights was criticised for incorporating traditional African ideals, Makaw wa Matua raged against the 'internal inconsistency, ethnocentric moral arrogance' of the universalists. More recent regional human rights regimes, such as the Arab Charter on Human Rights or the CIS Convention, are under fire for not reproducing the universalist human rights prototype. Whether it be the 'Asian values' debate or the parallel 'Universal Declaration' adopted by Islamic countries, the universalist lobby would do better to address, rather than ignore, the challenges and the diversity.

The 1993 Declaration and Programme of Action adopted at the 1993 Vienna World Conference on Human Rights does acknowledge that human rights 'must be considered in the context of a dynamic and evolving process of international norm-setting, bearing in mind the significance of national and regional particularities and various historical, cultural and religious backgrounds', but it does not reflect the ideological challenges to universality of human rights that preceded the Conference. As Caroline Moorehead wrote at the time in *Index*, the line on universality was held in the fear that authoritarian governments were using 'cultural relativism' as a screen for their own violations of the UD. But the challenges to it persisted, as do demands that it reflect more fully the cultural and ideological diversity of the world's people. To dismiss alternative views as merely the design of authoritarian governments to perpetuate abuse and impunity is to miss the point. Only dialogue can achieve a shared human rights ethos and with it a greater commitment to enforcement.

A truly 'universal' framework for human rights must be broader than the western narrative; must reflect competing philosophical perspectives. As the new UN Human Rights Commissioner Mary Robinson says, 'It's time to listen.' ❑

***Siraj Sait** is an Indian lawyer and human rights activist*

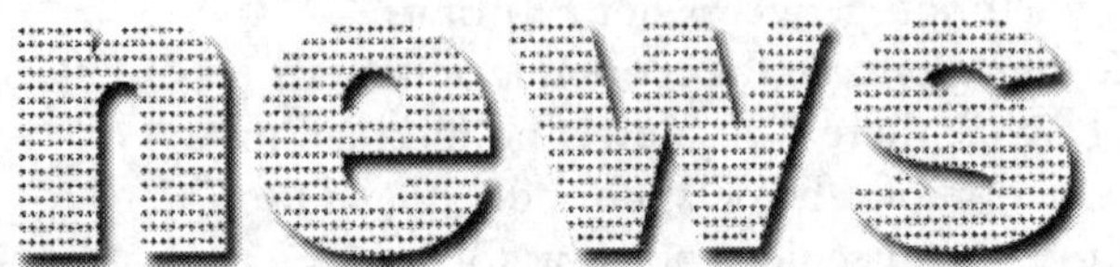

LATVIA

Gross allegations

Juris Kaza

On 10 March, Latvia's prosecutor-general filed criminal charges against a publicist for a series of articles criticising Russia. The charges, alleging that Juris Rudevskis violated Article 69 of the Latvian Criminal Code forbidding the incitement of racial or ethnic hatred, carry a three year sentence.

Writing in the political weekly *Nacionala Neatkariba* (National Independence), Rudevskis refers to Russia as a 'savage' society and cites numerous examples of massacres, court treachery and murder from Tsarist times to the Communist era.

A student and specialist in international law, Rudevskis said: 'This is a gross violation of my freedom of expression and a deliberate attempt to intimidate the press.' The charges, he said, were 'rushed and suspicious'. His articles also make reference to the present-day rise of chauvinist and fascist movements in Russia and discuss the role of the Russian Orthodox Church in supporting 'state tyranny' through the ages. Rudevskis concluded that while Russia can be considered a dangerous, anti-democratic society, he hopes and believes it will come to its senses.

Latvia is in the midst of a political crisis over the citizenship and language rights of over 700,000 Russian-speaking residents.

UMIT OZTURK

Anything to declare?

Fifty years ago the environment was not high on the agenda – today it's a different matter, and with good reason

'Somoza's men also destroyed
lakes, rivers and mountains.
They diverted rivers for their estates.
The Ochomogo dried up last summer.
The Sinecapa dried
because of the great landowners' tree-felling.'

Ernesto Cardenal

Throughout history, the impact of war on human lives has been measured only by the body count. The level of outrage is commensurate with the numbers of dead. War's destruction of the environment is never taken into the reckoning. Nor is compensation for those who remain alive on a desolate landscape ever discussed.

The Universal Declaration of Human Rights has no provision for the protection of the environment: individuals have no environmental rights, nor are their binding rules enjoining governments to protect the environment. As a result, a decades-long ecological tragedy has been inflicted on the land and the people who inhabit it. The main victims of this are often indigenous groups against whom their governments, or companies with the collusion of government, wage political and commercial war.

During the Vietnam War, over 80,000 tonnes of the defoliant Agent

Orange were dropped by the USA on Vietnam. Thousands of acres of forest were burned and villages destroyed; the long-term effects on the health of the local people has been disastrous. Yet no charges of 'crimes against the environment' – let alone against humanity – have ever been brought against the USA.

Wars waged by governments against their own indigenous or minority peoples have frequently been even more devastating. The fate of the Kurds in the Middle East is one instance. For decades, the regimes under which they live – Turkey, Iraq, Iran – have enjoyed impunity for acts that violate not only their conventional human rights but also their right to live in their traditional environment.

Since 1925, there have been 29 Kurdish popular revolts against the Turkish government. In the course of the most recent war with the Turkish army, begun in 1984, more than 3,000 villages and hamlets have been forcibly evacuated; some have been totally obliterated from the map by Turkish security forces. The number of homeless is estimated to be as high as 3 million. Thousands of acres of forest, arable and pasture land, livestock have been destroyed by fire; the ecosystem that had sustained the Kurds for centuries, and which they in turn had nurtured, is no more. (*Index* 1/1995)

The commercial and industrial policies of transnational corporations, often with the collaboration of national governments, can be equally destructive. Since the indigenous people of a country, frequently a minority whose interests are not represented by their government, have neither minority rights nor any 'right of environmental self-determination', they are defenceless against assaults on their land.

The Yanomami people of Brazil had no 'rights' to protect them from the massacres that accompanied the arrival of gold-mining transnationals in pursuit of the wealth that lay beneath their native forest. The Ogoni of Nigeria were slaughtered once they began to protest against the destruction of their environment by transnational oil companies. Nor was there anything in the Universal Declaration to deter the mining giant Rio Tinto Zinc from polluting Bougainville's ecosystems by dumping its waste on the island.

There have been atttempts to plug the environemental gaps in the Universal Declaration: the UN Conference on the Human Environment in 1972 resulted in the creation of the UN Environment Programme (UNEP); the Stockholm Declaration that accompanied it was the first clear definition of humanity's 'fundamental right to freedom, equality and adequate conditions of life, in an environment of a quality that permits a life of dignity and well-being'. This was followed in 1992 by the UN Conference on Environment and Development in Rio de Janeiro, Brazil. The secretary general of both conferences was Maurice Strong, formerly a director of one of the world's leading nuclear reactor manufacturers.

In 1995, when Turkish anti-nuclear activists were stopped at gunpoint by the police during a demonstration at a proposed nuclear site near Akkuyu village, soon after Strong's company had tendered its bid to the Turkish government, the value of the Stockholm Declaration was called into question.

During the UN Conference on Human Settlements (HABITAT-II), hosted by Turkey in 1996, the Turkish authorities banned any discussion of the impact of Turkey's war against the Kurds on their lives and environment. The UN responded with a deafening silence to the ban. Cynics could be forgiven their question: 'Does UN have anything to declare?' ❑

***Umit Ozturk** is a journalist from Turkey living in London where he edits* Newsline, *the newsletter of the Kurdish Human Rights Project.*

ISRAEL

A door opens

Marie Stone

On 12 March, the door of a cell in the Ashkelon Prison near Tel Aviv was left open and Mordechai Vanunu's 11-year spell of solitary confinement was ended. A former technician at Israel's nuclear reactor in Dimona, he had provided the London Sunday Times with information proving that Israel had secretly accumulated the world's sixth largest nuclear arsenal.

Lured to Rome by a Mossad agent, drugged, kidnapped and sentenced in camera to 18 years imprisonment, Vanunu has always claimed that people in a democratic society have a right to know if their government is building weapons of mass destruction.

Vanunu has served two-thirds of his sentence. His lawyer Avigdor Feldman who says he has sensed misgivings among Israel officials about the way in which he has been treated, adds, 'I wouldn't say it's a totally fantastic possibility that he would be released.'

Into the future

Views from around the world on the successes and failures of the Universal Declaration, and thoughts for the future

THE SENTIMENTS

The tragic situations in Palestine/Israel, Iraq and Bosnia are stark reminders that the UN has not lived up to its overblown Charter and Universal Declaration of Human Rights.

The UN must cease to reflect the interests of those who run it so that it can practise what it preaches; otherwise, its noble sentiments could end up like those in the divine books: fine on paper and nothing else.

Abdullah al Udhari *is a writer, poet and translator from Yemen*

THE PRINCIPLE

The Universal Declaration of Human Rights is the most important achievement of the United Nations.

Previously, rights were generally considered to be an attribute of, or to derive from, citizenship in a particular state. The universality of rights has encouraged people everywhere to demand their rights; and has legitimized efforts by inter-governmental bodies, governments, non-governmental organisations and individuals elsewhere to protect the rights of their fellow human beings, not only those of their fellow countrymen and countrywomen.

The international human rights movement owes its development to the legitimation of this principle, and the rights revolution that, in the past decade and a half, has contributed to significant changes in many governments in Latin America, the countries of the former Soviet Empire, East Asia and certain countries in Africa, also derives from it.

Aryeh Neier*, president of the Open Society Institute, New York*

THE RECKONING

Up to the mid-1980s, you would have been pushed to find a copy of the UDHR anywhere in the Soviet Union. It's only since *perestroika* that the Declaration, like other pieces of international legislation, has been used to further democracy in Russia.

Our President has decreed that 1998 is our 'Year of Human Rights'. It seems an appropriate moment, therefore, to remember those who suffered from the repressions of the totalitarian regime. We live in a country where fundamental crimes against basic human rights remain unpunished. Nor have the criminals made any genuine act of repentance before their victims. Worst of all, perhaps, there has been no acknowledgement of the crimes, the savagery, the lawlessness.

Our presidential Commission for Human Rights has already prepared a mechanism whereby Russian citizens can take cases concerning their rights all the way up to the European Court. However, according to our press, this is going to cost them US$10,000: this is too much.

Here's an interesting thought: it's only 50 years since countries came together under the UN flag; only a little over 50 years since the end of worldwide wars. For most of its history, humanity has managed perfectly well without without legal documents like the UN Declaration. The Declaration is an imperative of our age; the inevitable result of a nuclear world. Without such documents, conceived by and backed with the prestige of the UN, the death of humanity is inevitable: it will tear itself apart with nuclear confrontation, religious conflict and national prejudice. Unfortunately, the organisation has been rather too much under the US thumb of late.

***Vladimir Zhirinovsky** is the leader of Russia's Liberal Democratic Party*

THE TRIUMPH

Without the Declaration, the history of the second half of the twentieth century would have been even crueller. In the 1980s, the human rights world was politicised; without its campaigners the communist regime would have survived longer. For the first time in political history, a philosophical concept destroyed a totalitarian regime.

But measured against the status of human rights in the world today, the Declaration's failures are more obvious than its successes. For those who have had no experience of freedom, it's difficult to understand. Its principles need no expansion, but their effects should touch all people: it will have real impact only when everyone understands it, even the illiterate.

Since the Declaration is an official UN document, it would make sense for it to become a condition of UN membership that every member state includes it in its constitution.

Martin Simecka *is the editor of* Domino Forum *a recently founded magazine for liberal discourse in Slovakia*

THE ENFORCEMENT

The Declaration has changed the relationship between competing value systems. For centuries unquestioning priority was given to collective values, above all to state values and interests. By accepting the Declaration, states themselves recognised that the rights and freedoms of an individual were no less important than the rights, freedoms or interests of the state or the collective.

While this gave a strong impetus to the understanding and development of rights and freedoms in the modern world, it made them part of state policy and, as such, shifted the debate out of the domestic context and onto the international platform. It is easier to accuse another state of failing to protect human rights than to make these rights the foundation of one's own state.

It would be useful if, instead of assurances from UN members that they support the Declaration, they were made to sign a commitment of some kind to a minimal guarantee of human rights; an unconditional guarantee that would be monitored and enforced by, say, a UN commission. Such minimum conditions should guarantee the rights of the accused and the convicted. And it would encourage the spread of an individual human rights culture around the world. Without it, we run the risk that these notions will again become ancillary to 'state interests'.

Naum Neem *is chief editor of* Index/Dos'e na tsenzuru, *Moscow*

THE KNOWLEDGE

Having read – and signed – the Declaration is like having tasted the fruit from the tree of knowledge. Governments everywhere not only know that what they do suppressing rights is wrong – after all, no-one needed to wait for the Declaration for that – but they have to acknowledge the wrong and realise others are aware of it too. In this sense, the Declaration is indeed a watershed, and the results are clearly visible: more attempts to adhere to the principles of the Declaration – more lip-service even - and some practical implementation.

There is, however, no angel with flaming sword to expel governments violating human rights from their Eden of national sovereignty. Just as the Declaration has highlighted the obligation of governments to uphold the principles it contains, it also dramatically draws attention to its non-application, and the incapacity of the international community to enforce it.

Indeed, human rights seem often to be involved in trade-offs: murderous dictators are able to strike deals with patron states by giving up slaughter and having a blind eye turned to their 'ordinary' human rights record as a reward. In other trade-offs, human rights are offset against commercial interests, or Security Council voting patterns. Yet without the Declaration, all this would be considered just normal *Realpolitik*; now it is seen as shameful, and in need of justification. Thank God for small mercies.

But no, I would not like to see anything added to the Declaration, though some of my pet 'rights' are missing. As it stands, it is an outrage to dictators, and dictators are – or should be – an outrage to its signataries. This puts some signatories, dictators and their friends on the spot, makes them squirm, and sometimes even change. Again, thank God for small mercies. The greater ones seldom come.

***Konstanty Gebert** is a Polish writer and journalist*

THE WISH LIST

The effectiveness of the UD is hard to measure. It has provided authentic human rights organisations and advocates with the means to expose and address human rights abuses, but within limits that have to be recognised if we are to be serious.

The operative meaning of international conventions (and domestic law, for that matter) is not determined by words on paper, but by the ability to interpret and enforce them. In the international arena, that ability is not equally distributed, to put it mildly. The powerful do as they wish; the weak may complain. A dramatic example is the fate of the World Court ruling in the case of Nicaragua versus US, with implications too obvious to merit comment.

Another is the fate of the conditions on the threat or use of force in the UN Charter, the foundation of modern international law. These conditions are null and void for the powerful, as illustrated once again in early 1998, when the US announced with frankness and lucidity that it would violate the Charter at will to 'pursue our national interest'

(Secretary of State Madeleine Albright).

The same holds of the 'laws of war' and other conventions, and the privileges extend to client states. It is the task of 'responsible intellectuals' to suppress or angrily deny such truisms.

The UD is no exception to the principles of world order. It has been used to berate official enemies (often quite accurately); the powerful and their clients fare differently. However cynical, such procedures sometimes have a beneficial effect, leading to easing of terror and repression in the targeted countries.

The same was true of the Carter 'Human Rights programme' – in reality, a congressional programme reflecting popular pressures that developed in the 1960s, evaded in shocking ways by the executive branch. Though the programme reeked of hypocrisy, it did save lives and encouraged oppressed people to demand their rights. Much the same could be said of Communist Party condemnations of human rights violations in the American South, and the sometimes courageous actions to prevent them.

There are terror states that make no pretence of observing the UD: Indonesia since the western-backed mass slaughter in 1965, Saddam Hussein (particularly during the '80s, the period of his worst atrocities, with the assistance and support of the US and UK, among others), etc. Where popular struggle has led to observance of some basic rights articulated in the UD, the record is mixed. The world's most powerful and arguably most democratic state is a good example.

The official US position is one of extreme relativism: the socioeconomic provisions of the UD are largely dismissed. They are 'a letter to Santa Claus... Neither nature, experience, nor probability informs these lists of "entitlements"'. (US Ambassador to the UN Jean Kirkpatrick). Other provisions are violated at will; notoriously, Articles 14, 13 and 5. The US has one of the worst records in ratifying enabling conventions; the few ratified are qualified as inapplicable to the US. The intellectual classes laud US leaders for their courage and integrity in upholding the universality of the UD against Third World relativism. An impressive achievement, given the record.

On revisions and additions, I have my own wish list. But at the top is an end to hypocrisy. I admire Kirkpatrick's honesty, and think it would be a step forward if it were more widely shared. Then it would be much more easy to organize public pressures to overcome the contempt for the

UD and to give real substance to its provisions – not just as a weapon against others who happen to be out of favour among the powerful.

Noam Chomsky *is a professor in the Department of Linguistics and Philosophy at the Massachussetts Institute of Technology, Cambridge, Mass.*

THE EMPOWERMENT

The Universal Declaration is a living document. To commemorate it in the closing years of this millenium, the debate must give more priority to current complex human rights issues: the right to development, the recognition of the rights of indigenous peoples, the rights and empowerment of people with disabilities, gender mainstreaming and issues of benchmarks and accountability in furtherance of these and other rights.

The international system's achievements to date in implementing human rights standards cry out for fresh approaches. I do not see this as an occasion for celebration. Count up the results of 50 years of human rights mechanisms, 30 years of multi-billion dollar development programmes and endless high level rhetoric and the global impact is quite underwhelming.

We still have widespread discrimination on the basis of gender, ethnicity, religious belief or sexual orientation and there is still genocide – twice in this decade alone. There are 48 countries with more than one fifth of the population living in what we have grown used to calling 'absolute poverty'.

This is a failure of implementation on a scale which shames us all. So much effort, money and hopes have produced such modest results. It is no longer enough to hide behind the impact of the Cold War and other factors limiting international action in the past. It's time instead for a 'lessons learned' exercise.

One lesson we need to learn, and to reflect in our approach, is that the essence of rights is that they are empowering. Poverty itself is a violation of numerous basic human rights. Furthermore, the increased recognition of the feminisation of poverty makes it vital to link into the international protection of human rights the energies and approaches of the thousands of international and national networks of women's groups. This link between rights and empowerment is very much in my mind as I begin to identify my own priorities.

Mary Robinson, *UN Commissioner for Human Rights*

ALINA VITUKNOVSKAYA

Inner light

Die, Fox, Die

I will keep silence like a beast that can't speak,
in order to know what is inside me,
put me into the grass like a rag
and say 'Die, fox, die.'

Eyes rolled in the forest,
so as not to look at myself.
You said: 'Die, fox, die'
this means one has to die.

I will keep silence like a fish or the dead
so as not to be able to tell you calmly
after you put me in the grass like a rag:
diefoxdiefoxdiefox.

The scythe went through me like the rusty future.
The half-moon took out the sharp knife.
They all said to me: 'die, fox, die fox.'
All will kill me and you will too.

I no longer hear voices,
if you want , keep repeating
'iefoxdiefoxdiefox'.
oxdiefoxdiefoxdiefox'.

You can't recognise your own face,
falling again into the same rhythm,
it is not diefoxdiefox

but die and die yourself and yourself die.

Look at my beautiful eyes,
I would like to make a gift of them to you,
pray diefoxdiefoxdiefox
or die yourself and die yourself and die yourself.

And then I give myself to be killed,
to become a fur coat for you in the frost,
your hand could move
as my tail moved.

In front of the mirror
you have a ginger coat,
like an animal with a
monster inside.
Once you will be
reflected by me
and I will tell you: 'die,
fox, die.'

Credit: Russian PEN/P. Shop

Not Disappearing Anonymously

Not disappearing anonymously
under a train or a car...
To be... or to remain a has been?
When? Today or tomorrow.

Not disappeared finally,
but shouting and tense...
The dead man snagging the switch
will discover me when the light goes on.

I am a dwarf, mapped by cancer,
I am a fish spirit, already rotting,
a sick man will put me in a sack
to scratch, punch and croak.

The cook will search me out
and kids will take me to the market
and papa will lose me at cards
and my mother will not recognise her son.

Not allowing himself to notice himself,
to change into an attack of pain.
Senseless children,
noughts and crosses on him.

A Real Man's Story

No matter what I have in my pocket.
I have pistols in my brain.
But the shop assistant said: 'Oh God',
putting on an old coat like sweaty dreams.

She could only whisper 'get out' to the cashier.
I already started to shoot.
Some stupid bastards looked crookedly at death
to know.

Then some beetles in State uniform,
whose violence is funny like a running knot on the neck of a corpse,
in their interrogation room read me Sorokin's 'Norm',
and I kept putting my signature after each word, like a bitch.

Some mother brought me onion and dough.
From her loving care I felt disgusted and stank.
I had syphilis, soul and bride
were naked on the bristly stick with the rotting rag.

With this mop the pack of wild women washed the floor,

and she traipsed round the prison corridor,
swearing like a whore and finally asked
whether she had less time to live than the time that I'd do

sitting like a chicken on the eggs of death,
in a cell for 114 prisoners with brains and faeces,
or rather in a trap of 30 square metres.
and they did with the bride what she said.

When, angry with wrinkled passion, my only love,
dead, dragged herself to different hells through the morgue,
I saw how God leered
and understood his absolute desires. Until now

waking up at home after fifteen years of prison
I drink urine and Sorokin's faeces,
so as to go through the intervals of darkness
I come to the person who is looking for me.

I see in the heavens teeth, jaw and tongue.
I know who will eat my insides with an axe.
And some kind of mother with chunks of fat and sausage
is speaking with me behind the bars with her savage mouth.

No matter what I have in my pocket, after all
I will come out sometime and buy you a cunning knife.

Children, who are somehow bored
will cry and piss on me – I couldn't care less.

A beautiful girl with green drilling eyes
can never drill through into my savage brain.
When she, jumping out of bed,
whistles for some roses.

I will turn eyes and skin into zeros and cracks
with black blood like a shower.
Then I'll go to the voluntary tunnel of the firing squad,
because the world is as it was and is still boring. ❑

Alina Vituknovskaya *(b 1974) is widely considered one of the most talented young poets of her generation in Russia. In October 1994 she was arrested and charged with selling LSD, and was held in custody until October 1995 when she was freed on bail (*Index *1/1996) . Rearrested again in October 1997, she was tried and sentenced to 18 months in prison. She was released on Friday 24 April 1998, the court having decided she had served her term while awaiting trial.*
Translated by Richard McKane and Zeigam Azizov